Nathan Gray is a highly experienced and decorated test and fighter pilot, who has flown with the Fleet Air Arm for over two decades. His stellar career has taken him from the war zones of the Middle East to the United States. He has also qualified as a commando green beret, paratrooper, and forward air controller. Nathan featured in the BBC series *Britain's Biggest Warship*. This is his first book.

NATHAN GRAY

HAZARD SPECTRUM

TO THE LIMIT – AND BEYOND
WITH BRITAIN'S TOP TEST PILOT

HEADLINE

First published in 2023 by
HEADLINE PUBLISHING GROUP

First published in paperback in 2024 by
HEADLINE PUBLISHING GROUP

1

The views and opinions expressed are those of the author alone and
should not be taken to represent those of His Majesty's Government,
MOD, HM Armed Forces or any government agency.

Cataloguing in Publication Data is available from the British Library

ISBN: 978 1 0354 0254 0

IIMYLO_UMTW2U_ILY2TM&Bx∞
IITLD_S_DLP
IIMLULU_WUIWBN_URMSM_ILU4∞

Typeset in Sabon by CC Book Production
Printed and bound in Great Britain by Clays Ltd, Elcograf S.p.A.

HEADLINE PUBLISHING GROUP
An Hachette UK Company
Carmelite House
50 Victoria Embankment
London EC4Y 0DZ

www.headline.co.uk
www.hachette.co.uk

You've never lived until you've almost died. For those who had to fight for it, life truly has a flavour the protected shall never know.

Guy de Maupassant (attrib.)

Contents

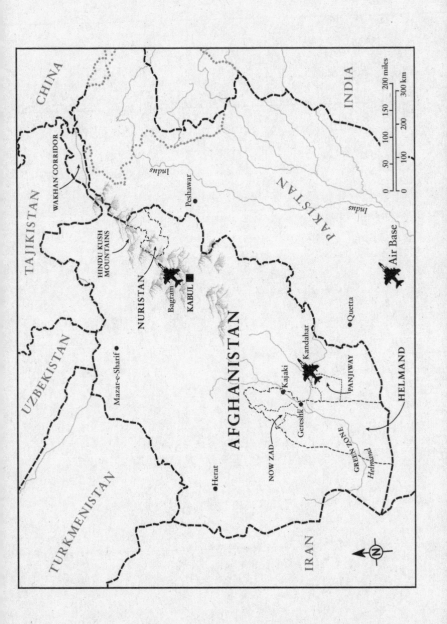

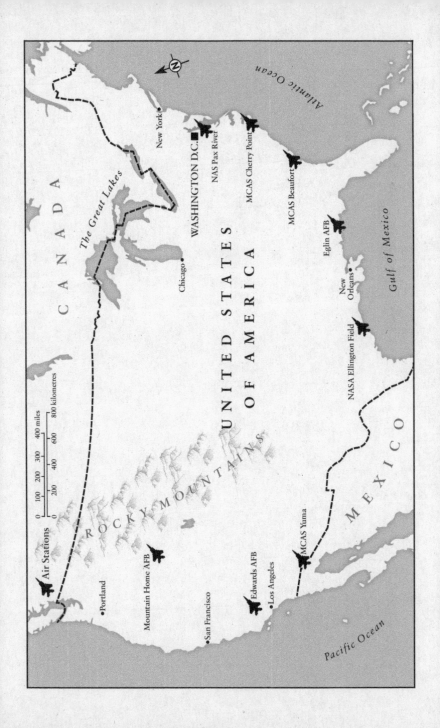

Author's Note

The names of some individuals have been altered to protect their anonymity. Some dates and precise locations have been changed.

1

5 December 2002

I hear the voice in my headset.

We're on hot mic and when he's not speaking, I can hear him breathing.

'OK, I think we're good,' says Lieutenant Commander Martin 'Jak' London, a man we all revered, a Fleet Air Arm fighter pilot who had seen and done it all and who was now my instructor for the day.

We have been airborne for 20 minutes, completing a couple of preliminary orbits of the airfield to burn off some extra fuel.

'Let's go back down and start the exercise.'

I glance at the flat farmland 6,000ft below us. It is one of those clear mornings in winter that make England look so beautiful. The early mist has gone, there is hardly any wind and the frosty patchwork fields glisten in the sunshine.

In the warm cockpit of our Sea Harrier T8 – the two-seater training version of the plane the British public fondly think of as the 'jump jet' – I can see the main runway of RAF Wittering, flanked by Stamford to the north and Peterborough to the east.

We start the descent, aiming for a conventional landing. No jump jet stuff this time. Just a normal approach, flaps down, like any other modern aircraft. I reduce power, push the stick forward and feel the Harrier ease down at about 350 knots. I get on the radio.

'Wittering Tower, Yeovil Zero Seven is now complete and in the descent, joining the circuit to land.'

Their response is instant. 'Yeovil Zero Seven, circuit is clear – you're clear descent and join downwind.'

This is a regular landing in terms of the configuration of the aeroplane, but instead of aiming for the main runway, we are heading for the stretch of tarmac alongside it. It is the start of a training sortie, in which I am required to show that I can execute a short take-off and equally short landing within the narrow confines of the taxiway.

I bring the jet down and we come to a halt about halfway along it. As usual, the crows are strutting around the airfield, oblivious to the whining, manmade bird of prey in their midst.

'OK, that was good,' Jak says. 'Now let's do the short take-off again. This time we'll go straight into the landing pattern and come back here for the rolling vertical landing.'

'Roger. OK. Happy,' I reply.

I focus my mind on the task ahead, which requires getting the Harrier airborne using just one-twentieth of the space required by more conventional fighter aircraft.

For the second time that morning I run through my pre-take-off checks and the routine emergencies brief, speaking it out loud so Jak can hear that I have it off pat. 'From zero to STO, we'll abort take-off for anything.' STO, or 'short take-off', deploys vertical thrust via the Harrier's four swivelling nozzles.

'From take-off to 150 knots, we'll eject for any major loss of thrust or control.' We both know that in those first few seconds of flight a Harrier in trouble is a dead-man zone, and there is nothing else you can do.

'If we get to 150 knots or above, we will have time to carry out emergency actions like selecting manual fuel, dropping weapons or fuel tanks, before turning downwind and coming back to land.

'Happy?' I ask the man who had more than 5,000 hours in his logbook and who had avoided being shot down over Bosnia by inches when a surface-to-air missile whistled past his wingtip.

'Happy,' comes his confident reply.

'Yeovil Zero Seven ready for departure from the northern intermediate,' I tell the tower.

'Yeovil Zero Seven, you are clear for take-off.'

I do my final checks and then slam the throttle all the way forward, taking my feet off the toe brakes as I do so. The noise level rises to a deafening roar as the Rolls-Royce Pegasus engine reaches full power, and I feel my body being thrown back in the seat as the aircraft hurtles forward. Two seconds later we are travelling at 65 knots and I pull down the nozzles to their pre-assigned position and the Harrier leaps into the air.

With the nozzles angled towards the ground, the soundtrack is incredible, like the all-encompassing barrage in your ears when you plunge into water from a great height.

After a short take-off, the Harrier is going too slowly to

fly conventionally, while still being subject to all the elemental forces and dynamics of aviation. I have to gather it, using the rudders to point the nose into the wind, at the same time ensuring the wings are at the correct angle to continue down the centreline of the taxiway and climb away.

I move my left hand from the throttle to the nozzle lever alongside it. It's a lot thinner and shorter than the throttle and not quite as glossy in texture. 'Grab that,' I am thinking, 'and move it forward, to push the nozzles back, to keep the plane accelerating.' Then it will be time to raise the landing gear and the flaps as the jet hits 250 knots and starts to fly away 'clean' – in conventional configuration.

But we never get to that point. Instead, something happens that is beyond my wildest imagination, and that no amount of training could prepare me for. Instead of climbing, I feel a thumping pressure wave hit me from behind. The head-up display disappears and with it all the audio – including the hot mic to Jak. The acceleration that I was so used to has been brutally switched off and replaced by an equally powerful deceleration, which flings me forward in the cockpit.

With the head-up display gone and the engine suddenly silent I've got no reference to the outside world, other than looking beyond the canopy. All I can sense is that I've been jolted forward. There is no communication with my instructor and the aircraft has started rolling to the right and is falling at the same time. I sense that we are about to turn on our back, so I instinctively apply full left stick to try and correct it. Warning and caution lights are flashing in front of me, igniting the instrument panel in a way it can only do in a massive crisis.

At that instant, all my emergency drills seem irrelevant – certainly the process of going through checklists and safety protocols. I have no idea what's happened. Is this a major loss of thrust or control? Must I eject? It's like, what is this? What the hell's going on? I didn't expect this ... this is *inexplicable*.

It has all happened so quickly that adrenalin has barely had a chance to kick in. I am in a state of disbelief, complete disbelief, as I attempt to correct the aircraft. I wonder if this is my fault. Because I'm so inexperienced – this is only my sixteenth flight in a Sea Harrier – I'm half-expecting Jak to take control from the rear seat and fly away. 'What on earth were you doing?' I can hear him say. Or, 'What the hell was that?' Or maybe he would explain it, as if it were routine. 'Oh yeah, jets sometimes do that – just turn everything off and back on again. Don't you worry about it, it's all pretty standard stuff.'

I am thinking all these things because my brain cannot comprehend that I'm at the sharp end of one of the most catastrophic failures that could ever happen to a Harrier and its pilot.

Full left stick is doing nothing.

I look up – it's only natural to focus on the threat – and because I've got no display, all I see is grass coming up to meet me. I see it and to my mind I'm already upside down. In that one, brief second, I am already upside down and I don't know what's going on. And that's when it hits me that I have to eject or, at least, I *should* eject.

The right thing to do is to eject, but I've never thought through the possibility of ejecting to my death.

Of course the right thing is to eject, and we are always taught to eject in time. But I have no time. I haven't had time. At no point has there been any time. In that millisecond, my brain recognises that this is now unsurvivable. If I eject I'm going to be catapulted into the ground; if I don't eject I'm going to land on my head, upside down, and I am going to die. So it's eject and die or stay with the jet and die. There is no good outcome here.

I decide that I've got to get out at all costs. That's what I've briefed to Jak in what seems like another lifetime, less than a minute ago. And that's what I've always been taught. I can't stay in the plane – this is unrecoverable and I am going to land upside down and the aircraft is going to explode and I will be part of the wreckage.

That's a fact.

I will eject and I will go into the ground and I will die. That's a fact too.

So I have to choose which way to die.

I know this is going to be a worthless effort, a pointless one, but I go down to the handle and think to myself, 'Well, you better at least make sure you pull the right thing, rather than just pulling on the kneeboard on your leg or something else.' So I look down and I consciously focus on the handle, a thick rubber loop with yellow and black stripes.

I grip it with my gloved right hand and pull . . .

I expect instantaneous violence and massive explosive force, but nothing happens.

Nothing.

I am still looking down because I don't want to look up at what's about to meet me . . .

And then my whole world changes.

Because I'm looking down, I've pulled with my right hand almost up to my shoulder. As the seat begins to move at unfathomable speed, my head goes down even further and I can see the rocket motors firing underneath me. I see white heat turning to a mix of white, orange and yellow as the explosive ignites and the rockets detonate simultaneously. The correct ejection position is supposed to be head up and back in a straight line with your spine. But that isn't going to happen.

The rockets firing is the last thing I see because the power of the ejection has forced all my blood into my legs. I don't black out, but 'grey out' – a state of semi-consciousness when you are aware of what is happening around you but your faculties are compromised. I feel the otherworldly force and violence of the ejection, as my body is propelled through the canopy like a crash-test dummy going through a car wind-screen. Then everything goes very quiet and very cold, as I swap the warmth and chaos of the air-conditioned cockpit for the freezing air of that still December morning.

That coldness, the biting coldness, hits me like the shock you feel when you dive into the freezing ocean. I am still conscious and my eyes are wide open, desperately trying to find a visual reference point. I feel like I am tumbling as time stops in the four seconds it takes me to travel between the plane and the ground.

I am waiting to die with my blind eyes wide open. 'Why do you want your eyes open? You don't want to see this. You are about to be hammered into the ground. Do you really want to see this? No, I don't. Yes, I do. Eyes wide open. But I can't see anything.'

'Is it now? Is it now? Am I about to hit the ground? When am I going to die?' I can't see what's happening and what's going to happen, but I want to see it and I don't want to see it all at once.

That grey blanket that has completely enveloped me feels like the threshold – a dim passage through a doorway – and I am about to emerge at the other end. The wrong end. I'm on a tightrope, on that boundary, and I know I can fall either side ...

2

The day that changed my life forever started routinely enough with my alarm at 6.30am. I was sleeping in the tiny room allotted to me at the end of a windowless corridor in the officers' mess at RAF Wittering in Cambridgeshire.

This was not our permanent training home. Along with two other student Sea Harrier pilots and four instructors, I had come up from the Royal Naval Air Station at Yeovilton in Somerset for a three-week detachment at one of the RAF's main Harrier bases and an airfield regarded as the playground for Britain's iconic jump jet.

Aside from the main runway, the base featured numerous short landing strips and narrow taxiways as well as a selection of vertical take-off and landing pads, some of which were in woodland. It was the perfect place to develop the complex array of skills required of Harrier pilots in the most demanding plane operated by the British armed forces.

Prior to this challenge, I had practised conventional flying techniques at Yeovilton, on sorties when we rarely touched the nozzles that control vertical take-off and landing. That led to our first 'press-up' when we launched vertically, established a stable hover and then landed in the same place for the first time. But now we were going to develop the full gamut of skills in a plane that had up to 20 different configurations on landing and take-off.

Sitting up in bed, I felt the bitter cold in a building with Second World War-era central heating that was always off when you needed it and on when you didn't. I grabbed a towel and began the long walk to the showers where hot water came in lethal spurts and then went icy.

Back in the room I shaved at the sink and quickly dressed, pulling on my olive-green flying suit, and spent 10 minutes going through my aircraft emergency drills and procedures for the day's flight. This was another big one – the second consecutive day when I would be demonstrating a short take-off and rolling vertical landing – and I was determined to nail them. That meant safely and precisely executing potentially dangerous manoeuvres with no input on the controls from my instructor.

We all knew that we had to master each skill in an exceptional manner; the Harrier had a well-established reputation as a dangerous aircraft even in experienced hands – it could bite you or take you over the cliff edge at the slightest slip-up. Not for nothing was it known in the Navy and the RAF as the 'widow-maker', a jet fighter in which scores of pilots had been killed since its introduction in the mid-1960s in accidents induced either by pilot error or by equipment failure.

Like all young fast-jet pilots I'd sometimes thought about the dangers and what it would be like to eject. During my time on the Hawk trainer, one of my fellow students had had to leave his cockpit in a hurry after miscalculating a landing approach, so we knew something of the experience from his recollections. One of my instructors hit a bird when taking off in a Hawk and ended up using what we called his 'bang-seat' – something I heard as a gentle 'pop-pop' from my room at RAF Valley on Anglesey, as the rockets fired and he was launched through the canopy.

I tried to imagine being catapulted out of the cockpit myself and thought of what might happen that could prompt that kind of emergency. In training we would pull an ejection handle on a rail next to our seat and it would pump us up, maybe a foot or two, to give us a jolt. In the simulator there was even less of a response – a little bump to register that the ejection had been successful. So we had no real-world preparation for something all of us hoped would never happen.

That beautiful winter's morning, it was the last thing on my mind. As a 26-year-old lieutenant on 899 Naval Air Squadron, my focus was entirely on taking the next step in my flying career – the next step on my way to becoming a fully fledged Royal Navy fighter pilot.

I set off for the dining room. It was like a journey through the RAF ranks. In the corridors the doors progressively changed from hospital green and reinforced glass in the junior-officer accommodation, to ever more grand affairs. By the time I reached the central section, heavy oak and polished brass were the order of the day. Underfoot, vinyl tiles had been replaced by worn brown hard-pile and then plush burgundy embossed carpet.

I'm not a breakfast person, preferring to fly on a mug of tea or coffee and an empty stomach for maximum alertness. But I wanted to put in an appearance with my instructors and fellow student pilots. Among them was my good mate Andrew Neofytou, who we called 'Scrabble' because his surname was a jumble of awkward letters, two of which were worth four points. Deep down he's a bit of a softie, but he'd found the steely outer armour that he needed to cut it in the military and make it as a Harrier pilot of exceptional talent.

Alongside him was another of my best mates and friendly rivals, Simon 'Scranbag' (Navy slang for a bag of rubbish) Rawlins. Tall, floppy-haired and a red-socks-wearing preppy, 'Scranners' is one of the most disorganised people I've ever met, but he's an absolute natural in the cockpit of a fighter jet. One of the most gifted pilots I know, he went on to fly nearly 200 combat missions during four tours in Afghanistan. That morning he was flying a sortie in the RAF training variant of the Harrier – the two-seater T10, a ground attack aircraft that features, among other things, a more powerful wingspan and a bigger cockpit than the plane I was flying.

Jak, one of the senior instructors on the course, was also there. He had agreed to go up with me that day after his colleague Gary Langrish, with whom I had originally been tagged, had taken a leave of absence to visit his gravely ill father. I had never flown with Jak before, but his reputation was as well known to me as it was to everyone else in our world.

A fighter pilot to his fingertips, Jak was a warm, modest and charming 43-year-old who relished passing on his skills to younger generations. Born and raised on the Lizard peninsula in Cornwall, he had flown everything from helicopters to Harriers and had seen active service in the Gulf, the former Yugoslavia and Sierra Leone. He had also come to wider attention in a recent BBC One 999 episode. This featured his near-miraculous recovery of a Harrier after its canopy shattered at 40,000ft over the Gulf of Aden in 1998.

Despite undergoing rapid decompression and being pelted with shattered Perspex, which littered his freezing cockpit, Jak immediately threw his plane into a steep dive, dropping 37,000ft in about 45 seconds, an experience that he compared to driving an open-topped sports car at 300mph. It left him with severe windburn around his eyes, but he still managed to get back on the deck of HMS *Illustrious* in one piece, for which he received a Queen's Commendation for Bravery and an MBE.

A real gent around the mess, Jak was quite a character; a snappy dresser, he famously drank only 'matured' cold black coffee that he had brewed the day before, smoked Marlboro cigarettes, enjoyed red-hot curry for breakfast and was very particular about his favourite wine, of which, on occasion – in fact on many occasions – he would consume quite a lot. He could be wild, and the stories about his escapades when he was younger were legion. But he seemed to have the knack of breaking the rules and getting away with it; even if he was caught, it never seemed to matter much, because he was Jak.

We looked up to him because he had experienced pretty much everything that fast jets could throw at you, and because he had thousands of hours on carriers, out at sea where we knew the dragons lurked, ready to catch us unawares. All the things that we junior pilots regarded as potential threats, Jak took in his stride. Of course, the Navy wanted to promote him, but Jak had no intention of swapping the cockpit for a desk, and his scruffy flying boots for polished shoes.

Breakfast at Wittering in those days was an elaborate

affair, with silver service at the enormous mahogany dining tables and stewards waiting on your every whim. I gave them little to do, sipping tea poured from a silver pot and nibbling at a piece of toast under the watchful eyes of the Queen and the Duke of Edinburgh, whose portraits dominated the room.

Scrabble and I chatted about the day ahead and compared notes on what we had learnt from the day before.

'So, you're up with Jak today?'

'Yeah, mate . . . yeah.'

'Well, you're in safe hands then, Nath – enjoy the ride.'

'As if . . .' I thought.

'If you get it right, it'll be very quiet, like flying on your own,' he said. 'But if you get it wrong, you'll certainly know about it.'

Scrabble filled the silence that followed with laughter.

I knew what he meant. If you heard nothing from your instructor, it was what we called a 'chuck-up' or thumbs up. You did not want to hear corrections from the back seat or, worse, the instructor taking the controls, because that meant a fail. You would have to do the exercise all over again and you could be on your way to being 'chopped' from the jet world and sent to helicopters.

At 07.30 precisely the minibus taking us to our hangar left from outside the mess and woe betide anyone who was late. 'Wheels are wheels,' was our watchword. It was the way the Navy instilled discipline into everything we did. Flying jets is about absolute precision and, at 30,000ft, rules and instructions are inviolable. In mid-air, if you are a second early or a second late, you are probably going to collide with somebody because they will be on time. We operated by the same principles on the ground, and none of us had any doubt that if we weren't there on the dot, our mates would simply close the door and drive off.

The hangar we used was on the periphery of the airfield and it looked like something out of Chernobyl. It had been abandoned by the full-time RAF occupants at Wittering and us Fleet Air Arm pilots only used it every now and again. It was cold, damp and empty, had bits of litter lying around in the corners and was covered in bird shit from the pigeons roosting in the eaves.

Jak and I found a couple of chairs and sat down to check the forecast from the Met Office on the fax. Then we got on the hangar phone to the tower and checked what runways were in use that day and let them know what we were planning. Jak pulled out a small squadron laptop and we went through a PowerPoint presentation on the tasks for the day, and the aims and objectives. Clicking on each subject heading, he left it to me to fill in the blanks.

We talked through the rolling vertical landing that I would be doing for the first time on a taxiway, a far narrower stretch of tarmac than the main strip.

'OK, Nath, the goal is all about safety and precisely executing the manoeuvres,' Jak said. 'It's all about precision – precise speed on touchdown and ensuring you touch down at the right point.'

'Yes, got it.' I tried to sound confident.

'You've got to get your line-up coming in correct,' he continued. 'It's like flying through hoops – imagine you have different hoops at different points in the profile.' He gestured at the laptop diagram. 'So, at this hoop you need to be in this condition with nozzles here, speed here – at this point you need to be ...'

As I listened, I couldn't help succumbing yet again to the feeling that I shouldn't be there, that I wasn't good enough and that I was a hopeless imposter trying to master a £20 million jet fighter. Some days I would go from hour to hour, wondering when my bubble was finally going to burst. Maybe it's about to happen at this briefing right now. Was Jak about to give up and say: 'Nah, mate, what are you doing here?' and expose me for what I was?

Partly because of this, I always prepared as well as I possibly could to try and stop it happening. But right until the end of my career, when I was the Navy's test pilot, entrusted with trialling the new F35 stealth fighter worth hundreds of millions of pounds, I was still under the impression that someone was going to walk in and show me the door.

'... the same final checks – weather, take-off speed, nozzle angle ...' Jak continued, as I nodded away.

The bedfellow of my vulnerability on this score was my nervousness about flying, and about flying the Harrier in particular. Although I had been an aviator for five years and had progressed through six types of plane, I had never lost the nagging feeling, each time I climbed into the cockpit, that I did not have what it took to do the job.

That anxiety was never more acute than in the Harrier. When you've slammed to full power and lowered the nozzles, so that all the thrust is hitting the ground, you are incredibly exposed, sitting just a few feet away. The power is overwhelming and there are so many forces, noises and jolts in play. In the back of your mind, you know that if something goes wrong, you will not be able to control it – up there, in that exposed tiny cockpit, you are there for the ride, whatever happens next.

The briefing was over and Jak and I checked in with Scrabble, who was the duty officer for the day, and told him what we were about to do.

'All looks good, Nath,' he said. 'Your jet is on the flight line, ready to go, serviceable. Just so you know, it has got a little more fuel on board than you need for the sortie, so you may want to do a couple of circuits first to burn it off.'

'Roger that,' I said as Jak and I headed off to grab our flying gear. I pulled on my G-pants, over my flying suit. Tightly fitting trousers, they have inflatable bladders that press on your legs and abdomen during periods of high G-force to help prevent loss of blood to the brain and black-outs. Next came my kneeboard, with my flight instructions for the sortie, then my life jacket, oxygen mask, helmet and finally my gloves.

'You go and do your walk-around while I sign for the jet with the engineers,' Jak told me. He was the instructor on the flight as well as the official aircraft captain.

Our all-black two-seater T8 training Harrier had 'Royal Navy' picked out in large white capital letters at the base of its tail. Every time I approached this remarkable feat of British engineering, I felt enormous pride and a sense of privilege. I have no doubt that I had a big smile on my face that fateful day as I greeted the ground crew, who welcomed me with a respectful 'Morning, sir.'

After a quick tour of the airframe, checking the engine intakes, nozzles, flaps, wheels and undercarriage, and anything else that caught my eye, I climbed the ladder into the cockpit and took advantage of the delay to start my pre-flight checks and settle in. It was easier doing this without the pressure of hearing Jak breathing in my ear over the internal comms system. With friends from one end of the base to the other, he loved chatting to the engineers, so I knew I had plenty of time.

Eventually he appeared and I could see him doing his own walk-around before climbing the ladder into the rear cockpit and strapping himself into his Martin-Baker Mk9 ejection seat.

'Hey,' I said. 'You up?'

'Yeah, I'm up.'

We formally checked our internal radio. 'You're loud and clear,' I said and he repeated it in turn.

Then I heard him sucking on his oxygen supply.

'My oxygen is good,' I told him.

'Yeah, oxygen is good,' Jak replied.

'OK, ready for canopy?'

On his assent, we took the locks out and closed the big Perspex cover that operates like a giant clam shell on the two-seater Harrier. The next step was to make our seats and the canopy itself – which incorporated an explosive jagged black line that shatters on ignition – live. We pulled out our pins to arm the system and popped them in the holders on the glareshield of the cockpit where the ground crew could see them.

Our seats that day incorporated a 'zero-zero' ejection system. At ground level, and with the jet at a standstill, wings level, you could still expect to be fired high enough into the air for your main parachute to open and give you a good chance of coming back down to earth without incurring massive injury. Other models might be capable of achieving that sort of result at ground level only if the plane had reached 60 knots, or 100 knots at 1,000ft, and so on.

Martin-Baker had developed a special seat for the Harrier, to deal with the unique possibility of an engine failure in hover mode, when a pilot would be forced to eject as the plane was plummeting to the ground. Tests had shown that pre-existing seats did not have enough juice to overcome the forces driving the pilot downwards. They solved that by adding more rockets and more explosive. So Jak and I knew that, if we ever needed it, we would be leaving our Harrier at a hell of a rate of knots, with an estimated 50Gs of acceleration force.

I plunged the engine start switch and the Pegasus power plant came to life. It grew in strength, whining, spooling and growling in the way that only a Harrier can. We moved out to the long taxiway, just ahead of Scranners in his T10, who was due to take off after us. I completed my final checks before running through the in-cockpit emergencies brief with Jak. We both knew we were sitting on independent ejection systems and that we would each have to pull our own handle. At that point it would be, as we termed it in the brief, 'every man for himself'.

After receiving clearance from the tower, I lined the jet up on the centreline, filling the engine fuel galleries with three quick slams of the throttle from idle to full power. I held the aircraft with my foot pedal brakes and checked the nozzles were functioning correctly by deflecting them down momentarily before resetting them. After a final check that our seats were live, that the take-off run was clear and that the orange windsock on the edge of the runway was still doing what I expected, I went for one last check with Jak.

'Happy?' I asked.

'Happy.'

We were good to go.

Then I slammed the throttle ...

3

Tumbling towards the ground like a rag doll, with the cold air piercing my skin, I walked the threshold.

Then comes a massive tug from my shoulders. My seat separating in mid-air maybe, then my canopy opening above me, though I can't be sure.

The moment I feel that wrenching force, my eyesight returns, and for a split second I see the ground coming up to hit me. On reflex, my training kicks in and I try to pull my legs together to execute some sort of parachute roll. But I'm heading sideways and it's too late anyway.

Underneath me, and still attached, is a big yellow pack that you would normally kick away after an ejection at altitude. Inside it was my life-saving stuff – life raft, axe, fishing rod and all sorts of other irrelevant gear in this situation. I'm stuck with it and, despite my best endeavours to execute some kind of roll, I land in a massive heap.

The local farmer at Wittering, bless him, has recently ploughed his field and it has been raining. Having been speared over the top of the 10ft wire fence guarding the perimeter of the airfield, I come to a juddering halt in a small trough between ridges of soft brown mud.

Momentarily stunned, I lie there for a few seconds, feel

something tugging me and begin to realise it's a parachute. Again my training takes over. I instinctively go for my life jacket activation ring. 'That's what you are supposed to do when you eject, otherwise you're going to drown,' I tell myself. When it's inflated, what little movement I have is restricted even further as I lie pinned to the ground in land-locked Cambridgeshire.

What has just happened is beginning to dawn on me – I have left my fighter jet in the fastest and most violent way imaginable, save for being shot down in mid-air.

Could I feel my extremities?

Yes.

Can I see any injuries that would stop me from moving?

No.

I manage to deflate the life jacket and start slowly moving my legs and arms. My head is still encased in my flying helmet with my oxygen mask clamped to my face. I try to sit up, but fail. All the equipment I'm attached to makes sure of that.

I take off my life jacket and then find the Martin-Baker quick-release connector on my waist and twist it to jettison the survival box and the parachute. At last I can push myself up into a sitting position. My seat lies a few feet away. In the distance, on the other side of the perimeter fence, I can see an inverted Royal Navy Sea Harrier, engulfed in flames. There is no noise – it's like a dream when the only things you hear are your own breathing and the ringing in your ears.

I take off my helmet and mask and get to my feet and watch the plane burn. I'm on my own here, I think, but where's my instructor? Where the hell's Jak? Where is he? Jak?

I can see the edge of a wood not far away. Having seen where the plane is lying, I'm expecting to find Jak there. I imagine he recognised the unrecoverable situation a long time before me and had ejected earlier in the take-off sequence. Perhaps he's going to saunter casually out of the trees, laughing and joking and saying: 'Wow, that was some ride, eh, Nath?' Or cracking jokes about fighter pilot reaction times. Or maybe there will be more of the kind of accusatory questions that haunt me: 'What on earth did you do that for?'

I stand there waiting for him with blood trickling down my face from damage to my head and neck that I am barely aware of. Then I start shouting his name. 'Jak! ... Jak? ... *Jak!*'

I keep doing it, certain that he'll hear me and, as I do so, I start walking towards the perimeter fence, for the first time feeling excruciating pain midway down my back. As I draw closer, I see something lying on the ground near the base of the windsock, on the far side of it.

My eyes are stinging with sweat and blood, but after another couple of paces I can see that it's an ejection seat. But how? How can there be two ejection seats and only me here?

As I get ever closer to the fence, I start to pick out more detail. The seat is facing away from me and towards the ground, with its drogue parachute still attached. But there's no sign of the main canopy. And then I see a hand sticking out. It's lost its glove and is as white as porcelain. The thought registers that it's Jak's hand, that he's there, slumped in his seat, not many feet away but beyond my reach.

I start shouting again ... shouting and shouting for Jak to acknowledge me. It feels like time has stopped and that this finely choreographed moment on the stage of my life will go on forever.

It was then that I started to hear sirens, and could see the Transit van we called the 'Popemobile' racing across the grass. The crudely adapted vehicle with a Perspex dome was normally used by the instructors to monitor Harriers landing at precise points marked out on the taxiways. I had never seen it move at speed and it looked like whoever was driving it was going to break its axles before getting to me.

Even though I was behind the fence, I raised my arm to warn the driver to slow down as it approached and not crash into Jak's seat. When he jumped out alongside it, I immediately recognised my good friend Scrabble. When the crash alarm went off, he had ignored protocol, leaped into the van and – without contacting air traffic control – had tanked it more than a mile across the air base in a beeline to where I was standing.

Because he had come in from a different angle, he could now see what I could not. He looked down at Jak for a second or two and the expression on his face when he glanced back at me will be seared on my memory forever. At that moment I knew that Jak must be severely injured at the very least, but I hadn't given up all hope.

Scrabble then ran over to me.

'Mate, are you OK?' he asked breathlessly, through the fence. By the time he had climbed it and jumped down onto my side, he was in full first-aid mode.

'Mate, don't move, we need to protect your back,' he said. 'Stay where you are – in fact, you need to lie down.'

'What's happened to Jak?' I mumbled. 'I don't know what's happened to him . . .'

'Don't think about that right now. You're OK. Sit down – that's it. Now ease back. Everyone's going to be here in a minute – and then we'll get you sorted.'

He paced up and down alongside me, agitated and impatient, as a fire engine followed by an ambulance made their way towards us. The firemen asked me to walk round to a gateway some distance away, but Scrabble would have none of it. He ordered them to cut through the fence right there. Then the doctor arrived and triggered the protocol of putting me onto a spinal board and a stretcher.

'Hang on, wait,' I told the doctor as I was being strapped down. 'You check on Jak first; check on him and tell me if he's OK.'

I saw him go and crouch down and reach underneath Jak's seat. I could tell by his body language that this was not good. There was no urgency, and when he stood up he was covered in blood. He looked at me, shaking his head, and slowly and silently mouthed the word 'No'.

At that moment any hopes I had that Jak might still be alive were extinguished and I knew too that nothing in my life would ever be the same.

While they were preparing me for medevac by rescue helicopter, cutting my clothes off and taking all my things, I remembered my parents back home in Stoke-on-Trent. I knew this was going to hit the news, and that the Ministry of Defence might be slow to get their act together, and I wanted someone to let them know I was alright.

'Hey, hey,' I called to one of the other pilots who had rushed to the scene. 'My phone is in my jacket on the Ops Room desk, please use it to dial my parents and tell them I'm OK.'

'Sure, buddy,' he said. 'Consider it done,' and I felt that weight lift from my shoulders.

I lay there for a while waiting to be loaded up, trying to think everything through. Was it my fault that my plane was now a burning wreck and my instructor had lost his life? Did *I* do something wrong? Had *I* been found out in the worst way imaginable before my career as a fighter pilot had even started? I kept running through what had happened, trying to understand what I could have done that caused the engine to cut out and the plane to flip, but I had no answers.

When you eject from a fighter jet there are strict medical protocols, and once I got to the A&E department at the Queen's Medical Centre in Nottingham, I was subjected to a barrage of tests; every bone and sinew in my body was examined. I eventually started to feel sorry for the doctors and nurses because they knew, and I knew, that most of it was unnecessary.

But it was during those first few hours, as the adrenaline started to ebb away, that I finally let myself go – when the tears flowed, releasing the tension that had built up in my subconscious as images of the crash and its tragic aftermath flashed through my mind. You might think this would have happened in response to a gesture of concern by a nurse or doctor, but the trigger was being loaded into the narrow confines of a full-body MRI scanner.

As I lay in that sterile, narrow, grey tube, unable to escape its incessant tapping and beeping, it seemed to transport me back to the cockpit, and I went into free fall. Suddenly I was still flying, then landing, then ejecting – why had I done that? The ground was coming for me. I had to get out when I did, didn't I? Where was Jak? Did he go before me or after me? Am I in hospital? Or am I still walking the threshold between life and death in that grey half-world between the cockpit and the ground?

By the time they slid me out I was in a real state, and it took me a while to find my bearings again and remind myself that this was the here and now; the accident was over, I had survived it and I was in hospital.

The worst part in A&E was the work on my eyes. As I blasted through the canopy, I was splattered on my right side – on my face and upper back – by lead from the minia-ture detonation cord built into the Harrier's windscreen. This turns molten within a thousandth of a second of the ejection handle being pulled. Because the plane was rolling to one side, I got covered in it as I smashed through. It had left me with superficial burns on my face and neck and lead in my eyes.

With my head strapped tightly in place and my eyes bathed in iodine, the doctor told me to stare straight ahead and not to blink and then started picking out the fragments. I saw the syringe coming right in and all the while I was fighting the urge to shut my eyes. Twenty years later I still have lead embedded in my arms, back and all over my face. And every time I undergo a dental x-ray, I get asked whether I have ever been blasted in the head by a shotgun.

But the most serious injury was to my back. The force of the ejection, and the fact that I hadn't been able to assume the correct posture before pulling the handle, had shattered a bone in my spine where it joins the ribcage, with hundreds of hairline fractures. I still thank my lucky stars that my spinal cord was not affected and the bone eventually repaired itself, stronger than it was before.

When the tests were finally over, I was wheeled into the spinal unit's intensive care ward, a six-bed room bristling with high-tech machinery, where I was to spend the next two days. It was a surreal experience because I felt I didn't deserve to be there and the people in the beds around me made me realise how lucky I was. A young guy to my right, with burns and spinal injuries from a car crash, was completely wrapped in bandages. All I could see of him were his bloodshot, frightened eyes.

Opposite was an 18-year-old who looked OK from a distance, but had lost the use of his legs permanently. Sitting right in his eyeline, I watched him break the news to his girlfriend and then to his parents, and saw them try to work through it with him. And this was just the daytime stuff. At night that ward was one of the saddest places I have ever experienced.

On that first day, my parents and brother jumped in the car as soon as they'd been told about the accident. My dad and brother had not told my mum the full extent of what had happened, but said that I had been involved in a mishap at the airfield and that I was going to be fine. Unable to contact me, they were anxious to find out the nature of my injuries for themselves. On the way, they turned on the radio to see if there was anything about it on the news.

When she heard the headlines, my mum hit the roof. 'A

Harrier fighter jet has crashed at RAF Wittering in Cambridgeshire, killing both pilots . . .' Naturally, she thought they had been trying to shield her from the reality of what had happened that morning. They too were in a state of shock, wondering if the powers that be had decided to save the bad news until they got to the hospital. After some frantic phone calls, my dad tracked down a Ministry of Defence family liaison officer who reassured him that I was still very much alive and being treated for my injuries.

One of the hardest parts of those first few hours in hospital was the nagging anxiety about my role in what had happened on that taxiway. I was desperate for an explanation. Had we been hit by a bird strike? Or had I done something really stupid that undid the plane? Had there been some kind of technical failure? I still had no idea, and the not knowing was gnawing away at me.

Gary Langrish had driven straight to the hospital after spending a few hours with his father. We both knew that he had dodged a bullet that day, as the one who was supposed to have been in the back seat. 'Gazza', as he was inevitably known to all of us, was in overall charge of flying training at Yeovilton, and he was one of the best – a softly spoken, gentle, wonderful bloke who after he left the Navy emigrated to New Zealand, where he spends much of his time on his boat.

'Hey, Nath, how are you feeling?'

'Hey, Gazza, I'm OK, I'm OK. Good to see you, mate,' I said.

There was pause as he drew up a chair alongside my bed.

I knew it didn't take a genius to spot that I was far from

OK. 'I just can't believe what happened,' I whispered. 'Jak . . . and on my watch. I feel so guilty . . .'

He took a deep breath.

'Look, Nath, we already know quite a bit about this, and you've got nothing to feel guilty about. There were fan blade fragments all down the runway, leading up to where the plane came to rest. It looks like a blade broke off for some reason and then destroyed the engine which catastrophically exploded. There was nothing you could have done.'

'Yeah, but I was at the controls . . .'

'There really was nothing you could have done. Pilots can't make blades separate from a Rolls-Royce engine. This is *not* on you.'

I turned away to let this sink in. What he was saying made sense, of course, but it didn't explain why the Harrier had flipped over. We both knew that if it had simply pancaked back onto the ground, Jak and I would have ejected safely. But I did feel some relief, because for the first time I was getting an explanation I could rely on. Maybe this wasn't actually my fault after all . . .

That night, as I lay in the ward listening to my neighbour moaning as he tried to adjust his body position, I saw my hospital phone blinking in the dark. Military tradition has it that when someone dies on duty, there's a massive piss-up to celebrate their life and career. Back at Wittering, everyone from the Royal Navy and the RAF Harrier fraternity – pilots, former pilots, officers of all ranks, ground crew, the lot – had turned up to honour Jak, and the booze was flowing freely, as he would have wanted.

I started to get messages from my Harrier pilot mates, then

station commanders, even air chief marshals and admirals, all telling me how great Jak was – which made me feel even worse – and thanking God that I was OK. To start with, the voices were serious and coherent; by the end of the evening, I could barely make out their slurred words against the barroom cacophony. As I lay there mulling over what Gazza had told me, it felt like I was listening to voices from another planet.

The following morning my lieutenant commander – my senior pilot – called. It made me quickly realise that, as far as the Royal Navy was concerned, it was business as usual, whether I had just ejected from a fighter jet or not.

'Hello, Nath.' His tone was clipped – the kind that some officers use to underline how busy and how important they are. 'Hope you're well.'

'Yeah, thank you,' I replied slowly. 'I'm in –'

'Just so you know, the accident investigation board has convened, and they want to get cracking tomorrow.'

'Oh, OK –'

'So I need you to get in a car and drive back to Wittering so they can meet you and do a preliminary interview.'

'I . . . I'm sorry . . .' I stammered. 'What are you saying?'

'Yeah, that's it – get yourself to Wittering, if you can, please.'

He was in full military mode, but rank and hierarchy couldn't have been further down my list of priorities. I'd already turned down a visit from the secretary of state for defence during my initial admission. And, in any case, I couldn't quite believe what I was hearing.

'Can't they come and see me here in the hospital? I'm

still in the ICU, and I'm not sure the doctors will allow me to travel.'

'No, no, *no* – there's a captain on the board, and I simply cannot ask a captain to go and see a lieutenant. That's not how it works.'

That was it, as far as I was concerned. I had never knowingly been insubordinate in my entire time in the Royal Navy, but everyone has a breaking point, and this was mine.

'Well,' I said, 'you can tell the captain from me to ram it. I'm not going anywhere to see them. If they want to see me, they know where to find me.'

I got the impression from the stunned silence that followed that my message had well and truly hit the mark. Within a few hours I had them at my bedside, and later the admiral of the Fleet Air Arm, and a few other military bigwigs, all eager to talk to me.

Later that day some of my best mates, Scrabble and Scranners among them, turned up to offer a bit of morale-boosting good cheer. They were under strict instructions from the nurses not to bring in any alcohol, and promised to be on their best behaviour.

Also with them was another pilot we all knew as 'Tinsel'. Always smiling, mischievous and full of energy, he was holding a bottle of something that looked like blackcurrant. He politely and earnestly asked the nurse whether it was alright for me to have it. Ribena, after all, is the perfect thing for hospital visits.

Yes, it was fine, she told him with a knowing look.

Then the others produced their own little bottles of the same health-giving elixir, and stashed them away on the nightstand next to my bed. I joined in the banter: 'Thanks, lads, but where are my flowers and grapes?'

Long after they had disappeared I thought, 'You know what, I could use some of that "Ribena" after all.' And I wasn't wrong. Bright-red rum, red port, red whisky, you name it, just what I needed. 'Good lads, good lads,' I thought to myself, as I let the alcohol do its work.

Jak's funeral was held five days after I got out of hospital. There was a huge turnout on an overcast day, with mourners filling the lovely medieval Fleet Air Arm Church of St Bartholomew at Yeovilton, and spilling over into the churchyard. Just about anyone and everyone from the Royal Navy was there, and even the toughest and strongest fighter pilots I know were in tears when his coffin was brought in. That was when I first got sight of Jak's partner, Maria, and their six-year-old daughter, Jill. I knew I would have to meet them at some point and I had no idea what we might say to each other.

I didn't want to be at the front of the congregation – I felt it wasn't my place – so I stood with those at the back, thinking about a man whom I did not know well, whom fate had determined I would be with in his final minutes. It was a strange experience to be around so many people who knew Jak far better than I did, and knowing that they were aware that I was the student pilot who had escaped without serious injury from the crash that had killed him.

Commander Tim Eastaugh, the Sea Harrier senior officer at Yeovilton, gave the eulogy for a fighter pilot he had known for years. He described Jak as a legend. 'He was a character,' he told us, 'who was larger than life, and extremely humorous, but also totally unselfish. He was always the last to leave and totally dependable. With Jak, aviation was a way of life, he wouldn't have felt complete without it.'

Jak was buried with full military honours in the immaculate churchyard, where many other aviators lie, and we each stepped up to the graveside to salute him. When it was my turn, I stood to attention and, after saluting, stayed for a while, not saying a prayer but silently talking to him. Time stood still. I said I was sure that he would have some words of guidance for me . . . and then my mind blanked out, overwhelmed by the force of emotions swirling beneath the surface. I turned on my heel and stepped back.

At the wake in the wardroom at Yeovilton, I met Maria and Jill and Maria's mum, also called Jill. They could not have been warmer and more sympathetic as I shared my feelings of guilt and responsibility for Jak's death.

'There was nothing you could have done, and you have absolutely nothing to feel bad about,' Maria told me. 'If, given the choice of the two of you, Jak would have wanted you to survive, so we're just grateful that you're alright.'

Honestly, you couldn't have asked for more understanding from a family coping with the shock of sudden bereavement.

Later that afternoon, something happened that I will never forget. Jak's daughter had been running around at the wake, diving in and out of groups of people and generally letting off steam. When I got to the wood and glass-panelled door on my way from the bar to the toilet, Jill was in the corridor, holding the handle shut, as small children love to do.

And that's how it was when time froze. Both of us were holding on to the door and we were staring into each other's eyes through the glass while, behind me, the wardroom came to a standstill. Jill had the fighter pilot stare, just like her father, and it was as though she was telling me I had shut a door on a part of her life. The feeling was unbearable as I looked at her and felt all those eyes on me from behind. Eventually my agony came to an end when Jill let go and pushed the door open.

I said thank you to her on the way through, as she ran off into the bar.

4

I won't lie. I haven't found it easy to get over the accident. It invades my subconscious most days, even now, two decades later. Despite knowing conclusively that it was not my fault, survivor guilt still plays its tricks. And I never forget Jak, someone I have got to know better in death than I had the chance to in life.

In the weeks following his funeral, I didn't discuss the crash much with people outside my own family. Some of my flying colleagues who were there that day, or saw it from a distance, seemed to struggle to know what to say to me. Perhaps they were battling with their own demons.

The events of that early December day reminded most of us that what we were doing was some of the highest-risk – and potentially lethal – stuff possible in the service of our country. We liked to convince ourselves that it would never happen to us, that our training and the protocols and safety equipment would get us off the hook. But when something like this happens, you get exposed for what you are – not an invincible fighter pilot so much as a fragile, flimsy human body. That's all you are – you are not a superhuman Top Gun after all.

Though, that wasn't the case with everyone I came across in those first few weeks leading up to Christmas in 2002.

Testosterone-fuelled fighter pilots live in a rarefied world – many of them think they are the best, and believe they can cope with just about anything. They are also used to speaking their minds, whatever the consequences.

Having been out of circulation for a couple of weeks, recovering from my injuries, I accepted an invitation to a seasonal gathering at my old Hawk training base, RAF Valley on Anglesey. It was important, I felt, to get out and see some friends and try to put the accident – at least momentarily – behind me. I found myself talking to a slightly worse-for-wear ex-Harrier pilot who had previously instructed me on the Hawk.

'D'you know something?' he said, as we stood, pints in hand in the packed officers' mess bar. 'When I heard about the accident, and that there was one unnamed fatality, and I knew it was you and Jak who were flying that day ...'

'Go on,' I said cautiously.

'Well, I knew Jak better than I know you, so, to be quite honest, I wished it was you who had died and not Jak.'

I must have looked stunned, because then he said: 'You get that, don't you?'

'Oh ... oh, OK, yes ... yes, I do. Um, I suppose so,' I managed to say, trying to sound both completely unfazed and not totally offended.

I wasn't sure what else I could say. I remember thinking: 'Some days we all have thought bubbles above our heads about things that are best left unsaid.' I understood where he was coming from, but I still couldn't quite believe that he was prepared to stand there and say it to my face. I guess everyone deals with grief in their own way.

But the accident did something else that proved positive and helped me throughout the rest of my career in the Navy. It changed my frame of reference about good decisions and bad ones, good days and bad, and acceptable levels of risk in situations of danger. I had experienced one of the worst things that could happen in the cockpit of a fighter jet, so almost anything else seemed manageable. The polar extremes had been reset – my definition of where the boundaries lay had been expanded, as had my tolerance of imminent threat. This would prove useful in combat in Afghanistan; it did not make me a more reckless flyer, but one with a little bit more time when under pressure.

Anyone who ejects – who becomes an 'ejectee' – is routinely grounded for three months, so there was no return to the cockpit for me until March, whether I wanted to or not. During those weeks I made two appearances before the official accident investigation board who interrogated me in fine detail about everything I had done and not done during that disastrous attempted take-off.

Gradually they established a full narrative of what had happened to my Sea Harrier, which fitted broadly with what Gazza had told me at the hospital.

It was well known in those days that the Rolls-Royce Pegasus engine had something of an Achilles heel. Its two large air intakes sit just behind the cockpit. The outer rotor blades that you see – the largest in a turbo-fan engine that features several sets of progressively smaller blades inside – were vulnerable to any damage at their base, an area known as the 'z-zone'. If anything hit them and caused damage at that point, they were liable to break off. The design also incorporated a titanium cage around the blades, so that if one did fracture it would not fly out and puncture the fuel tanks.

As we were taking off, and developing huge forward momentum, our jet picked up something from the runway – perhaps a small stone or a piece of other debris. This was then sucked into the air intake, chipping one of the big blades in the 'z-zone'. The blade broke off and was ingested into the engine, where it smashed its way through the other blades inside, many of which ended up being spewed out, in pieces, on the runway. At the instant when I was demanding most power from the engine – when it was rotating at its fastest – the damage was devastating, as the power shut down completely and the ruptured fuel tanks exploded.

However, what made the accident so uniquely dangerous was something less foreseeable. When the broken blade parted company at high speed from its root, it bent the titanium retaining ring by an inch or two, as the ring absorbed the force of the impact. This, in turn, dislodged a small air-conditioning unit underneath the control rod for the ailerons, the movement of which, on the trailing edge of each wing, determined the aircraft's roll rate and angle of bank.

With the air-con unit pushed up a couple of inches, the rod was now distorted and jammed in position at one end of its range. The effect of this was to put us into a hard and rapidly accelerating right-hand roll which, unchecked, made the Harrier flip upside down. Of course, I could not have known any of this when I applied full left stick to try and correct the roll in my futile attempt to keep the wings level.

The engine had failed catastrophically and was producing no thrust and the plane was already engulfed in flames before it hit the ground. This was something that Scranners confirmed to the tower as he watched the crash from the cockpit of his own Harrier. It then skidded about 100 metres after it landed on its back before coming to rest on the grass, with its undercarriage pointing skywards, where it was engulfed in a series of explosions.

Detailed analysis of my ejection and of Jak's, together with data collected from the plane's black-box flight recorder, established that I left the cockpit at an altitude of around 50ft, when the wings were a few degrees short of being at a perfect right angle to the ground. This gave me just enough leeway to establish a positive trajectory and for my main chute to open. Jak, on the other hand, almost certainly ejected a few thousandths of a second later – something I have thought about a lot.

With greater experience than I had, he may have paused, momentarily considering whether we had any other options before he pulled his handle. Either that or he pulled at the same time as I did, but the sequencing of the ejection initiation caused a fractional delay. In the event, he exited the canopy when the wings were past being at right angles to the runway – probably at 91 or 92 degrees. The critical difference between us gave him irreversible momentum straight into the ground, with no time for his seat to separate or his main chute to deploy.

The hardest part of the accident to envisage is not the destruction of the engine and the rapid loss of altitude, so much as the Harrier's violent deceleration and the fast roll rate. These extremely disorientating forces combined to convince me that I was already upside down, when in fact I wasn't and was still at right angles to the grass. And it was the roll rate and bank angle that sadly proved fatal to Jak.

I was lucky in so many ways. I didn't hit the wire perimeter fence of the airfield while being propelled over it, or any trees in the nearby wood. I would have been unlikely to have survived the impact with either. I did not land on a hard surface but on soft plough. But perhaps the biggest stroke of good fortune was what happened to my main chute.

Parachutes with canopies without vents, of the type our seats were fitted with, tended to fill out completely for a second or two – so-called shock-loading – and then collapse as the initial pressure in them became overwhelming. Then they would gather themselves and set again. In my case, my main chute had just enough time to shock-load, but not to collapse, because by that time I had already hit the ground. In effect, I had ejected at a low enough height for my weight to be momentarily taken by the chute, even though my trajectory was broadly sideways. If I had ejected at, say, 100ft, my chute would have collapsed on me and I may well have hit the ground so hard it would have been fatal.

One of the many remarkable aspects of this whole affair was the accident investigation board's conclusion. There was the official version and the real one, as I discovered when a member of the board called me the night before the report was published.

He said I was completely exonerated.

'But, we think it is important you know,' he continued, 'that, from our point of view, we believe the accident was not survivable. No one could have got out of that plane alive.'

'But I did,' I replied.

'Exactly,' he went on. 'In the military, as I'm sure you are well aware, Nath, we work on fact, not hypothesis or abstract theory. The facts say you survived, so we can't officially say this accident was unsurvivable, because clearly it wasn't.'

'Hmm, sounds like you've got a bit of a problem then . . .'

'Well, we've found a way round it. Instead of saying "unsurvivable", we have had to write the words "barely survivable" into our report, to take into account what actually happened. But, to be honest, the word "barely" in this context is about as far-fetched as it ever could be when you see it in print.'

Many months later I paid a visit to the Martin-Baker company on the outskirts of London, where I met the men and women who had designed and built the seat that had saved me. They too had looked in great detail at my ejection and come to the same conclusion. This should have been a fatal event for me, as it was for Jak.

They ran all sorts of iterations of my ejection, altering the key parameters to try and produce a positive outcome. They changed the precise timing of the rockets firing, the windspeed, altitude, angle of bank and so on. But to no avail. Each model ended with a flat line on their monitors, and the single word 'FAIL'. In each case they could not achieve a successful opening of my main parachute. 'There is no way you should have survived it – our sequence says that is impossible,' I was told yet again.

I was unbelievably lucky to be alive. I only had to think about Jak to know that. But that day at Martin-Baker was when it really hit me. Although I'd heard it from the board, here were the people who knew every last detail about the

seat I had used, and they were telling me that in my particular circumstances, it was useless. Mulling it over, as I drove
home, I couldn't help thinking I was getting a second chance
that I had no right to. How could I possibly turn away from
that? But equally, had I not been given the ultimate warning,
the ultimate let-off, and should I not heed that and think of
doing something else?

Early in the new year, Tim Eastaugh called me into his office
at Yeovilton. My three months' grounding would expire in
early March, when the principal medical officer at the base
would have to decide whether to sign me off as fit to resume
'bang-seat' flying, and he wanted to know what was on my
mind.

He closed the door and we sat down on either side of his
desk. He noted that I looked to have made a good recovery,
physically at least, then asked me how I was. I told him I
was on the mend.

'Look, it's completely understandable if you don't want to
come back to flying,' he said. 'It was an awful thing that happened and it may well be a watershed for you. I understand
that. And I understand too that you may not want to come
back to fly the Harrier. In that case we can look at placing
you as an instructor somewhere. And then again, every job
in the Navy is open to you too, if you don't want to fly.'

He paused.

'So where d'you think you will be at the three-month
point, Nath? What is it that you want to do?'

I didn't hesitate.

'I want to be here, doing this, flying the Sea Harrier,' I said with as much conviction as I could muster. 'That has been my dream all the way through, and I still haven't achieved it yet. There is no way I can turn away from it now.'

I was thinking to myself, if I give up, what would Jak think? What would have been the point of Jak and me being in the Harrier on that fateful day? He died training me to be a Harrier pilot, and I must complete that process. What more motivation do I need? His sacrifice can't be for nothing.

Looking back, I think I was still in shock to some extent, and found it hard to think of changing course. I see myself then as like a man running and stumbling towards a target, and when someone shoots his arm off, he keeps on running. Then someone shoots his leg off and he starts crawling. In other words, nothing was going to change my destination in life. The momentum and drive were still there to prove to myself that I could join the elite – the cadre of fighting-capable, single-seat-jet pilots at the controls of a Harrier, the most bewitching plane in Britain's air armoury.

I have always stuck to the philosophy of never turning down an opportunity if I think I might regret it. But there was something else in play: I wasn't mature enough to even consider changing direction. I had spent the last five years building up to this life-defining achievement, and I didn't have the guts to walk away.

There are people who love to criticise those who quit and decide to do something different, but some of the 'quitters' I've seen in the military are the bravest people I've met. People who fire a weapon for the first time and say, 'No – that's a path I do not want to be on,' and then leave and find a new course in life. It takes bravery to say, 'This is not for me' and face your own frailty and possibly regret.

I carried on. But thankfully it became the right decision, because once I had been through those early, dark times, I quickly discovered more focus, more passion, more dedication to my vocation than ever before.

A former fighter pilot with a tough outer shell, but with caring and compassionate qualities beneath the surface, Eastaugh took me under his wing from then on. He knew the Navy was keen to post me away from Yeovilton during my rehabilitation, to jobs that had no relevance to flying. There was talk of me doing a course to learn how to become a divisional officer, or to go and work at Navy Command at Portsmouth, but the man we all knew by his nickname – 'Stiggins' – wanted me to stay right there in the heart of the Harrier world. So he found me a temporary job in his office and I spent a couple of months working on the squadron's forward-planning programme, helping to organise student pilot training and instructor postings.

As the appointment with the medical officer drew closer, Gazza got back in touch. He was still in charge of training and wanted to look after my reintroduction to flying in person. He called me one evening at my home, a little stone cottage in a village near Yeovilton.

'Hey, mate, I hear you are coming back to us, which is great news.'

'Yep,' I said. 'That's the plan.'

'Well, maybe we should have a chat about what it is you think you need to do to get back to where you were. Do we need to start the course again at Wittering? Do we need to do an introductory flight with you in the back seat, so you can get your bearings? What d'you reckon?'

'I'll tell you what I'm thinking,' I said. 'I feel like I need to break through that moment of the accident. I need to get past that point, and it seems to me you can either have a long lead-in to get to that stage, or you can just smash it and get straight into it. What I'd really like is to do exactly the same flight again.'

I paused to let it sink in, for me as much as for Gazza.

'I want to replicate that flight, but this time hopefully with a different outcome. I want that to be my first flight back.'

'I get that, Nath. But in what capacity? You can sit in the back, where you will not have to worry about all the switches and starting the jet and all that nonsense, and you can just sit back and enjoy the ride and see how you feel.'

'No. No chance. I want to fly it from the front, Gazza. Being in the back seat is the worst place for me right now.'

Although we both knew he should have been the one in the rear seat on the day I lost the aircraft, Gazza had no hesitation in volunteering for the position once again.

'I'm doing that flight with you,' he said firmly. 'I'm flying that flight with you.'

What I was proposing for my reintroduction was not really within the spirit of the rules for returning ejectees, but Gazza got the plan approved and came back to me within 24 hours.

'Right,' he said, 'it will be me and you. I'll be in the back, you'll be in the front. We'll start up on the flight line in exactly the same place as you started last time, and we'll take off from exactly the same spot on the taxiway.'

'Cheers, Gazza, thanks, mate,' I said, thinking how lucky

I was to have such an understanding and accommodating instructor. 'Thanks, mate.'

'You will start the jet,' he continued. 'You will do all the checks, you will do everything as if we're stepping back in time. We won't necessarily do the whole sortie, because that's not important. This will be an exposure for you, but you'll take off and we'll then go and fly around for a bit. It's all against protocol, but if that's what you want to do, then that's what we'll do.'

I didn't want to fly into Wittering from Somerset. I wanted to fly *from* Wittering, as I was trying to do three months earlier, and Gazza understood that too. So he flew a two-seater T8 up from Yeovilton while I drove.

This was a big ask for the Navy because they were effectively putting a jet at my disposal, rather than having me jump to their tune and do the flight where a jet was already waiting, or as part of an existing aircraft movements plan. I was being indulged, but I guess they could see that losing a pilot at my relatively advanced stage of training would be a disappointing outcome following Jak's loss.

When I got to Wittering on the night of 12 March 2003, the staff in the mess were waiting for me. They had assigned to me the same room, at the end of that long set of corridors. I had asked them for it, because I wanted to dispel any hint of giving in to superstition; at all points, my strategy was 'Confront this thing head-on. Draw a line under it so you can move forward.'

That night I lay on my single bed, complete with its crappy springs, waterproof mattress and itchy sheets, in my tiny room with its little sink – the officer's privilege that we used to call the 'night-heads', Navy slang for toilet. I barely slept a wink as I ran through everything that had happened since the last time I was there. Someone had told me that I must have angels on my shoulder to have walked away from the accident; I needed them now more than ever.

'You're a fool,' said a voice in my head. 'You're giving the Grim Reaper a second chance to get you.' And, in a way, that is exactly what I was doing. I was saying: 'You know what, here's your chance. Take it now, because I'm not giving you another opportunity.' That didn't turn out to be strictly true, but it was how I'd move on, how I planned to stop it plaguing me every time I took to the air.

The following morning was uncannily similar to the day of the accident. Another pristine, cloudless sky, with Wittering bathed in winter sunshine.

Gazza greeted me at breakfast with a simple question that we both knew plumbed huge depths.

'You alright today, mate?'

He looked me straight in the eye.

'Yes, mate,' I said, looking straight back.

And from that moment on, nothing more was said. This could have been any other standard training mission. There was no emotion and no extra chat. We both knew the wind direction was coming from the opposite side of the airfield to where it had been three months before. We both knew it did not support taking off on the taxiway to the west. But we did it anyway.

I went through my pre-take-off checks, including the full emergencies brief, running through all the possible circumstances in which we might use our ejection seats. When I'd finished and we were ready to go, I paused for a second, looking ahead through the windscreen, framed by the jagged lead detonation line. Then at the taxiway stretching in front of me, and on to the orange windsock in the distance, where Jak had ended up. I thought to myself: 'This is it; this is where you take me or you forever hold your peace.'

I slammed the throttle and held my breath. And I carried on holding it as we reached take-off, as I nozzled out, brought the landing gear and the flaps up – waiting all the while for the Reaper to come and grab me ...

But there was nothing ...

And nothing ...

And still nothing.

We hit 300 knots, then 350, and I started pulling up to 6,000ft. For the first time in about 40 seconds, I started breathing again.

'Well done, mate,' Gazza said quietly on the hot mic, as I pulled the plane into an easy banking manoeuvre, watching the ground below me and allowing myself a moment of satisfaction. I had done what I said I was going to do and faced down all the doubts. This felt like the ultimate vindication of my self-belief. I had no illusions about the fact that the accident would always stay with me, but I knew I had taken the first big step away from it to the rest of my flying career.

Just over a year after that flight, I attended the inquest into Jak's death at the Hilton Hotel at Corby in Northamptonshire, alongside Maria and Jill, Jak's mother. We were there for a couple of days and we stuck together.

I knew I would have to be cross-examined as part of the

process, and once again I found it hard not to feel I was in some way responsible, and that my head was on the block. Maria – who was in the Navy herself – was a huge source of strength, as she had been when I first met her at the funeral.

The tribunal heard that the damage that ultimately caused the crash was unimaginably small. The tiny nick at the base of a fan blade had been eight-hundredths of an inch deep and eighteen-hundredths of an inch long. So small it was almost invisible to the naked eye; and so small it was hard to believe that this alone could have been the undoing of my jet.

In the wake of the crash, blades, redesigned by Rolls-Royce, were introduced to make them more robust and less vulnerable to impacts from foreign objects. The crash also prompted new protocols on runway management at Wittering and Yeovilton, which became two of the cleanest airfields in the country.

Presided over by Anne Pember, the Northamptonshire coroner, the inquest turned into quite a heated affair as the Rolls-Royce lawyer sought to remove any hint of blame from the manufacturer and place it firmly on the shoulders of the Ministry of Defence. His cross-examinations of senior Royal Navy engineers focused heavily on previous incidents in which, he claimed, engine damage had not been properly repaired. Among them was one incident when a plane had been lost and the pilot had ejected.

He was equally aggressive when it was my turn, and started digging down into exactly what I had or had not done that morning before we took off. Had I examined the engineering logs prior to the flight to see if there was any damage noted on that engine? Was it not possible that I had missed the damage to the fan blade during my pre-flight inspection of the aircraft? Had I not noticed any change in engine temperature which might have indicated possible problems? Did I notice any change in the engine note at any stage?

I did my best to tell the truth as I was sworn to do, until Ms Pember stepped in and suggested we take a break. Outside the room, I told the Ministry of Defence lawyer that I felt we were being held responsible for the crash. It was a relief that, when proceedings resumed, the Rolls-Royce lawyer rose to inform the inquest that he had no further questions and I could stand down. Ms Pember paid tribute to Jak, describing him as an experienced pilot who had served his country loyally for more than 20 years, and went on to direct the jury to return a verdict of accidental death.

Whenever I fly in a plane with an ejection seat, the first thing I do once I have settled in is look down and find the stiff rubber ejection handle with its yellow and black striped marking. With the pin that prevents the system from initiating still firmly in place, I grasp it and bend it to a position that comes easily to hand at a moment's notice. Carrying out this visual and physical examination means I know I can pull it without having to look down.

Some military pilots never touch the handle, let alone run their hands over it. They want to pretend it's not there and they are never going to need it. As far as they are concerned, it's never going to happen. But I know how important this piece of kit really is, and how much the infinitesimally small periods of time that elapse between thought and execution can delay a process that can mean the difference between life and death.

5

They used to say I was a 'trailblazer' in the Royal Navy. That was the term for people who came to the service without a military background. It was true in the sense that neither of my parents had military experience, but both of my grandfathers had served their country.

The one on my mother's side had been in the Navy until invalided out after an accident. My dad's dad had been a private in the North Staffordshire Regiment, representing the county where I was born and brought up in the English Midlands.

One of his jobs was to look after the engines of vehicles that were transported on landing craft across the English Channel on and after D-Day in 1944. After that he joined the infantry as they fought their way through rural western France against the retreating German army.

He never talked about the war much, and certainly not during family gatherings. But once I had established myself in a naval career, he opened up about some of his experiences. He told me about his platoon commander, whose bravery had impressed him.

'When the men became paralysed with fear and stopped because of mines or snipers, he would move forward and lead them from the front,' he said. 'He would stamp the ground with every footstep in defiance of the enemy and the risks.' It was a powerful image of selfless commitment to the nation's cause that made a big impression on me.

The eldest of two boys, I was born in Leek in Staffordshire and brought up in the Sneyd Green suburb of Stoke-on-Trent, at the heart of an area known as 'The Potteries' because of the many ceramics companies that are based there. My dad worked for several of those companies on the shop floor, attaching handles to bowls and spouts to teapots, while my mum worked as a shop assistant in a department store in the city centre. Later my parents bought our local newsagent's, which served the huge housing estate close to our home, a business that gave them a prominent role in our community.

Mine was a happy childhood. I wasn't bullied at school, my parents were loving and supportive, and me and my brother spent our free time kicking a football about in our garden. We went to church on Sundays, under gentle persuasion, and on a family holiday each summer – usually by coach – and I earned my pocket money by doing a paper round. Like most boys in our leafy low-rise suburb, I had fairly realistic ambitions: I wanted to be a postman, then a fireman, and finally a policeman.

Until one day, aged seven, I looked up and saw something that stopped me in my tracks. There, seemingly just above the treetops, was an enormous aircraft rumbling slowly across the sky with what looked like another one sitting on its back. I cupped my hands around my eyes to focus better and help me see through the glare of the summer sun. 'Wow, look at that!' I shouted across the back garden to my brother.

We were watching a Boeing 747 carry the NASA space shuttle *Enterprise* on a promotional tour that had already included stops in Germany, France and Italy. These were about to be followed by a visit to Stansted airport in Essex, where 200,000 people turned up to see it.

It was so low over our house, we could read the markings on the side of the shuttle's fuselage, but it was like seeing something from another world. It was *so* big and it seemed amazing that a jumbo could fly with a spaceship perched on top of it. 'That's impressive, that's cool,' I thought to myself as we returned to our re-creation of the FA Cup final.

A couple of years later, I had another seminal experience that pointed in the direction that my life was to take. After years of coach trips that had taken us as far afield as Italy, my parents announced that we would be going on holiday to Majorca and, for the first time, by plane. While my brother was terrified at the thought of flying, I was buzzing as the day dawned and we set off to Manchester airport, each wearing a bright-blue travel shell-suit.

I grabbed the window seat on board our Monarch Airlines 727. We were just in front of the engines and my face was glued to the view as we took off. For the first time, I felt the thrust and experienced the sensation of being in a plane as it was released from the ground. My stomach tumbled as we began climbing through the grey cloud and drizzle of an English summer morning. We emerged into the spectacular sparkling blue and white wonder-world of aviation, as we climbed into the sunshine and levelled off. I scanned the horizon, imagining flying my own aircraft in that endless free space that I never knew existed until that moment.

My mum picked up on my enthusiasm and asked if I could visit the cockpit. 'These guys can do this for a living, so that's what I am going to do,' I thought as I was ushered in, met the pilots, and saw banks of unfathomably complex switches and dials.

I didn't pay much attention at school in my early years. I couldn't see the point. I wanted to leave at the first opportunity and get a job. But one moment of revelation came in my early teens when I was introduced to algebra in our maths class. Here was a way of thinking, a way of describing the world, that I could relate to. As soon as there was an equation involved, with an 'x' and 'y' to balance, everything seemed to fit into place. I loved it and everything that flowed from it.

During secondary school, aged 13 or so, our teachers organised a careers session where each of us had to say, in turn, what we wanted to do in life. I discovered for the first time what I was up against. We were told that every job becomes dull and mundane eventually and were asked to come up with occupational ideas that would never become boring. Among my friends were would-be hairdressers, pottery workers, mechanics, bus drivers, teachers and nurses.

Then it was my turn.

'What do you want to do, Nathan?'

'I'd like to be a pilot,' I replied firmly.

The class went silent. Then there were a few sniggers, and someone made a noise that sounded like a plane crashing. I knew there was no one else in that room who shared my passion; it was just me, but I was happy to plough my own furrow.

'Yes, Nathan, what an interesting idea. That would certainly not be a boring job.' The teacher grinned as everyone laughed.

And then came the gentle push-back.

'It's a great ambition to have, Nathan. But, to be honest, people from round here don't go on to do things like that,' he said. 'Have another think and come back tomorrow and let's try another idea.'

The next day I went through the motions of saying I would like a job as a skilled technician of some sort – a machinery operator in a factory, for example – but underneath I was more determined than ever that flying would be my life.

To start with, I thought flying just about anything would do, but gradually my focus tightened on the idea of becoming a pilot in the RAF. My mum used to take us to the library at our local town centre in the Hanley area of Stoke, where I would look for books on aviation.

I studied pictures of military planes of all kinds, but I especially liked the SEPECAT Jaguar, an attack aircraft then in service with the RAF and the French Air Force. To me its slender lines – like a big paper dart – were exactly what a fighter jet should look like, and I would draw it over and over again, trying to get the angle of its anhedral wing just right.

Many years later, before it went out of service, I had the chance to fight Jaguars in air combat training. Only then did I discover that the star performers of my childhood dreams were underpowered and had nowhere near the Sea Harrier's manoeuvrability.

The library's real showstopper was the big glass dome outside which contained a Spitfire. It was on display in honour of its designer, R. J. Mitchell, who was from Stoke-on-Trent. That was an inspiration, and it was not lost on me that someone from my city had had such a major impact on British history, and on the evolution of military flying.

This was also the era of the first *Top Gun* film, and then the first Gulf War, when British Tornado pilots played a prominent role, with several ending up on TV after being captured by Saddam Hussein's Iraqi forces. There were plenty of cues pointing me in the direction I had chosen.

But I was up against it, and it was probably to my advantage that I did not know how far I would have to go to make my dreams come true. Despite my earlier antipathy to studying, I had worked out that to be a pilot in the RAF I would have to become an officer. That meant I would need A-levels, and possibly a degree. So I went to sixth form college, where I combined maths and physics with geology.

I applied to the RAF for a 'sixth form scholarship'. This was a scheme in which the service would fund basic flying training for students, which would put them on their way to securing a berth as a full-time trainee pilot later on.

I headed to the Royal Air Force College at RAF Cranwell in Lincolnshire for a day and a half of interviews and got another shock. For the first time, I came across an echelon of well-spoken, entitled young men, many of them from military backgrounds, who seemed completely at home in the RAF environment and behaved as if becoming a fighter pilot was their destiny.

They were confident, not to say arrogant, and had a worldliness – a familiarity with politics, history and world affairs – that I couldn't begin to match. I was out of my depth, and although I did well on some of the practical tasks, the examiners knew it. They made me feel very uncomfortable as I struggled to answer their questions. Unsurprisingly, I was rejected.

At a subsequent visit to my local military careers office in Stoke, I came up against another raft of patronising indifference to my ambitions. When I arrived and announced that I wanted to be a pilot in the RAF, the Air Force officer smiled and, looking at his fellow recruitment officers from the Navy and the Army, said sardonically: 'A pilot? Wouldn't we all like to be pilots.'

When they had finished chuckling, they made it clear that in this catchment area, at least, there wasn't much history of people joining the forces as officers. I could be an enlisted man in the RAF, they suggested, and think of a career as a mechanic.

They offered one positive piece of advice: if I was still determined to fly, I should join my local Air Training Corps, where I could wear a uniform one evening a week and march around a parade square. I took them up on it and then failed with another application to the RAF – and that involved another humiliating grilling at Cranwell – this time to be a full-time trainee pilot.

But the Air Training Corps was not a complete waste of time. It delivered a key moment in my evolution from Stoke-on-Trent schoolboy, with dreams of a life in the sky, to Royal Navy single-seat fast-jet pilot. 'Air Experience Flights' was a scheme which offered cadets the chance to go up in a Chipmunk two-seater, single-propeller aircraft, to see if they liked flying, and if it was something they should pursue. My chance came at RAF Ternhill in Shropshire, with a pilot-instructor who spent his weekends sharing his passion for flying with youngsters like me.

'Oh, you're Royal Navy?' I said, when he greeted me on the tarmac.

'Yeah,' he said, 'we have pilots too, you know. I'm actually a helicopter instructor.'

'Oh, right,' I replied, considering, for the first time, the role of air power in the Navy.

He was the best guide I could have wanted on my first flight in a small plane. As we took off, I was grappling with all sorts of anxieties – the fear that I might not like my calling, that I might be sick or, worse still, I might not have the aptitude for it. I'd been in an airliner, of course, but not this, and I had no idea what might happen. But as we took off, my concerns melted away. It was intoxicating – a sense of sheer joy and freedom flooded my consciousness as we 'broke the bounds of earth' in our little red and white plane and climbed above the airfield.

'Do you want to take the controls, Nath?' I heard the man in the seat in front of me say on the cockpit voice frequency, after he had settled the Chipmunk on a steady heading.

'Yes, *please*,' I replied enthusiastically, and then listened intently as he talked me through the way to use the stick. Then he surrendered control and for the first time in my life I flew an aeroplane wings level, then banked it left and right, and then climbed and descended again.

It felt so natural, and just as I was thinking 'I can do this,' the instructor echoed my thoughts.

'You can fly, young Mr Gray,' he said. 'Yeah, you've got it . . .'

It was a beautiful clear day and luckily, not being the tallest on the block, I was pushed up a bit in my seat by my parachute, so I could see for miles. Compared to an airliner, there wasn't the same sensation of acceleration on take-off in the little Chipmunk, but this felt like uncontrolled free flight. You could do what you wanted, and soon I had a go at an aileron roll and then a barrel roll. They went well, so well, in fact, that the instructor asked if I would like to try a loop.

'Why not?' I thought.

Again he explained what was involved, the levels of G-force I should use and how to correct the plane's attitude relative to the horizon at all points. After demonstrating the most famous manoeuvre in aerobatics, he then let me loose. I set off, up and over, with him coaching me all the way round the circle we were describing in the air.

'Yeah, good correction,' I heard him say as we went through the top. 'Yep, keep pulling, keep pulling, keep pulling,' he advised as we came back out. 'Great – really good job,' he concluded as I brought the Chipmunk back level with a big grin on my face.

We had only been airborne for 20 or 30 minutes, but it felt like I had already travelled a million miles in the right direction. I had come to grips with the three-dimensional flying space. This was my eureka moment; I had found my playground.

Some talk about 'natural talent' or 'ducks to water' – perhaps they are true in my case, though I know far more gifted pilots than me. It's certainly true that I had an instinctive affinity with the airborne environment. I felt very comfortable learning from the instructor, as he demonstrated each manoeuvre, explaining how to do them as he did so and then letting me try to replicate what he had done.

'So, how was your first flight?' he said, as we taxied in.

'Wow, just fantastic,' I beamed.

He revealed that he had never let a cadet try to do a loop on one of those flights before, and he offered me some timeless wisdom.

'It's a long journey, Nathan. And it's tough to make the grade as a military pilot,' he said. 'But don't let anyone stop you, because you can do this. You've got the talent for it and if I've managed to get there, then you can too. Good luck.'

6

I never saw the barriers I had to overcome to gain acceptance in the RAF as class-based, even though I was coming at it from a working-class background.

To me, it was more a case of being behind. The other young would-be pilots I met always seemed to be two or three years ahead of me in their development and I needed to bridge that gap. The message had come across loud and clear: I had many of the right attributes technically and in terms of my practical ability, but I needed to broaden my horizons.

The first step was further education and the University of Manchester Institute of Science and Technology, where I read aerospace engineering. I wanted to do that course because the brochure for it had a jet on its front cover. I might not have made the grade with my expected results at A-level, but I confidently informed the interview board that I was going to be sponsored by the RAF. Though this wasn't quite true, it was enough to open the door to secure my place.

Arriving in Manchester as a wide-eyed undergraduate, I went to the freshers' careers fair and met a Navy recruitment officer. He was a real old salt, whose windblown features suggested years at sea. At that stage I was all in for the RAF and there were few pointers indicating that I would eventually find my home in the Senior Service.

'Oh, I see you are looking at the RAF,' he said as I stood at the adjoining stand, leafing through their promotional literature. 'Have you thought about the Navy?'

'No, I'm good, thanks. It's the RAF for me. I want to be a pilot.'

'We have pilots too, you know,' he replied, using the same phrase I had heard from my instructor on that memorable day in the Chipmunk.

'Yes, I know you do, but an RAF pilot is what I'm looking at –'

'Fine. You go on your way, young man, and join the Air Force, and try and be a pilot,' he said. 'Because the last thing you will want to do is face the challenge of the toughest aviation in the world.'

At this, my ears pricked up.

'Why would you want to try and land on a small postage stamp that has been tossed around in a storm on the ocean at night – something that is too difficult for most pilots – when you can do it all on land? So by all means go and join the Air Force, where you'll always have a two-mile-long runway that never moves to work with. And I wish you all the luck . . .'

It was a clever way of catching my attention, and it planted a seed in my mind. If someone says I can't do something, then, sure as hell, I will try to prove them wrong. And if it's not hard, or nearly impossible, then it's hardly worth doing.

My time at Manchester was spent working for my degree – my final year included a dissertation on parachute design, something that would become a matter of life and death to me five years later – and flying in the University Air Squadron. Based at RAF Woodvale in Southport, the unit played a critical role in securing jobs for graduates with the RAF, so it was vital that I flew regularly and did well in all my tests.

At the end of my first year, I went solo. I was flying a Scottish Aviation Bulldog, a similar design to the Chipmunk with a top speed of 120 knots, but with its two seats arranged side by side. I remember the lonely feeling in that little cockpit as I prepared to take to the sky on my own for the first time. I had flown a circuit of the airfield with my instructor as normal. Then, after we had landed, and with the engine still running, he climbed out, leant back in to tighten his seat straps so they would not flap about, gave me a thumbs up and walked off.

It was up to me from now on, and there would be no one to check next moves with, or take over if I made a mistake. As I taxied out, I felt slightly sick. That fragile feeling in my stomach continued as I lined up and then let her go down the runway. But as soon as I got off the ground, the nerves disappeared. I felt comfortable at the controls of the Bulldog, to the point that I wanted to stay up there and not have to come back in after one circuit. The high point was the landing, as I 'greased' the little plane onto the tarmac with barely a bump. What a feeling ...

By graduation I knew exactly how to approach my next interview with the RAF, my third attempt to join Her Majesty's Air Force. I knew how to hold myself, how to talk and how to deal with the sorts of questions they would ask. Despite flying less than many of my peers at Manchester, I was considered one of the best pilots in my year and could do almost anything in the Bulldog, including solo aerobatics. The interview – once more at Cranwell – was a breeze. Finally, I had made it. I had a letter formally accepting me as a trainee pilot officer, and they sent me a pair of boots so I could begin breaking them in.

At the same time as I had made that final application, I had also written to the Navy. They had sent me details of when to travel to Portsmouth for a three-day assessment for a job as a pilot. They also sent a warrant, to cover my train fare there and back, that I had cashed in for two tickets at the station in Stoke-on-Trent.

Once accepted by the RAF, I couldn't see the point of going to Portsmouth and called the Admiralty to tell them I would not be coming. That was fine, they said, but in the meantime could I send the travel warrant back? I told them I had already used it to buy my tickets and was amazed to hear the woman on the other end of the phone tell me, in that case, I would have to reimburse the Navy for their cash value.

Blimey, what a joke, I thought. I am being asked to pay for an interview I am not even going to attend ...

Then she made a suggestion. 'Look, Mr Gray,' she said, 'you've got the tickets, and you'll get three days of free board and food and the chance to see what we do down here, so why don't you just come anyway?'

I thought about it and could see her point, but I decided I would do nothing to prepare for my interviews and tests. They would have to accept me as I am, warts and all, and if they didn't like me, too bad.

The practical tasks and leadership tests were far more demanding than I had experienced at Cranwell, but somehow

I excelled at all of them. In one task I had to lead a group of four trying to cross a swimming pool, with only a few ropes and some pieces of wood to work with. We managed to get everyone across, something the instructor quietly informed me he'd never seen before.

Then came the formal interview with a board made up of a naval captain, a commander pilot and a school headmaster. The captain asked me various questions about my flying career and then moved on to wider issues.

'I notice, Mr Gray, that you have filled in the section of the form detailing your regular reading, not with a national newspaper, but with a magazine entitled *Loaded*.'

'Yes, sir,' I said.

At that point the pilot sitting next to him started to laugh, and that's when I realised that this was the place for me; this was my future military family right here. I think they appreciated that I was telling the truth and not trying to be someone I wasn't, something I always felt I was doing with the RAF.

At the end of the three-day assessment, my overall performance, together with my flying reports from uni, had placed me in a strong position. I had done well, they informed me, and they would now consider whether to accept me as a pilot and on what type of commission.

'Well done, Mr Gray. We will be in touch in two or three months' time, if that's OK,' the captain said.

'Actually, sir, that isn't going to work,' I told him. 'Because I already have a letter from the RAF saying I start officer training at Cranwell in three weeks' time.'

'Right, I see,' he said before clearing the room, so it was just the two of us. 'Look, I am prepared to stick my neck out here,' he said conspiratorially. 'You've done really well – really quite well indeed. So shall we try and make a deal? What would it take for you to join the Navy and walk away from the RAF, if I could make it happen?'

'Well,' I replied, trying hard to hide my growing excitement, 'I want a commission as a pilot only – not a navigator, observer, or air traffic controller or anything else – and I want the best commission you have available.'

'OK. Step outside and I'll see what I can do.'

Five minutes later he called me back in with the two other board members once again sitting alongside him. After all my years of trying and being rejected by the RAF, this was going to be a tumultuous moment, and I couldn't help a faint smile breaking out on my face.

'Mr Gray, I am delighted to inform you that we can offer you a position as a pilot on a sixteen-year commission, beginning in January at Dartmouth,' the captain said. 'But given the unprecedented circumstances around this offer, you will have to accept it right now or it will be withdrawn. What d'you say?'

I didn't hesitate for a moment. I had found my home, somewhere I could be myself and excel. I was going to take on the toughest challenge in military flying and it would not be with the RAF. I would be a naval aviator.

'I am happy to accept,' I told him.

A few weeks later, in January 1998, having posted my boots back to Cranwell, the newly commissioned Sub-Lieutenant Gray turned up at the Britannia Royal Naval College at Dartmouth in Devon to begin a year of naval officer training.

*   *   *

My first year in the Royal Navy was pretty standard stuff. I went out on the famous P-1000 class 'picket' boats, learning how to be a seaman, to navigate and tie my knots. Then I completed a two-week flying course at Roborough near Plymouth on a Grob G 115 two-seater prop aircraft. This was a German-built, slightly more svelte version of the Bulldog.

The course was a way for the Navy to check that I had the right physical and mental attributes to be a pilot. I passed with flying colours and then moved on to the aircrew survival and interrogation course at Gosport. This involved being subjected to quite tough physical and psychological stress to help prepare me for the eventuality of being captured in war.

During my year at Dartmouth I met Lucy, a student at Exeter Uni, through her brother Joe with whom I was sharing a room at the college. She was attractive and fun and we hit it off immediately, though neither of us thought anything could come of it. But one night after a party, sitting overlooking the harbour, we made a little pact: if we both got to our thirtieth birthdays and remained unmarried, then we'd be each other's fallback option. Little did either of us know how that would play itself out ...

Then came an unexpected fork in the road. There were too many young pilot officers waiting to start training and, as I was one of the youngest of my intake, I was asked to stand aside for a year. Instead of moving on to the next flying assignment, I was sent to 40 Commando Royal Marines, the Navy's elite ground troops, an experience that proved invaluable for a future ground attack fast-jet pilot. I would later come across quite a few of the men I trained with during my time at Norton Manor camp at Taunton in Somerset on deployment in Afghanistan.

I completed the gruelling ten-week All Arms Commando Course during my year there – climbing 30ft ropes, tackling the infamous Tarzan assault course and running 30 miles with full equipment – making me a proud Commando Green Beret. By the time I left and headed back to the next step in my flying career, I had gone native.

This time I was flying the Firefly T67M, another notch along the curve from the Chipmunk, but still a single prop twin-seater. I passed the course without much difficulty, but I surprised my instructors by telling them I had changed my mind about fast jets and wanted to be a commando helicopter pilot, so I could support the Royal Marines on the ground. I had been in the mud with those guys and my respect for them was boundless. Surely the best way to return the favour after a year with them, I reasoned, was to use my flying ability to offer them direct air support from the most flexible platform in the British military arsenal?

The instructors were not expecting this. My flying progress had firmly indicated a future in jets, and they were not going to let me deviate from the plan.

With that in mind, they sent me for my first visit to the Royal Naval Air Station at Yeovilton. The idea was to show me around and give me a feel for the machinery I would go on to fly. It was a smart move. Up until then I had only ever seen a military helicopter up close. The Sea Harriers were as big as the helos, but a lot more shiny. As I stood next to one and ran my hands over the fuselage, I got the message – this was going to be my chariot. They didn't let me sit in one, but occupying that single seat in the cockpit was now my goal.

But my time in the Harrier was still some distance away. After the Chipmunk, Grob, Bulldog and Firefly, next on my list was a year in the Short Tucano, at RAF Linton-on-Ouse in Yorkshire. This was a two-seat turbo-prop trainer that could reach speeds of 300 knots. I was going faster than ever before and flying one of these felt more like the real thing, with an ejection seat for the first time, and an oxygen mask clamped to my face.

Like the previous ones, the course was dominated by the same progressions and exercises, with the emphasis on mastering them in the new plane. I knew my performance had to be immaculate in all departments – the Navy only had Sea Harrier fast jets, so I had to make the top grade of single-seat fighter pilot or there was nothing.

Then came the big one – the move to RAF Valley and the conversion to the Hawk trainer. Promoted to lieutenant and armed with awards at every level, this was the moment of truth as I attempted to master jet power for the first time in the cockpit of a plane that could fly at 500 knots, 200 knots faster than the Tucano.

My first flight was unbelievable: it's the only word to describe the feeling. When you fly in a relatively slow plane you are buffeted by the air, and the whole thing feels like a bit of a struggle. When you strap yourself into jet power, you get the sense that the airframe is cutting through the wind – slicing it like a super-sharp knife. And the faster you go, the easier it gets.

The Hawk was like a little sports car – fun, nimble and

agile. No wonder it has been the aircraft of choice for the Red Arrows since 1979. But it is a deceptive beast, and the challenge for trainee pilots using it for the first time is to understand exactly where its aerodynamic limits lie. While all the other aircraft I had flown had conservative airframes that gave plenty of warning of an impending stall, the Hawk – with its more radical delta wing profile – gives you no warning at all, and it can be lethal. When you make your final turn coming in to land – the slowest you'll ever be in that plane – any misjudgement on airspeed will see the aircraft depart and crash.

I was driving to Bangor the day after I had completed my first solo in the Hawk, and saw a plume of black smoke rising from RAF Mona on Anglesey, which was our relief landing ground for Valley. When I got back to base I discovered that one of my course mates, on his second solo, had stalled his Hawk at exactly that point – his final turn – and had had to leave via his ejection seat. Luckily he was fine and enjoyed his notoriety that evening in the mess bar.

The Hawk was the perfect prelude to the Harrier and I went through the various stages of training without incident. But I never felt cocky or confident at any point. In the back of my mind were insistent voices that reminded me that I might not be good enough, that I might be spotted as the fraud that I was, and that this could all come to a sudden end. It was classic imposter syndrome, and not even finishing each course at the top of the list could suppress it.

I was awarded my wings at Valley. I was now officially a qualified pilot, which also meant I could receive flying pay – effectively danger money. That was a huge moment.

Whatever else you may be feeling, whatever doubts continue to lurk beneath the surface, at that point you know you are pretty good at your job. At the end of the Hawk training, me and my mate Scranners finished at the same time and our commanding officer gave us a choice: one of us would go to Sea Harriers at Yeovilton, the other to the newer version, the GR7 being flown by the RAF at Wittering. It was up to us.

I had been consistently top in ground attack and weapons deployment while Scranners, with his innate natural flying ability, was top dog in the air combat arena. Given that the GR7 was exclusively a ground attack aircraft, it seemed the obvious choice for me, while he would go to the Sea Harrier. But we talked it over and Scranners, bless him, wanted to be the first Royal Navy pilot to convert to the GR7 and trail-blaze a route that all of us would eventually follow after the creation of Joint Force Harrier. I made it clear I wanted to go to the Sea Harrier – it had been my focus for some time and I was committed. So we agreed a sort of upside-down deployment that surprised our seniors, but they were happy to go along with it.

When it was time to move on, I headed to Somerset while Scranners headed to Cambridgeshire. And that is why he was watching me from the cockpit of his T10 that fateful day a few months later when, as a visiting training pilot in my Sea Harrier at Wittering, I lost my plane and my instructor.

7

I had survived one of the worst things that could happen to any aviator. My multimillion-pound Harrier had flipped at less than 100ft and then exploded on impact. I had ejected almost parallel to the ground, and by some miracle lived to tell the tale. My legendary instructor Jak had not been so lucky.

The accident would leave a permanent scar and I knew I would be haunted by Jak's loss. But as I returned to the Sea Harrier, I felt confident I could cope and still fulfil my dream of becoming a single-seat, fast-jet pilot, capable of flying from postage stamps in storm-tossed oceans.

After the reassuring success of my sortie with Gary Langrish at Wittering, I was back at Yeovilton, where my commanding officer, Dickie Payne, decided the best thing for me was to forget that I was 17 flights into my training and go back to the beginning.

All was well with my world as I raced through the early stages. Having already done my first hover and my first solo before the crash, I was given plenty of time to enjoy the Harrier on my own, and my confidence increased with my flying proficiency.

But this was not to be an easy ride. The first sign of the

trouble ahead came when my friend Scrabble suffered a serious technical emergency as he was delivering his jet back to Yeovilton from Wittering after completing two air combat training flights.

He was at 24,000ft, just north of London in the Oxford area, when he heard a low rumble followed by a big explosion. His aircraft had suffered an engine failure, and in an instant he lost his head-up display. The Harrier was now vibrating and shaking so much Scrabble could barely read his standby instruments.

As he dipped through a busy commercial airway into heavy cloud and poor weather, he declared a Mayday and began a series of five or six attempts to restart his engine, which was dangerously overheating. At this point, Scrabble was facing the terrifying possibility of having to eject from a jet overflying areas of dense population in central England.

But having dropped to 9,000ft, he finally succeeded in getting the engine restarted. He had only 69 per cent of his full power, but it was enough to maintain level flight. He was diverted back to Wittering, where he executed a 'fixed throttle landing' on a power output that no training manual had prepared him for. This involved setting the engine revs at a fixed level, so there was no need to alter it, then using the Harrier's nozzles to trim the plane and bring it down.

Scrabble did a superb job of getting it back on the ground and, as he did so, he selected power nozzle braking – using the nozzles, this time pushed forward, to act as brakes. But as soon as he increased the power output to slow the aircraft – the first time he had touched the setting since the restart – there was another huge bang and a big fireball exploded out of the back, as the Pegasus engine seized and then disintegrated.

It later emerged that a fan blade had broken off and wrecked the inside of the power plant, a scenario that was similar to mine. Scrabble's stricken aircraft eventually came to a stop at the end of the runway, not far from the windsock where Jak and I had ended up four months earlier.

Scrabble wears his heart on his sleeve, so I could tell he was pretty stunned by what had happened and how close he had come. To start with, when he called me from Wittering and told me what had happened, I thought he was joking because he loves to take the piss. His favourite trick was calling the squadron operations desk anonymously and asking the duty officer for me, knowing that a Tannoy request would catapult me from my desk, at the opposite end of the building, to answer the call.

'Hello, Lieutenant Gray here,' I would answer breathlessly.

A snort of laughter, then 'You're a cock' was what I would usually hear.

But not this time . . .

'No mate, gen dit, twelve clips,' he said curtly. This was Navy slang for a true story – a genuine dit – and a major scare – 12 clips being the number of safety catches we used to secure hatches on ships when coming into harbour or heading into a storm.

'At 9,000ft I thought I was going to have to bang out. Imagine if I had had to leave the cockpit over Oxford?'

Listening to him, it made me think again about my theory of probability. I had convinced myself that what had happened to me and Jak was a once-in-a-lifetime event and the probability of it happening again, or something like it, was vanishingly small. But the fact that this had now happened to Scrabble seemed to upend that logic and reminded me that probabilities are just numbers. The same thing – or something equally life-threatening – could easily happen to the same person twice when flying this amazing piece of vertical take-off technology that had such a chequered safety record.

I went back to my day job and tried to put it out of my mind. But a few months later something else happened that increased my underlying feeling of unease. Rob Schwab was one of the most experienced Harrier pilots in the squadron. He was from Jak's generation, and had helped mentor me after the crash and encourage me to get back in the air. He had ejected twice during his flying career in the Navy, once as a flight instructor in a Hawk, when the undercarriage collapsed on landing, and once over the Bristol Channel, when his Harrier entered a spin and would not come out of it.

On this occasion, 'Schwabby' was doing a routine maintenance test flight in a Harrier that had recently undergone extensive engineering work. He was up high doing his stuff when, without warning, his control stick jammed across to one side, triggering a downward out-of-control spiral. Schwabby tried everything to free it, and was in danger of having to jump out again. But somehow he got the stick moving, and the plane level, and then took his turn to declare a Mayday.

Down below at the squadron, we heard 'Emergency State 2, Sea Harrier' on the airfield Tannoy system, and we all stopped what we were doing to watch the drama unfold. 'Emergency State 1' means a plane that has crashed; State 2, one that is about to.

I abandoned my preparations for my next flight and ran to the ops desk. I knew it was Schwabby because there were not many of us flying at any one time and word quickly spread that it was him who was in trouble.

On the radio we heard him calmly describe how the stick had locked hard to the left and how he had managed to free it. He said that other than the fact that he couldn't steer it properly for a few seconds, the jet seemed to be flying OK.

'I am keeping it steady and I am just going to bring it in for a straight approach,' he said, as he prepared to land on the runway we called '27'.

The ops room's massive glass window gave us a panoramic view of the airfield, and we watched the Harrier as it came into view.

The Tannoy broke the tension: 'Emergency State 2 Harrier is on long finals to land on runway 27 ...'

Schwabby was on a three-degree glide slope with his landing gear down, coming in slowly and smoothly in ideal conditions, with a gentle westerly headwind. It looked pretty much perfect. Then, at about 200ft, he must have put in a small correction on his heading and the stick jammed again, because there were gasps as we watched the plane start rolling off track. It banked hard to the left and then disappeared behind the roof of the hangar directly in our line of sight.

I had seen enough.

'Get out!' I shouted, not that Schwabby would have heard me. 'Get out! *Eject, eject!*'

I was sure that the next thing we would see was a mushroom cloud of black smoke rising from behind the hangar. But we did not hear the pop of an ejection seat and there was silence on the radio. A split second later, out of nowhere, we saw the Harrier rear up, scream over the roof of the hangar, then come down on the runway with a thump and come to a stop. There was a stunned silence in the room.

After we had watched the jet taxi in, most of the others went back to whatever they were doing, but I went down to the flight line. My personal experience informed my reaction here. I knew that even the swashbuckling Schwabby wouldn't be able to laugh this one off.

He was ash-grey when he walked in, and had completely lost his mojo. As he reached me he gave me a big hug, which was not his normal style.

'Are you alright, mate?' I asked him.

'I'm not doing this again,' he said in a monotone and with unmistakable finality, and trudged off.

A missing protective cover for the base of the stick on his Harrier had allowed dust to accumulate, which created small tracks that the mechanism jammed into geometrically. A subsequent investigation demonstrated the same thing could have happened on many of the other jets in the squadron, and that it was a miracle Schwabby had been able to work his one free. I believe it proved a turning point for him, as he exchanged his career with the Royal Navy to one in commercial aviation.

I started to wonder how I had found myself in this corner. We all knew that military flying was dangerous, but no other aircraft in service was having such close calls as this. Somehow, it had to stop. Were we just having our fair share of scares, before it went back to plain sailing? I elected to hope that was the case, and carry on.

I'm sure that most of my 20 or so fellow fast-jet pilots at Yeovilton weren't feeling like this at all. They were still happily operating on the mantra we learnt in training – that if we practised for every bad eventuality, we would ensure they didn't happen, and if they did, we would know how to deal with them. But for me and Scrabble it was slightly different; I had been in a fatal accident and he had been the first on the scene after it happened. We both knew that real life could be far more complicated than the training rule book would have us believe.

My flying was still going well, although the nerves and doubts were starting to creep in as the first anniversary of Jak's death approached. The triggers were not only from incidents in the air. I was getting regular letters from the Navy medical centre in Portsmouth. PTSD was very much in everyone's mind, as a likely consequence of experiences that involved extreme psychological stress, and they were doing their best to follow up with me.

I would sit down and fill in leaflets and tick the boxes as required.

'How often do you think about the traumatic event. Never? Sometimes? Often? Always (every few hours)?' *Always*. That was me. Tick.

'Does it affect your sleeping? Yes? No?' Yes, tick.

'Do you enjoy your job? Yes? No?' Hmmm ...

'Does your job remind you of the event? Yes? No?' Affirmative.

I answered truthfully in all cases and duly sent back the forms, but never heard another word from them. The main impact was to remind me, more than my subconscious was already doing, about the accident.

Even if I had wanted to escape the anniversary, that would have been impossible. The Sea Harrier Force organised a big memorial service for Jak to mark it. I had been to the windsock at Wittering on my own to have a chat with him, but this was an event at which just about everyone turned up. They cancelled flying and opened the gates from the airfield so everyone could drive directly to the church in Yeovilton, where, after the service, we all gathered around his gravestone.

It was like reliving the funeral again, with loads of people coming up and talking about the accident and what had happened and how I must be feeling. It was as if the last year hadn't happened, and I was going straight back to that December day all over again. It seemed that the first time round it hadn't really hit me because I was numb – probably in shock. But this time all my senses were fully alive and the memories were crashing in, one on top of another.

At the graveside, Scrabble and I stood at the back, as we had at the funeral. It began to feel very raw – I wanted to be there, but alone. After the service there was a big piss-up in the wardroom, but I didn't go. It felt like it had taken every one of the past 12 months to even begin to process the severity and sadness of the accident, and this felt like a setback.

Dickie Payne called me in for a career chat after New Year. I was a month away from finishing my training on the Sea Harrier and he was keen to talk through where I was headed.

He painted a rosy picture of my future, as I sat listening to him in silence.

'You're doing great, Nathan,' he said. 'You're a naturally gifted pilot with bags of resourcefulness, and we are very pleased with your progress. The way I see it, you will finish here and then go to the frontline – do three years operating off the boat and then come back here and become either a flying instructor or a weapons instructor. Then I see you getting promoted to lieutenant commander, so it's all positive.'

He paused.

'Obviously, you've had a hiccup,' he continued, perhaps sensing that all was not quite as it should be. 'And you are delayed by about six months compared to your peer group. But I like to think that we can catch that up.'

Then he asked me my preference: flying instructor or a weapons instructor?

I shrugged my shoulders. 'I don't really care,' I heard myself saying.

'What?' He gave me a look of serious concern. 'You must care about your career, and make a choice ...'

'No, really, I don't right now ...'

'Well, do you enjoy the flying?'

'To be quite honest, no. It's not enjoyable. I constantly think the aircraft is going to kill me. I think something is going to happen on every single trip.'

As I said this, a Harrier roared towards the office window and went into the hover. The noise was deafening and it meant the conversation had to pause awkwardly until it landed, and we were left with the whining of the Pegasus engine in the background. Seeing that Harrier over Dickie's shoulder seemed poignant. Was I really going to stop flying that amazing machine, or front up and carry on?

'Right,' said Dickie, picking up from where we left off, 'er, well, why don't we ...'

I interrupted him.

'It's knackering to come into work every day and wonder if I am going to make it, and if I am going to come home,' I said, sticking to my guns.

I told him that I cycled to work every day from my cottage and had got into the habit of leaving the number for the bike's combination lock in my locker with my stuff, so at least it could be moved if I didn't make it back.

'The thing is, I regard coming to work every day as a terminal event at the moment,' I added.

Neither of us spoke for a few seconds as that statement hung in the air. I hadn't planned to say any of this, and I think Payne was surprised, not so much by what I was thinking, but that I had admitted it to him so openly and honestly.

He was a kind boss, full of understanding and care for his subordinates. 'OK, Nath, you're only a month away from finishing, and you *are* going to finish. Let's keep going and we'll take it steady,' he said.

I hesitated for a beat. 'OK.'

'Come and see me if you really don't want to carry on, but let's at least get you to the end, and we'll see where we take it from there.'

A few weeks later I was flying an exercise over the Bristol Channel, where we practised identifying an enemy plane by merging with it at high speed, prior to simulating shooting it down. I was coming in fast from 40,000ft when I felt my Harrier start to shake, gently at first, but then more and more insistently. Within a few seconds, I could no longer read my head-up display as the whole aircraft started rattling around.

My first thought was that it was a problem with the engine, so I pulled out of the dive, called my wingman, told him what was happening, and took the speed off.

'I've got a vibrating aircraft – it feels very rough,' I said before declaring an emergency and heading back towards Yeovilton. My wingman, an instructor, flew alongside me and inspected my Harrier.

'Your plane looks good,' he said. 'But I see your tail plane at the back shaking quite a bit . . .'

That seemed to fit with what I was experiencing. Something was wrong with my airframe at the rear. Despite all the worrying events leading up to this moment, I felt calm and self-aware in the cockpit. It seemed to me that I had a head-start in this sort of predicament. I was able to steadily assess the situation and mentally prepare for a sudden deterioration in my plane's flying characteristics, primed to pull the handle and leave in a hurry if there was no other choice.

Down on the airfield, the mood was much as it had been for Schwabby's emergency, with everyone watching as I made a long, straight approach. This was another 'Emergency State 2, Sea Harrier', and I was determined to get out of it alive. I brought the plane down onto the concrete, with the vibration still shaking me around, and shut down a mile from the squadron as the fire engine and ambulance headed towards me. After an initial inspection showed nothing dangerously untoward, I climbed out and hitched a ride in the tug towing my Harrier back to the hangar.

A detailed inspection revealed that the nut on the long single bolt attaching the tail plane to the fuselage had started to unwind. In fact, it was only about one full revolution from falling off, along with the tail plane itself. It was never clear why it had started to undo itself, but it seemed like a self-perpetuating route to disaster – as the nut dropped further, the vibration grew stronger, ensuring that it unravelled even more. But this, I was told, was yet another one-off event.

Even before I knew what the problem was, I stood looking at my plane, helmet in hand, wondering how many more incidents of this kind I could take. The angels on my shoulder had to be working overtime. Something fatal was starting to feel like my destiny – the Grim Reaper I had confronted at Wittering was still waiting for me, and I was presenting him with all the opportunities he needed. I couldn't help but conclude that I needed to break the pattern and stop offering myself to him on a plate.

Dickie Payne was already on the case. He called me in even before I put in a request to see him.

'I know what's just happened, and I know you are in a different place to most,' he said. 'How has this affected you, Nath? How d'you feel about moving forward?'

I told him I thought I still wanted to fly in the Navy, but that I was at the point where I would also like to take a break for a while.

'I feel there is a pattern of accidents and near misses and I want to disrupt it,' I told him. 'I know I'm close to finishing, and I don't want to jeopardise my flying career, but I also know I need some breathing space.'

Payne was all ears. Within 24 hours he had discussed my situation with the overall Sea Harriers commander, and called me back in with his proposal. I would pause my flying career to spend a few months at the Forward Air Controller and Standards Unit at RAF Leeming in North Yorkshire. This, he said, was the perfect follow-up to my experience in the Royal Marines. I would learn how ground forces talk to, and use, air assets like the Harrier, something that would broaden my understanding of my role in the cockpit, and help me in my mission to support the guys on the ground.

This was also a smart move from his point of view, as the Joint Force Harrier concept increasingly became a reality, merging pilots from the Royal Navy and the RAF into one force. We would be flying only the GR7, the ground attack Harrier variant, which was a far safer plane than the Sea Harrier. So understanding how to work with Joint Terminal Attack Controllers, otherwise known as JTACs – soldiers who specialised in talking to pilots – would be invaluable.

I took him up on it. It seemed a good distraction and a change of pace, which is what I needed, even though I was concerned that my flying career might be over.

But Payne reassured me.

'Get yourself trained as a forward air controller, get yourself embedded within the brotherhood of those guys, and then, when you return, you will have the bit between your teeth,' he said. 'I am convinced that sending you away for a while will restore your appetite for what you do best, and you'll come back and get straight into it.'

He said that even though I was a handful of flights short of my full training requirement on the Sea Harrier, he would treat that course as finished. I would be able to return and start my conversion on the GR7. On that score I could relax; my Sea Harrier days – my days on the 'widow-maker' – were over.

In case I had any doubts about the wisdom of getting away for a while, a few weeks after this meeting, Scrabble had another emergency when his canopy failed while he was carrying out the same exercise as I had been doing over the Bristol Channel. Despite the explosive decompression, he managed to get his jet back on the ground having suffered windburn to his eyelids and with the broken detonator cord from the shattered Perspex windscreen flapping around in front of him.

It was another piece of remarkable flying by him to save his aircraft, having overcome the shock of storm-force wind at icy temperatures and knowing that his engine could fail after ingesting shards of Perspex. It was the first canopy failure on a Harrier since Jak's recovery of his jet to a carrier five years earlier in the Gulf.

Dickie was right on all counts. I thoroughly enjoyed my time in Yorkshire, learning how best to communicate from the ground with fast-jet pilots in combat scenarios and understanding the difficulties they have talking to people who are looking down from 15,000ft.

If I learnt anything there, it was about patience, humility and understanding when dealing with those guys in the future. The key to safe and efficient close air support is assessing what the situation is like for the troops on the ground, and

I vowed I would always put their interests first – especially in perilous situations. Within the fast-jet pilot world I always promoted the view that we were in the *supporting* role, subservient to the interests of our mates on the ground, not the other way round.

During my sabbatical from the cockpit, I also completed the parachute jumps course at RAF Brize Norton in Oxfordshire, where I was awarded my paratrooper wings. I was now qualified not only to act as a forward air controller, but to be inserted into a combat scenario from the air. This was a unique skillset, which made me a better ground attack pilot than I might have been otherwise. Predictably, with all these extra qualifications, I took a lot of flak from my pilot mates for being a 'badge collector', with a mess uniform adorned with more badges than a Boy Scout's.

Dickie was as good as his word. When I returned to the squadron, I was sent back to Wittering to begin my year-long conversion on the GR7. Compared to the old Sea Harrier, this was another world. It wasn't like a better, more modern Mini than your first banger; this was a Roller – a five-star hotel compared to a shanty town. While the old planes were out to get you with their quirkiness and unreliability, the GR7 felt like it was welcoming you with open arms. It was still a Harrier by name, but completely different by nature.

In the hover, for example, the Sea Harrier was twitchy and untamed, keeping you constantly on edge and waiting to catch you out. The GR7 incorporated a new stability augmentation system that helped the aircraft stay level. Developed in the US as the Harrier II, it was in all respects a more refined flying machine.

Whereas its predecessor was designed as a multirole aircraft, and included a radar to detect enemy planes, the new variant's sole job was delivering things that went 'bang' in the ground attack role. The GR7 was also equipped with something called a 'thermal imaging airborne laser designator', a small pod with a digital screen on the console that you could use to guide laser-controlled bombs onto a target.

With more aerodynamically efficient wings – the so-called 'super-critical' wing design – and big 'barn door' flaps that produced improved lift at low speeds, the GR7 was a superb flying machine. The upgraded Pegasus engine performed well both in hot weather and at high altitude, qualities that would make it ideal for deployment in Afghanistan. It also had a skilfully designed cockpit, with a much bigger dome canopy than the Sea Harrier which gave an excellent view of the ground.

It felt like the test pilots and designers had really thought this aircraft through and considered the needs of the pilot. The first time I flew in one, I had so much space to move around in, I thought I was going to fall out. After landing in the old plane, you would open the canopy and your forearms would come to rest over the cockpit edges, because there was nowhere else to put them, something that could not happen in the GR7's wider and brilliantly designed 'office'.

In some respects it was so different that it barely felt like a Harrier. And it was easy to think that Wittering was a completely different base to the one where I had crashed. But that only worked up to a point. I knew what had happened there, and the staff in the officers' mess knew too. They even offered me my old room again, which was kind of them, but this time I moved on and requested one in a different wing.

If this was going to work, it would have to be a new chapter, a clean break, with no baggage.

For the most part, I could keep the flashbacks in check. But I still had to walk out of the same mess doors as I had done two years earlier, and take off on the same stretch of taxiway that Jak and I had used, and look at that windsock every day. Every time I lined up ready to ask for clearance for launch, I would experience a momentary hesitation as it all played itself out in my mind.

'Right,' I would tell myself, 'I am going to call the tower and ask for take-off.' Then I would hear that inner voice tapping away with the flimsy old argument about probabilities, now reinforced by a clear mind, rested and refreshed by my time away. 'This happened to you. Because it happened, the chances are it is not going to happen again. In fact, the chances are it is not going to happen to anyone, so the chances of it happening to the same person twice are really slim. But just make sure you've got it square in your mind: you are going to launch, gather the aircraft, and if there is a big bang, you are going to eject. OK?'

In those fleeting moments that were barely detectable by an instructor or anyone else, I would see the aircraft rolling upside down and exploding on me. I visualised the ejection not as a violent explosive force propelling me into the sky, but a slow process that could – and should – have been quicker. 'So this time,' I would tell myself, 'when you feel that again – when you feel the aircraft start to flip – there's no question; you pull that handle and get out. This time there may not be angels on your shoulder, making the impossible possible and the unsurvivable survivable.'

This was how I coped, and it worked as I made my way through the course, learning the GR7 and becoming familiar with every landing pad and taxiway that Wittering had to offer, including the short strip next to the windsock – a stretch of tarmac known as Delta 29 North.

When the course ended, I transferred to the frontline Harrier base at RAF Cottesmore, just across Rutland Water. This was where RAF pilots of 1 and 4 Squadrons and Royal Navy fliers of 800 Naval Air Squadron came together as Joint Force Harrier.

I was ready.

8

We were going to take off with a 30-second split, one after the other. Then we'd head away from the airfield at low altitude, as fast as possible and on agreed – and randomly selected – headings before climbing high over the desert.

We knew the Taliban had the potential to shoot us down using old Stinger ground-to-air missiles. The question was, had they got the batteries to match the hardware? If they had, we would have little option but to eject if hit ... if we were lucky enough to still be alive, that is.

I sat in the cockpit of my Harrier inside the camouflaged sun shelter on a sweltering day at Kandahar Air Base. This was the home in southern Afghanistan of the six Harriers supporting British and NATO troops engaged in a bitter counter-insurgency campaign that followed the US-led invasion of late 2001.

All around my GR7, the maintainers were completing their checks as I prepared to head out onto the main runway for the first time. Among their final duties was a check on my electronic warfare warning system – the box of tricks that would alert me to a missile being fired in my direction.

I had been in the country for only 48 hours and already I was on my first mission, flying as wingman to a war-weary

RAF pilot looking forward to handing over and going home after four or five months of relentless combat flying.

It was late September 2006, nearly four years since the accident and six months after I had transferred to Cottesmore; 800 Naval Air Squadron was taking over from 4 Squadron RAF, and I had been sent out two weeks early as point man for the rest of my team.

I had arrived on a huge Boeing C17 transport aircraft with a load of Special Forces guys who melted away as soon as we hit the ground and, despite all the preparation and all the briefings I'd attended, Kandahar airfield still came as a shock. Not least because of the stench from the large open sewage tank at one end of the runway that invaded my sense of smell and taste, my clothes, my bedding and my flying suit. Even now, the smell of sewage anywhere takes me back to that airfield with its cratered runway (thanks to the efforts of the US Air Force during the invasion five years earlier) and its pockmarked terminal buildings.

There were never more than eight Harrier pilots at Kandahar at any one time. Our job was to provide support for NATO troops on the ground across the whole of southern Afghanistan. In practice, this mainly meant Helmand province and Panjiway district, to the west of Kandahar, which were the centres of the Taliban insurgency in the south. The north of the country was covered by American A10 Warthog 'tankbuster' aircraft based at Bagram, close to the capital, Kabul.

Of the pilots at Kandahar, at any one time, two would be on night duty, four on day missions and one sitting on the authoriser's desk that deals with secret operational chat. The remaining one would be involved in mission planning or debriefs and finding time to make calls or send emails to loved ones back home. It was a case of arriving and hitting the ground running.

We lived in rudimentary, container-style buildings with a series of six bedrooms occupied by five people each, with camp beds divided by towels hung from ropes. There was a corridor down the entire length of one side that led to the showers and toilets. The water-spitting, wall-mounted air-conditioning units ensured that the fragrance from the 'poo pond' was with us 24 hours a day.

With light corrugated roofs, these buildings offered no protection against Taliban missiles. There were air-raid sirens, but we would often hear them only after the crump of incoming fire. These attacks killed or injured Coalition soldiers and air base personnel fairly regularly, and destroyed a Harrier just before I deployed.

Although I was an outsider to the battle-hardened pilots from 4 Squadron, we were all mates from Cottesmore and they could not have been more accommodating, as they showed me the ropes, passing on pre-mission routines that would remain unchanged for years. Their commanding officer made it clear they were there to help with a transition that they were looking forward to completing.

'Welcome, Nath,' he said when I went in to see him on my first morning. 'You are part of our squadron now, and part of our team. There is no difference in the way we operate here and the way we will treat you. So ask any questions you may have. You're our ticket out of here basically, so whatever it is you need, you will get it, because you're going to pass it on to your squadron when they arrive.'

He paused.

'The fighting is relentless and fierce, and nobody back home understands just how all-consuming this war is.' I got the message loud and clear. We'd need all the help we could get.

One of the pilots gave me a useful tip. 'If you've never seen someone who has been blown to pieces, try to avoid taxiing past the medical tent when you land behind the medevac helicopter,' he said. 'On occasion, these will be individuals that you will have been supporting that day, which in some ways is good, but be careful, because the images you see will stay with you forever.'

We had briefed in exhaustive detail our mission for my first sortie, which involved heading north to support Dutch soldiers occupying a hill in Helmand that was the focus of regular Taliban attacks. I was ready to help, and committed to the idea that my role was to do all I could to assist Coalition soldiers on the ground, and try to prevent as many of them from being killed or wounded as possible.

I was clear in my own mind about the big-picture rights and wrongs of the war at that stage. This was a counter-insurgency campaign in which we were fighting the Taliban, but also al-Qaeda, who were the driving force behind them. I thought by going in, with our expensive equipment and high-end tactics and training, we would be engaged in a short war that would be successful and we would be able to get back out quickly. If only ...

The hours leading up to the moment I climbed into my jet were a blur of new people, new procedures and new tactical concepts, and not much sleep. For the first time in my flying career, I was preparing to take off in a war zone, ready for combat – that meant wearing a combat survival waistcoat over my flying suit that would never be issued during training back home. In it I carried my Walther PPK semi-automatic pistol plus three magazines, laser pens for helping guide fire from rescue aircraft, a tourniquet and two morphine pens. These might be needed if, for example, I needed to run on a broken leg after ejecting.

I was carrying a block of $10,000 in cash to help buy my freedom in the event of capture, and a so-called 'blood chit'. This was a rectangular 'document' made in silk which confirmed in various languages that I was a UK national. It included a message to the effect that I should be treated as a prisoner of war if captured, and that the UK government would reward those who aided my safe return.

For the first time in my service life, my dog tags were around my neck, hanging from a chain wrapped in a shoelace to prevent hot metal burns from the sun, magnified through the cockpit canopy. These carried my name, service number, blood type and date of birth. I also carried a personal radio that worked on a secret frequency, which would allow me to contact search aircraft, and a small hoist with a carabiner clip. This was an improvised piece of kit that we had developed. The idea was that we could strap ourselves to the outside of an Apache helicopter in seconds and be lifted out of a fire-fight if it was too dangerous for a bigger, personnel-carrying chopper to come in and land.

A lot of thought had gone into what would happen if we were shot down and managed to eject. We always flew in pairs, so if one pilot went down the other would be flying orbits above, doing everything in their power to keep their colleague safe and calling in every air asset they could find to ensure a swift extraction. But we all knew there was a strong chance we could end up fighting for our freedom and that we might not succeed.

In common with most other pilots I discussed this with, I took the view that I would never allow myself to be captured. Having seen what the Taliban did with enemy prisoners, I had no plans to be taken alive. We knew there would be no negotiation, that from their point of view this was not a 'normal' war governed by the tenets of the Geneva Convention, and that captured combatants, especially pilots, would almost certainly be killed, but only after experiencing a very public display of hell on earth beforehand. My plan was to fight until the last bullet, and that slug wasn't going on the enemy unless the target was the last man and I could guarantee the outcome.

Apart from all the rescue stuff, I was also carrying maps of southern Afghanistan. These were marked up with scores of points of interest – buildings, road intersections, bends in rivers, odd field shapes and so on – that had been picked out by our troops during patrols, and that helped us identify targets and locations. These were stored in map 'buckets' on the side of the cockpit, with the maps in use stored in clips on the canopy glareshield. They were alongside a pair of stabilised binoculars that would prove invaluable for spotting people on the ground.

While I was kitted up in a way I had never been before, my jet was also war-ready. It was carrying two 540lb bombs – one airburst charge that detonated just above the ground and one impact bomb – plus 38 armour-piercing rockets stored in two under-wing pods. My GR7 was equipped with chaff – sheets of tin foil that were ejected from the missile launchers on the wing pylons and that were designed to fool radar-guided missiles – and flares. Released from the underside of the fuselage, the flares produced intense heat for a few seconds to distract infrared missiles that had locked on to the hot exhaust from the aircraft's engine.

I took a deep breath and then slammed for launch. I was on time, half a minute behind my leader. In a few hundred metres I was airborne. My Harrier felt heavy – fuelled up and loaded with weapons in the hot and relatively thin air at 3,300ft above sea level.

I stayed as low as I dared to minimise the chances of anyone getting a shot off at me. Just 50–100ft for the first 30 seconds, as the jet screamed over the perimeter fence and onto the fringes of the vast open desert that lay before me like a never-ending sandy beach. I watched my airspeed increase to 400 knots, and pulled hard on the stick while pumping out chaff and flares using a little toggle switch on the left-hand side of the console. With the aircraft climbing at 50 or 60 degrees, I headed to my pre-planned altitude of 14,000ft.

With an initial thousand feet of separation between us, we continued climbing until we could see each other. Then we flew in battle formation northwest towards our rendezvous with the Dutch near the town of Kajaki, close to the dam on the Helmand River of the same name. But then, as so often happened in Afghanistan during a war when a small number of air assets were spread over a vast landscape, our mission was abruptly changed.

'Stand by for re-task . . .'

The command and control desk at Kandahar issued the instruction after we had checked in and identified ourselves. We were given a new target using the coded 'kill-box' system that divided the country into easily identifiable operational sections. We tapped in the co-ordinates. This box was around 90 miles away, northeast of Kandahar, and east of the main highway that ran south out of Kabul, parallel to the Pakistan border.

At this point I was feeling fairly relaxed. As the new boy, I reckoned I was probably along for the ride, and would get the chance to watch my leader do the business, whatever that might be.

Now at 18,000ft and 20 miles from the target, we selected the radio frequency we had been instructed to use and heard the American voice of a forward air controller. This was normally a soldier on the ground trained to communicate with pilots who would be in visual range of the target. He may have been Special Forces of some kind – we never knew – and it was also possible that he was not physically in the vicinity below us, but watching the operation remotely through the eyes of a Predator drone. Again, that was a detail we would never know, nor need to.

He told us that our target was a cave complex which was occupied by the enemy. It had an opening to the west, which meant attacking from that direction, and he used a special code that I knew from my many pre-flight briefings amounted to confirmation that we had pre-clearance to attack it.

After a short pause, as we flew across the largely featureless desert, the voice came back on the same frequency and gave us our final orders. He read out the co-ordinates of the target, the line of attack we needed to use, reconfirmed the nature of the target and then detailed the weapons he wanted us to deploy.

Two 540-pounders, backed up with rockets.

Hang on a minute, I thought, these are the munitions I am carrying, while my leader has two 1,000lb laser-guided bombs which have not been called for.

It took a second or two for this to hit me. I was going to have to pick out this cave entrance in a never-ending brown landscape and hit it with three attacks, while my infinitely more experienced colleague watched me do it from above.

'Oh Christ,' I thought. 'Shit . . .' I added, muttering through clenched teeth.

'I've got this – you watch from high,' was what I'd been expecting to hear from the cockpit of the other GR7. But the American had specifically asked for the smaller munitions, probably because the US Air Force do not generally fly around with 1,000-pounders.

'OK, mate, this is over to you . . .' was what I actually heard, as I felt my heart rate increase and beads of sweat form on my forehead.

'Copied, I'm south of the target, request switch,' I replied, trying to sound as confident as I could and giving nothing away. At that moment me and my leader swapped altitudes and I assumed the lower level, ready to attack.

On the 'back-box' radio frequency, a separate communication channel between the Harriers, which could not be heard on the ground, I went through all the targeting detail with my RAF counterpart to make sure I had everything correct. Then he mentioned something else that, up until that moment, had not remotely crossed my mind, so focused was I on the task ahead.

'Yep, that sounds all good,' he said. 'Good luck, mate. This could be the big one, you know. This could be Bin Laden.'

So there I was on my first sortie about to attack a cave complex where the head of al-Qaeda and the mastermind of 9/11 might be hiding. He was one of the main reasons why we were out there in the first place and his death would cause a sensation around the world. But this barely registered. I didn't have the bandwidth to think all that through. Of course it was added pressure, but I had compartmentalised my mind to focus entirely on the technical aspects of my first job in combat, and I needed to shut everything else out – including the wider significance of who I might kill, if I managed to hit the target.

'Please don't mess this up,' I muttered to myself in the privacy of my cockpit as I prepared to put years of training into practice for the first time. 'Get this right, get it right . . .'

Getting a visual fix on the cave was not easy. The ground below was various shades of brown, and making out slight changes in elevation and occasional outcrops of rock through the desert haze was almost impossible. Spotting the dark scar of a cave entrance from above was a serious challenge, even though the diamond on my head-up display gave me a fix based on our American friend's GPS co-ordinates.

I needed to get visual confirmation and asked my leader, who had already spotted the complex, for permission to dive down so I could line up the diamond with the features he was describing. I tipped my Harrier in for the dive, started to make out a hazy ridge line and there it was – a black mark in the centre at the cave opening. Then I picked out the features to the left and right, slight kinks in the rock formations that would help me find it again when I came in ready to unleash the firepower under my wings.

I pulled up and circled round, ready to come in again 'hot and heavy'. I was being careful to be as economical with fuel as possible, to make sure I had enough for three good passes. All I cared about now was getting to the release point for my first bomb at about 9,000ft, which would give it the 10-second flying time it needed to arm itself before hitting the target.

I needed to be travelling at about 500 knots with my wings level for the weapon to head off on the right trajectory, and for all the parameters that governed its journey to that cave entrance to work.

I came down the slope towards the moment of truth, with the diamond and the cross hairs on the target. The dis-embodied American voice confirmed I was 'clear hot'. I had authority to drop. My speed built from 350 knots to 390, 410, 430, 460, 480, 490 . . . it was time to release the impact bomb and set it on its way.

I pressed the small round red weapons-fire button – we called it the 'pickle' button – on the left side of the stick, and felt the aircraft jolt as the bomb departed. Then I began to pull up and away, feeling the airframe shake as the Harrier tried to grip the thin air, dropping chaff and flares as I did so.

I knew my leader would be watching through his binocu-lars as he orbited above, and it felt like forever as I waited for his sit-rep. I just hoped I had not made a complete mess of it and missed by miles as I busied myself with the preparation for the next attack.

'Yeah, that was good – a DH,' I heard him say. Delta Hotel. Direct hit.

I refocused for the next run.

'Time to go again. That was good,' the leader confirmed. 'Let's use the airburst. Again, right on the entrance if you can, please, Nath.'

I delivered on target and then came in with all my rockets for good measure in a series of strikes that the forward controller deemed a 'mission success', releasing us to return to base.

I never saw any movement in or near that cave entrance, and there was no sign afterwards that I had killed anybody, let alone the al-Qaeda supremo. But I had broken my duck in Afghanistan and delivered weapons in anger for the first time. As we made our way back to Kandahar, I felt by turns numb, overwhelmed, and yet high on adrenaline. I had gone into a state of hyper-awareness during which I was able to focus on every tiny detail, and now I was releasing it all.

When I got back, I had to pinch myself. I had 'Winchestered' – a codeword we used for a jet that had expended all of its ammunition – on my first mission. I knew that some pilots took weeks to even fire a rocket, and there I was already feeling like I had made a contribution – however small – after one sortie. That helped me feel accepted in the close-knit society of Kandahar Harrier pilots. Like all the others, I had now done the deed. I had done something that is (and should be) outside normal human experience – dropped bombs on fellow human beings. Now I understood what we were about, and could sit comfortably in the silence along with the other pilots and, when we did chat, I could talk with them on a level, even though I had a long, long way to go.

It was probably fortunate that I saw no movement on that mission, and no indication that I had killed or injured anyone. Soon enough, it would be clear – via the pod or my binoculars – exactly who I was going to kill, what they were doing, what weapons they were carrying, even the clothes they were wearing, and when their lives were going to be dramatically changed or even brought to an end ...

9

We'd been scrambled – dashed to the aircraft, got airborne as fast as possible and over the 'green zone', the term we used to describe the narrow strip of fertile land along the Helmand River.

A company of Royal Marines, fighting alongside soldiers in the Afghan National Army, had been caught in an ambush near the town of Gereshk.

With my wingman in formation, we put the Harriers through their paces, climbing to 15,000ft, and then headed west-northwest towards the river, travelling fast above the expanse of empty desert. In 15 minutes we were on target and I made contact with the forward air controller on the ground.

From the cockpit, the vegetation on the eastern bank of the river looked like a dark green line that someone had painted on a vast canvas of light brown – a line that took us seconds to traverse. It looked deceptively peaceful, save for the wisps of grey smoke around the firefight.

I could sense the familiar tension in the forward air controller's voice and hear the background chatter of small arms fire every time he piped up on the radio. They had been patrolling an area of cultivated fields and had been pinned down by a large force of Taliban fighters operating along a hedge line with mortars and rocket launchers. The Marines had taken casualties and needed us to intervene to give them time to move back and regroup.

'Request immediate show of force,' he said rapidly and breathlessly, but trying hard to sound calm in the chaos of battle.

'Roger that,' I replied as we exchanged co-ordinates to establish exactly where they and the enemy were in the matrix of fields, ditches and treelines below us. We turned our Harriers away before banking round and making our approach. I was focused on doing whatever we could to help. We knew there were mortar rounds potentially in our airspace as we came in low, but the chances of being hit by one were vanishingly small.

I eased the stick forward, and with the radar-altimeter showing 50–100ft our two Harriers came smashing in over the desert, then across the fields and over the trees at high speed, with my wingman holding a separation of about half a mile. It was a classic fly-through in battle formation. Below me, I caught flashes of movement, a glimpse of three or four Taliban fighters running between trees, and then we passed them and were pulling up.

The show of force gave the Marines their first chance to try to get out. But incoming was still raining down on them and a few minutes later they had pinpointed the precise location of the enemy mortar team. It was near a haystack in the middle of a small field, midway between the treeline and the ditches and the irrigation canal where the Marines were holed up. They fired a smoke grenade into the haystack to make it visible from the air and I spotted it through the binoculars.

'We've lit the hay,' he told me. 'Hit that.'

'Yeah, copy.'

'You're cleared hot,' he said, as I tipped in again.

My wingman had only two 1,000lb bombs on board – too powerful for this sort of target and indeed for this type of close-quarters engagement, with our friendlies only a few hundred yards from the Taliban. So he flew overwatch as I went in to destroy the haystack and anyone around it. I unleashed all 38 of my rockets and watched it implode. 'Job done,' I thought, as the smoke cleared to show the stack burning fiercely and the flames spreading into the cut corn around it.

'Direct hit, good hit,' came the response from the controller, now running and gasping for air, as the Marines continued to move towards the desert, where they knew they would be safe. Then his voice went up an octave.

'We're missing some of our team ... we're missing some of our team ...'

I spotted a vehicle leaving the area on one of the rough dirt roads at high speed. A white truck of some sort, dust billowing behind it. This was an agricultural zone, without houses or compounds, so it was hard not to think it was connected in some way to the engagement below me. But that still didn't prepare me for what I heard next.

'There's a white Toyota Hilux heading north out of here,' the air controller was shouting. 'We reckon they've got three of our guys on board, and they've been taken – kidnapped.'

'OK, roger,' I replied. 'Yes, I have visual on the Hilux.' I imagined the driver thinking he was getting away, oblivious to the fact that I could catch him in two seconds if I needed to.

'Yes, that's it. You're cleared to strike.'

I was momentarily confused. 'Confirm? Are the guys in the Hilux the ones who have done the ambush?'

'Yes.'

'So where are our guys who have been kidnapped?'

'In the vehicle.'

'You want me to strike the vehicle?'

'Affirmative. They're as good as dead. They'll thank you for it.'

I guessed these were their mates – whether Afghan or British – and they must have had a pact: if any of them were taken alive, this is what they had agreed to do. They believed those men were going to be shamed, tortured, decapitated or skinned alive.

The radio had gone silent. Having worked with Commandos, I knew they would *say* they'd be prepared to call fire down on their own position in extreme circumstances, but I wondered whether they'd really carry it through. In any case, this was different. A cold-blooded attack on a vehicle that was leaving the battlefield, and carrying three of our own?

I knew I couldn't do it. There was no way I could drop weapons like this. There had to be a good reason to attack. Not least because I had to know I was acting within my rules of engagement. I was thinking, 'This is a decision I do not want to have to make; there has to be another solution to this, there simply has to be . . .'

I watched the Hilux gaining distance and looked back to where I could see the Marines on the move.

'OK,' I told them. 'I'm monitoring the Hilux, while I search the area.'

'Yeah, but take the Hilux ...'

'Negative. I'm searching the area ...'

I flew orbits around the target using my binoculars – the ordinary pair we routinely carried in the cockpit – to look for the missing men. I was hoping against hope they were not in the Hilux, and if that turned out to be the case, I could smash over there and take it out.

Another option was dropping a bomb ahead of the pickup, to make it stop. But doing that so close to a car with our own people inside was another course of action I wasn't prepared to consider. It would be dangerous for the captives, and probably fatal.

I was buying time because the guys on the ground wanted a decision. I knew I wasn't going to attack the Hilux; I also knew that not doing so would condemn their mates to something horrendous. But I had to make a decision that was both legally and morally correct, even if it meant consigning them to a fate worse than death.

I was on my own, with every second counting, alone in the cockpit, high above the drama being played out on the ground, with no chain of command to work through. And I knew that whatever I did, it would be post-mortemed by people in London, most of whom would never have had to take life-or-death decisions in the heat of battle.

With the aircraft on auto-pilot, I was holding the binoculars in one hand, the throttle in the other, to stop the Harrier stalling and falling out of the sky, and nursing the stick with my knees. I scanned the fields, ditches, treelines, tracks and any odd shapes I could find. I had almost given up hope when I spotted what looked like three silhouettes in the undergrowth, not far from the original ambush site. 'Thank God,' I muttered to myself. I kept staring at them, checking my airspeed and staring at them again.

'I've found three people,' I told the guys on the ground. I knew they could be three anybodies – ordinary Afghans hiding from the fighting, perhaps – but I was thinking, 'Please, please, please, let them be the ones we're looking for . . .'

I put the binoculars down to the right of my seat and started tracking the figures on the pod on my instrument panel. Once I had them in focus, I pointed my laser beam nearby to identify the spot and then got on the radio. I could see they were moving like drunks; one of them was probably injured and being carried or supported by the other two.

'It could be them,' I told the ground controller. 'But I can't be sure.'

We needed a helicopter to come in and get low down over them to confirm who these people were. The ground controller put in a call for air support and I made my own request to Kandahar, which fed through to Combined Allied Command in Qatar.

'Request helo support to identify potential friendlies,' I said.

Now we had to sit tight and wait, and hope these guys did not come under renewed attack before help arrived. By this time the Hilux was out of my visual range and was probably going to be difficult to find, but I couldn't have cared. All I was interested in was establishing whether or not these three were the guys the Marines had thought were missing.

Eventually a British Army Air Corps Apache arrived from Camp Bastion. The main body of the patrol had reorganised in the desert on the edge of the fertile strip and the helicopter went thumping over, circling above them like a giant hornet, effectively telling the Taliban to back off.

I gave the pilot the code for my laser and he used his sensor to locate it and lock on. Then I moved it towards the three bodies and his system tracked it, like a floating waypoint, as he flew towards them.

'OK, we're coming in – we've got a good spot,' the Apache pilot reported. 'Three friendlies confirmed, one looks badly wounded.'

We'd found them, but there was no time to relax. As the Marines moved back into the green zone to rescue the trio, a new firefight sparked up with Taliban in a treeline slightly further back, where they too had regrouped.

The Apache and my wingman had already been called away to another task and so once again it was up to me to 'deliver violence to the battlefield'. The forward air controller gave me the new target, and the Marines again used smoke to help me identify it. It was time for my two 540-pounders. I came in twice, first with the impact bomb, then pulled hard round and tipped in again with the airburst, which detonated fractionally above the ground.

They were both direct hits, but – and this is something I would never have believed if I hadn't seen it on several occasions in Afghanistan – even if you bang people right on their heads with big bombs, even 1,000-pounders, some of them always manage to walk away. I have no idea what state they are in, but they walk away.

And that's what happened. Three or four Taliban survivors were still taking the fight to the Marines, so my job was not done. I had no weapons left, but my blood was up. There was only one thing left in my armoury – the show of force that we had tried at the beginning.

I knew that if I flew over their heads at 100ft, our generally approved peacetime lowest limit, it wasn't going to make the slightest difference. These were committed men, fighting for their lives; I needed not just to scare them, but to try and take them out.

I had to weaponise the Harrier itself.

I flew away in a wide arc and brought the nose down, as the plane lost height, and set myself up to try and scare the living daylights out of the Taliban.

I was coming in low over the desert, the Harrier whistling and whining on a still Helmand day. The green zone was approaching, a thin dark line on my horizon. The target area was on the edge of the brown stuff before the vegetation began. I knew that, as soon as I'd overflown it, I'd have to pull up to avoid the trees.

I was barely above the surface of the earth, watching the distance to target counting down – 1.5 miles, 1.4, 1.3, 1.2. Then it came down to a mile. I was smashing in at full power and thinking I was going to take this flying bayonet as low as I could. Things were looking good. The radar-altitude meter was fluctuating in 5ft increments, as the dry desert floor undulated beneath the Harrier's belly; I needed to make sure there was nothing ahead that penetrated my lateral horizon.

If there was, I was going to hit the ground.

Now the desert was giving way to blobs of green – bushes and patches of grass. I was getting close. I deployed my speed brake – the rectangular baffle which drops down beneath the rear section of the airframe to help slow the plane on landing. I knew I couldn't hit the bad guys with my wing tip, but I could with the 'flying shovel', as long as I was coming in a few feet above the ground.

The green zone was coming up fast and I needed to get down even further. I eased the stick forwards, and focused on the little diamond in the centre of my head-up display that pinpointed the target co-ordinates I'd been given by the Marines. There were no low-altitude warnings or ground collision cautions in the cockpit, either audible or visual, because I'd turned them off. I was flying straight towards that diamond, and now the rad-alt was fluctuating in single digits, and anyone in my way was going to be killed out-right.

Now I was on it. A few more bushes, a drainage ditch, a low bridge. Three Taliban fighters were running across it, rifles in hand. In the snapshot of that scene in my mind, they are looking up, with wild eyes and bearded faces. I could only imagine the ear-splitting roar – a world of sound – that would have engulfed them at that moment, as my Harrier turned daylight briefly into darkness.

In a flash I was over them. I pulled hard on the stick as the vegetation became ever denser and more threatening to a jet flying parallel to the ground at, what felt like, head height. And it was only then that I was aware of my heart pounding in my chest. As always at times of real danger, I had been as calm as can be in the heat of the moment, focusing on what I needed to do to execute the manoeuvre. It was only afterwards that I felt the impact.

I took a couple of deep breaths, stowed the speed brake

and pumped out a few flares. I climbed high above the river, watching my instruments as I roared past the cultivated area and overflew the desert on the far side of it. As I eased back on the airspeed and began banking round again, I heard my friend – the forward air controller – on the radio.

'That's the gunfire over.' I could feel him relaxing, for the first time in this encounter. 'It's all gone quiet now, and we are in the process of extracting.'

A few minutes went by before he came on again to confirm that the contact with the enemy had now ceased. It was time for me to head for Kandahar.

I landed 20 minutes later, shut down the engine as normal and climbed out of the cockpit. I greeted the ground crew as if I had returned from a routine sortie.

'I see all your weapons are gone, sir,' said the crew chief. 'You still got all your flares in there?'

'Most of them. Oh, there's one thing you could do for me,' I added. 'Could you check the speed brake ... you know, give it a once-over.'

'Yes sir,' he replied. 'Did you have a problem with it? Is there something wrong?'

'Just check for any blood stains or impact marks.'

'What d'you mean, sir? Did you have a bird strike, or a problem on landing?'

'No, no ... I just tried to take some people out with it, that's all.'

I left them scratching their heads and walked off to do the debrief with the intelligence officer.

* * *

My airbrake tactic was to become quite controversial. About six months later, an air chief marshal's advice to pilots en route to Afghanistan was to remember, when they were Winchestered in combat, they were flying a weapon – the plane itself.

The UK press couldn't resist framing the story as if he was telling his aviators to go kamikaze, when, really, he was saying that this war was a real, grubby, dirty and hugely personal counter-insurgency campaign that we could not be detached from, sitting in our cockpits 20,000ft above the battlefield. He was trying to instil in us the commitment to engage and fight, as if we were Coalition troops on the ground.

I am sure he was thinking along the same lines as I was that day over Gereshk – use the plane to the limits of its hazard spectrum to either kill people or scare the hell out of them.

Our jets are basically high-tech muskets in a battlefield environment, and I was fixing bayonets as a last resort. Actually, this was not the last resort: that would be if there was a massive fight going on and the bad guys were about to overwhelm our troops.

In the most extreme scenario, the 'Winchestered' Harrier should become a £20 million flying bomb. I'd aim mine to pile in on top of the enemy, then pull the handle, and hope the ensuing explosion would turn the tide of the engagement sufficiently for our guys to dust themselves off and come and rescue me afterwards.

10

I had rarely been so intent on delivering firepower on target. I was not aiming to kill anyone; it was more about not destroying infrastructure – in this case a small but important dam on the Helmand River.

I had to be inch-perfect with my volley of rockets. I knew that if I damaged the dam, it could have long-lasting negative consequences for the NATO Coalition. We were aware that this was a war of hearts and minds, and messing up the water supply that serviced thousands of homes and farms in the Helmand Valley was a sure way to lose it.

As my Harrier screamed along towards the thin concrete wall, I could see muzzle flashes from my right where the Royal Marines had holed up in the trees. I came round a bit, to line up with the patch of ground on the opposite bank of the river, next to where the landward end of the dam started, and fired my warning shots.

The objective was to scare away the 10-strong group of Taliban, who had driven the Marines off and were now fighting their way across the dam towards them. I saw the impact – a cloud of dust and flying rocks – and, as I pulled up, I waited for my friend Bobby's verdict.

Had the Taliban taken the hint and legged it, and was the dam still in one piece?

I had no idea I would come across a guy on the battlefield that day I used to think of as 'Jackpot 06', and who knew me as 'Jackpot 07', our callsigns as fellow students at RAF Leeming in Yorkshire. We had spent a couple of months together there on the forward air controller course five years earlier.

We'd sat next to each other in class, and eaten together in the old portable cabin school building at the base. And we'd sloshed around in the mud of the North York Moors, as I helped him understand what the ground looked like from the perspective of a pilot travelling overhead at more than 400 miles an hour. There was a real knack to it, and I enjoyed helping him, using the experience I had as an almost fully fledged Sea Harrier pilot.

That sortie over the river had begun when me and my wingman had been called to a firefight in Nowzad, a few minutes' flying time from the Kajaki Dam complex in the rugged northeast corner of Helmand.

After intervening with a bomb attack on a Taliban position, we heard a ground controller requesting urgent fast-jet assistance in an ongoing firefight. He said Taliban fighters were in danger of taking control of one of the smaller diversion dams on the Helmand River, below the main one at Kajaki, and overrunning their position.

'We cannot lose the dam,' he said firmly, before going on to tell us that his unit of Royal Marines was under heavy incoming fire, and that time was of the essence.

I recognised his voice immediately ... and the call from fellow Royal Marines in need of help.

I decided to skip the formalities with fighter control back in Kandahar and responded spontaneously. I knew that if I went the official route, there would be a delay of 10 minutes or more, as permissions were sought and assessments made. We didn't have that time to spare.

I told my wingman I was going to fly 'split-ops' and break away. If the situation at Nowzad deteriorated, he was to let me know immediately so that I could return if required.

I wasn't sure if Bobby already had an inkling that I was one of the two pilots overflying Nowzad, but I decided to use my official callsign for that day's mission to start with.

'Widow 84,' I said, identifying him from his earlier transmission. 'This is Devil 55.'

'Devil 55, Widow 84,' came his response, 'you're loud and clear.'

I asked him for the co-ordinates of his position and tapped them in as I began the short trip to the new target zone.

Then I checked to see if this really *was* Bobby.

'This is Jackpot 07,' I announced briskly, expecting him to be properly confused if I'd got this wrong.

There was a delay of a few seconds, as the thought bubble expanded between us. Then he came back: 'Jackpot 07, Jackpot 06 ...'

Oh yes, we were back in business. But there was no time for niceties. The clock was ticking and I asked him for directions – exactly the sort of thing we had practised together in Yorkshire.

'I'm over Nowzad, I can see Kajaki and I can see the Helmand Valley – give me a quick talk-on, really big picture,' I told him.

He did a first-class job and we clicked like two cogs turning together, as I closed on his position.

On the way I informed fighter control about my diversion as a *fait accompli,* giving them no time to prevaricate or delay me. The guy on the other end got the message and let me get on with it.

I approached from upstream, smashing in at 50–100ft, and called Bobby at two miles' range, then one mile. He told me he had visual on my Harrier, as I came thundering through.

This was a tricky and fast-moving situation with few options for a safe and effective intervention. I could see the Taliban about a third of the way along the road cresting the dam. It looked like there was a fierce firefight underway with the Marines in the trees on the right-hand bank of the small reservoir behind the dam.

The other side, to my left, was mainly agricultural land and orchards. The question was, how did I convince the bad guys to back off and head back to where they came from? I didn't dare use my armour-piercing rockets on the dam itself, for fear of causing a structural failure, and my 540lb bombs were out of the question.

We needed to give the enemy fighters the impression they had no choice but to turn round and head for the bankside where, if they continued their assault, I knew I could attack them. Sometimes a show of force was all that was needed, but they'd ignored my initial fly-through. In fact, Bobby told me, the attack was intensifying and their lives were at risk.

It was time for plan B.

All I could think of was unleashing a big explosive impact

on the bank behind the insurgents with a volley of rockets, while the Marines delivered a sustained and intense barrage of fire from their side of the water. The hope was that, taken together, these would help the Taliban to realise their position was no longer tenable, and turn tail.

After sweeping round, I came in low for the second time and delivered 19 rockets as the Marines went for it with their heavy machine guns and whatever else they had. I sent the rockets in at 4,000ft slant range and the boys kept their end of the bargain up for as long as they could.

Then came Bobby's verdict. It was either going to work, or we would have a serious situation on our hands that would be difficult for me to do anything about.

The wait seemed to last forever.

I heard the click as he came on the radio.

'Rockets on target, dam still intact, enemy look to be moving off and regrouping . . .'

'Copy that!' I tried to sound calm and collected, but was mightily relieved. 'I'll remain overheard ready to hit them if they re-engage.'

But it looked like that would never happen, because, once they had regained the left-hand bank, the Taliban did what they did so often, so effectively. They turned themselves into ghosts, disappearing into the nearby orchards and becoming invisible to both Bobby and me.

I held off and closed my throttle to reduce engine noise. Perhaps they would come to the conclusion I had lost interest and departed. The minutes ticked by and, as they did so, the Marines moved forward again onto the dam, regaining the position they had lost.

Then came the moment we had been waiting for. The enemy couldn't resist the temptation to re-establish contact. The fire-fight started up again as they emerged from the orchard.

'OK, they've reorganised and we are taking fire again,' Bobby reported.

'Roger, I'm tally target, visual friendlies, coming in . . .'

This time there was no need to worry about the dam or anything else. The rules of engagement made the Taliban a legitimate target, an imminent threat to life, and I had the chance to make a decisive intervention.

I came in for the third time, and saw the Taliban firing across the water. I placed the bomb cross on their position and delivered a 540lb airburst right on top of them. Once again there was a big plume of smoke, dust and rubble, but this time the battle was over.

'Delta Hotel, stand by for battle damage assessment,' Bobby reported. And then a few minutes later: 'All enemy fire now ceased.'

'That's all copied, Jackpot 06,' I told him.

We were done for the day.

'This is Jackpot 07 signing off,' I told him, and I pulled the nose of the Harrier around the horizon.

On the way back to Kandahar, I reflected on a successful outcome to a tricky challenge and one that our training had not prepared either of us for. On the ranges at home, a target was a target and we just hit it. But the reality of war proved more complex, and this was a case in point. I needed to help protect our own troops, but without destroying the lifelines of hundreds of thousands of Afghans.

We had found a way to convince the Taliban to do the

one thing that would lead to their demise. On the following tour, I employed the same tactics on the main Kajaki Dam. An initial volley of rockets on the bank of the reservoir as a warning prompted the same reaction we had achieved on the smaller dam, as the Taliban retreated and regrouped. And the follow-up proved just as effective.

As Bobby had released me to rejoin my wingman and head for home, I'd wished him well and told him to look me up when he was passing through Kandahar on R&R. We worked a couple of other missions in Afghanistan, but I never saw him again.

11

It was the day *after* the sixth anniversary of my accident that someone tried to shoot me down. As on the previous five occasions, I had managed to avoid flying on 5 December.

This wasn't about superstition, it was a matter of focus and concentration. I knew that it would be almost impossible to clear my mind in the way I needed to in order to carry out a mission of any kind.

I'd dwell on all the nagging details in the time building up to it – 9.25am, the instant that my Sea Harrier flipped – and clock-watch as the minutes and seconds ticked by to the moment I pulled the handle with the plane almost upside down.

In the first few years, I'd be in thrall to my silent count-down. As each anniversary followed on, one after another, its grip gradually loosened. I would find that 10 minutes had passed and I had missed it. Then, as commitments at home and other distractions came into play, it would be gone by half an hour and I would look up to check the clock and breathe again.

But one way or another, I managed to avoid flying on that day for 12 years.

I finally broke my duck in December 2014 when I was

starting my training on the US Air Force Test Pilot School conversion course at San Antonio, Texas. I was scheduled to go up in a T38 Talon, a two-seater supersonic trainer, in the student role, taking my first steps towards becoming a test pilot.

That wasn't the right time to start making special requests; test pilots fly whenever and wherever they are needed, and they rely on raw data, not emotion. So that's how I took another big step towards overcoming the Wittering legacy.

During my three tours in Afghanistan, I was still going through some of the early anniversaries. While I tried not to make a big thing out of it, I would do my best to organise my rota so I was on a no-fly day on 5 December, or scheduled to fly only in an emergency. In that way, I managed to avoid being airborne and having to fight when my mind was elsewhere.

But 24 hours later I would be back, ready to rock and roll, and on this occasion we had been scrambled at midday to a 'troops in contact' in the Panjwayi district. This was a rural area close to Kandahar city, where the Canadians had been engaged in bloody exchanges with the Taliban that had cost many lives on both sides.

As I strapped in and punched the co-ordinates of our initial rendezvous point into the cockpit computer, the diamond showing the position of the firefight came up right on top of the airfield. 'We're already there . . . which means we could be under attack before we even take off,' I thought as I pressed 'zoom in' several times to see exactly how close this one was.

It turned out to be a few clicks west of the airfield, which meant we would be taking off right on top of the Canadians and the people trying to kill them in the fields of the green zone to the southwest of us. After a quick check with my wingman, we decided to launch over the open desert to give us scope to climb safely and minimise the risk of being shot at.

Once up at 15,000ft and 16,000ft respectively, we checked in with the Canadian ground controller. Their patrol had been ambushed not far from one of their forward operating bases. At least one armoured vehicle had been hit in an IED detonation, and they had sustained multiple casualties. They had called for a helicopter medevac and were now pinned down as they tried to reorganise and extract.

'We need you to get eyes on the enemy,' the controller yelled above the din of small-arms fire and rocket impacts.

'Yeah, roger that,' I replied as I looked down on a patch-work quilt of green fields. I could see the Canadians through my binoculars, fanned out in a cordon off an unmade track running along the centre of the valley. And I could see a smouldering black hole and what remained of their vehicle. But I couldn't spot either muzzle flashes or movement on the ground in front of them.

There was no way I could intervene with my rockets or the 540-pounders without being sure what I was firing at, or without the consent of the ground controller.

'I'm going to give you an escalation of force,' I told our Canadian contact. 'I don't want to put warning rockets down when I can't even see the enemy. So if that doesn't work, we'll try and work out a safe place to put some shots down that will convince them to move out.'

'OK, roger,' he replied as I got on the back-box with my wingman and we discussed our plan of attack. He'd fly overwatch as I came in low over the Canadians. If my presence prompted any movement by the enemy, he'd be ready to spot it.

My plan was to come in fast and low – 50–100ft – over the desert and then zip up the valley towards our friendly forces. Once there, I would break right, pumping flares as I did so. This tactic, using the Harrier as a noisy and menacing projectile, had often produced dramatic results because the Taliban had no idea whether I was going to open fire or not, and in many cases it had been enough to convince them to retreat.

Sometimes we used this sort of move as a morale booster with people we were trying to encourage to work with us. When remote villages were being scouted out by expeditionary troops for the first time, we would be called in to produce a dramatic demonstration of NATO Coalition air power to impress local elders. 'We're here to help you' was the message as we screamed over their heads, and 'we're here to stay.' Sadly, this would be a commitment we honoured only in the breach.

I could see the abrupt splash of flourishing vegetation ahead of me, against the browns and greys of the open desert, as I pushed down, levelled off and increased speed. This looked and felt routine enough as I approached the first fields, and the crops, irrigation canals and occasional compounds started whipping by in a blur underneath me.

Then something caught my eye.

To the right, at the entrance to the wadi, I saw a shadowy figure get to his feet and grab something from his waistcoat pocket.

He was starting to tap into it and, as I flew over the top of him, I realised that I'd been 'dicked'.

That's the term we used for what scouts or lookouts – 'dickers' in our jargon – did, warning fellow fighters that we were approaching. This guy was about 10 miles from the target, so there was every possibility he could get a call or a text to his mates further up the valley that I was on my way.

I exhaled into my oxygen mask, reset myself in my seat and pressed on. My spider senses were tingling, but there was nothing I could do except be extra-vigilant and watch for anything unusual as I came closer to the firefight.

About a minute later, a mile from the Canadians, I saw them . . .

'Whoa! Here we go – these have to be the ones he called . . .'

There were three of them, running towards the edge of the wadi, widening their angle to my direction of flight.

Not for the first time in my combat experience, everything seemed to slow down as I watched them out of the corner of my eye. Two had AK-47 assault rifles and one was carrying a tube. A Stinger anti-aircraft missile, or some kind of SAM ground-to-air missile? I had no idea.

As I flew towards them, I clocked the guy with the tube, as the others opened fire on either side of him, their Kalashnikovs held high above their shoulders, pointing straight at me. The one with the tube seemed to have been caught unprepared by the speed of my arrival. Was that a look of surprise on his face? But I was still 200 metres from him, giving him just enough time to react.

He brought his weapon up, but fired it from the hip.

Sitting in my Perspex bubble, I watched this bit of silent

theatre play itself out on the stage below. In slow motion, I saw a small black dot rising towards me. I seemed to be watching this siren of immediate and present danger for what felt like minutes, with its grey smoke trailing behind it. Then it was gone, disappearing like a passing planet in space, no more than 10–15 metres over my left shoulder.

'SAFIRE,' I shouted out loud to myself, using the military acronym for surface-to-air fire.

I could feel my blood rising. I couldn't believe I'd been directly targeted and shot at for the first time. I had spotted the dicker and they had nearly reacted in time, while I'd carried on regardless, assuming, hoping they would not. How dare they? These guys had tried to *kill* me. And I'd been their willing accomplice . . .

This was potentially a game-changing moment, not only for me, but for all Coalition air assets – fast jets, helicopters and transport aircraft alike. I had not heard of a Harrier or an American jet being picked out in this way before, and if the Taliban were now capable of using some form of ground-to-air missile against us, our tactics would have to change. We'd have to fly above a minimum altitude and change the types of weapons we carried, while shows of force would be out of the question.

I knew that if I got on the radio and uttered the S-word it would have an electrifying impact, sparking an instant and dramatic response, with an investigation launched immediately to establish exactly what had been fired in my direction. Was it a Stinger or a rocket-propelled grenade (RPG), of the kind that had regularly been used against helicopters?

But my priority at that moment was delivering for the

Canadians on the ground. In an instant I made the decision to hold off on telling the wider world what I had seen and concentrate on completing this show of force.

I sat tight, got to the target and banked right as planned, pumping out flares. I pulled up but kept my eye on the trio who had tried to take me down. I had spotted them running into a small hut, about 50 metres from where I had first seen them, and I kept a check on it from then on. I was determined not to let them get away.

I got on the back-box to my wingman, as my Harrier climbed through 10,000ft.

'Did you see that? I've just had a SAFIRE – two small arms, one missile.'

'Yeah, copied. I saw the puff of smoke and wondered what it was. You seemed to have flushed out the guys we were looking for.'

'Yeah, I've got eyes on a hut where they ran to . . .'

Switching frequencies back to the Canadians, I checked in with the ground controller.

'Did that have the desired effect?' I asked him.

'Yes, directly over the target, good effect. Enemy small-arms fire now ceased.'

'Roger that,' I replied.

'Halo' – the term we used for medical helicopters – 'now inbound,' he added.

This was excellent news. Maybe we had flushed out some of the main players who were pinning the Canadians down. It meant I was now free to talk about what had happened.

Keeping a close eye on that hut, I called up fighter control at Kandahar, gave them my callsign – which was either

Devil or Satan (we were told later to change both of those, because they were considered politically unacceptable) – and told them what they needed to know.

'SAFIRE, SAFIRE, SAFIRE,' I began, then gave my position, before going on to answer the first of a barrage of questions.

At this point, the pilot of a British Army Apache announced that he was inbound, coming up the valley, escorting a US Air Force Blackhawk medevac chopper. I recognised his voice immediately. He was another friend on the battlefield in Afghanistan.

This time it was a guy I had been with in the university flying squadron during my time at Manchester. I'd bumped into him at Timmy Horton's coffee shop in the Canadian section at Kandahar a couple of weeks earlier.

I told him I had received a SAFIRE and he confirmed he was aware of what had happened. I also told him my assailants were in the hut, and gave him the co-ordinates. I was operating under rules of engagement which forbade me from attacking them, unless they continued to present an imminent threat to me – by taking more pot shots, for example, should I come down low again.

The Apache was treated like a big infantry soldier, and worked to a different set of rules. He could attack whether they fired at him or not, as long as he could identify them as enemy combatants. I watched him heading towards the target using my laser to help him find it, until he piped up to say he was now receiving SAFIRE himself from the same three individuals who had attacked me. It meant their fate was sealed.

'We are setting up for an attack with Hellfire,' he said.

I watched from above. A few seconds later, a pair of lethally precise air-to-ground missiles shot out from underneath the Apache's stubby wings and almost instantaneously engulfed the area around the enemy fighters in a fireball. After a brief pause, the gunship pilot confirmed that the target had been 'neutralised'.

The firefight now over, the Blackhawk came in to pick up the most severely wounded Canadian casualties and we offered both helicopters top-cover for the short flight back to the Kandahar field hospital. We flew orbits overhead and then climbed high over the airfield ready to recover and land.

I had taken to heart the advice from that war-weary, homeward-bound RAF Harrier pilot not to land at the same time as the medevac helicopter. But this time I couldn't avoid it, having got down just before the Blackhawk came in. In fact, I was on my way back to our dispersal area when I was asked to wait on the taxiway as the Blackhawk approached.

The pilot came in fast, at right angles to the taxiway, pulled the nose up in the flare manoeuvre to reduce his speed, and then turned 90 degrees to line up and drop down. With no guns mounted, and big red crosses on a white background on its dusty black fuselage, the American helicopter sent a huge cloud of dust billowing in my direction.

Standing alongside the taxiway, the emergency medical team were already waiting dressed in their surgical gowns. As soon as the wheels touched the concrete, the loadmaster pushed the sliding side door open and motioned urgently for them to race forward.

I saw what I thought were two casualties, with drips attached, being carried out and placed on trolleys. There were silver and gold space blankets flapping in the wind from the rotors. In my mind's eye, I always see those broken bodies enveloped in red blankets, but I can't be sure why. Were they really red? Were they blankets, or were those blood-soaked bandages? My brain still plays tricks with me, as my subconscious and my memory fight to decide what I can live with and what I can't.

As I sat in my cockpit – canopy open and pushed back – watching this sad scene, I felt only admiration for the soldiers concerned, for the aircrew and for the medical professionals who performed miracles with even the most severely wounded. It made me all the more determined to do everything in my power to help men and women whose war involved, not the air-conditioned and comfortable cockpit of a modern jet, but putting their boots on the ground, knowing they could be ambushed or blown up at any moment.

As soon as the casualties were on the trolleys and moving off, with a phalanx of medical orderlies in attendance, the side door was slammed shut and the Blackhawk took off on another mercy mission to the battlefield. It was time for me to finish my taxi to the Harrier sun shelters at the bottom of the airfield.

After I had shut down, I thought about the minimal protection afforded by the canopy against bullets or worse. I placed my thumb and forefinger on either side of the Perspex; it was probably no more than five millimetres thick. We liked to feel invincible in our cockpits, but it struck me then that we would be a lot safer in a car, if someone was shooting at us, than a Harrier.

When I climbed out, I had a good look around the jet to see if I had picked up any impacts from the AK-47s, which were capable of bringing my plane down with one well-placed round in the engine.

'All OK, sir?' asked the head maintainer.

'Yeah, I'm just checking because I got shot at by two guys with AKs and another with a rocket of some kind.'

'Oh, right – interesting day at the office, then?'

'You could say that . . .'

'We'll take over from here,' he added briskly. And with that, four guys started crawling all over the plane, meticulously looking for signs of damage.

Much as I would have liked some time to reflect and relax, my debrief with the intelligence officers proved a long and arduous affair, as I was grilled on every aspect of the SAFIRE event. What did the warhead look like? What did the smoke trail look like? What colour was it? Was it straight or corkscrewing?

They were keen to send people out to examine the launch site, from where I had been attacked, but I was adamant that should be avoided at all costs. It was a dangerous and unpredictable area, full of enemy fighters and hidden IEDs, and it was no place for people trying to carry out a forensic investigation. I am pretty sure my advice was followed.

Within 24 hours the investigation had concluded that the most likely explanation was that I had been shot at by someone using an RPG. That meant the threat level remained unchanged. We could fly on the assumption that the Taliban still did not have a sophisticated surface-to-air capability.

We could continue as we were.

12

I was watching him on the pod using infrared – a little black two-dimensional ninja, moving nimbly between the rocks on the ridgeline. One foot wrong and he would have tumbled thousands of feet.

I couldn't believe how easy he made it look in terrain that would have challenged even the most experienced mountaineer. He ran, skipped even, across scree and between boulders, then stopped, pulled his rifle from the bag on his back, and took a shot.

I was flabbergasted that I had managed to find him as the shadows lengthened at the end of the day. This was the crest of a vast mountainside but there he was, moving in and out of the darker areas through pools of sunlight, several thousand feet below me.

Grabbing the binoculars, I could see his beard and caught glimpses of his shalwar kameez fluttering in the breeze. I could see that he was wearing flip-flops; an Afghan sniper in flip-flops, on his own, at 8,000ft above sea level.

I reckoned he was probably in his late twenties and I could tell that he was a master of his craft as he stopped again, steadied himself and sent another round towards the Australian Special Forces pinned down in the valley.

In all my experience I had never seen someone so at one with his tactical surroundings. 'How on earth do you fight somebody so agile, so elusive, ghostly even, to our Western eyes – how do you fight that, and, more importantly, how do you win?'

I put that thought to one side. Now he wasn't moving at all – perhaps catching his breath and reloading his rifle – sitting, crouching on his knees in a dark dip between rocks. He knew we were after him. He could hear the whine of our Pegasus engines above the wind, and I could sense him scanning the horizon.

We had a chance, but this was going to be far from easy. In that terrain a miss would be as good as a mile . . .

That day had started routinely enough.

My task, along with a wingman, was to carry out a photo-reconnaissance mission in the Chora Valley, an area of wide, fertile land overlooked by rugged mountains, about 115 miles to the north of Kandahar, where Taliban activity was increasing.

These missions required detailed planning, and we'd spent three hours with the intelligence officers, establishing exactly what waypoints we needed to fly between, our headings, altitude and so on.

We never knew the purpose of the intelligence. It could have been focused, for example, on a compound that ground troops wanted to target in a kill-or-capture operation. In that case, our pictures would help them understand all sorts of tiny but critical details – the design of a front door, the position of a door handle and hinges, the thickness of walls.

Another typical point of focus would be a rough road where Coalition forces suspected IEDs were being planted. Aerial photography on successive days could help establish whether there had been any change in the surface, or signs of freshly disturbed earth.

The camera on the GR7 worked automatically and was mounted in a pod on the fuselage, more or less bang under the pilot's seat. The key was to fly straight and steady to ensure the frames came out clear and crisp.

With the briefing finished, we got our kit and headed off to the jets at the other end of the airfield. We jumped into an old civilian jeep, our only form of transport at Kandahar, and drove slowly around to where the planes were waiting under their sun shelters. This was not a scramble, so we had to go the long way round, on the sand-covered road that came within metres of the perimeter fence.

In all my time in Afghanistan, I never felt so vulnerable to attack as I did when driving that route. In addition to its military role, the airfield was used by civilian passenger aircraft, and we knew suicide bombers would target the busy checkpoints on the main access road to the terminal building, just the other side of the fence.

Hundreds of people would queue to get in, and we would come dangerously close to them, with no body armour and no protection on the vehicle. I used to sit with my Walther PPK cocked and loaded on my lap, ready to use it at any moment, as we made our way slowly past the checkpoints. We had to make sure we did not attract the attention of the military police on the base for speeding – hard to believe, I know.

The photo-reconnaissance mission was going according to plan, as I flew pre-arranged headings methodically, one after another. On each pass, my wingman sat in battle formation alongside me, about a mile away and 1,000ft above, making sure no one was trying to attack us from the lush pastures of the Chora Valley.

But after we had been airborne for about an hour, we started to hear activity on our radio, the sort of rapid bursts of communications that could mean only one thing – our troops were in a fight with the enemy somewhere, and they needed help.

With just 50 minutes of 'playtime' left, we were re-tasked to an area south of us, in the Helmand Valley, where a Coalition ground patrol was under attack. Both our planes were carrying bombs, and my wingman also had rockets, but, after contacting the unit when we arrived overhead, we agreed to carry out our stock-in-trade – a show of force.

We came in loud, fast and low over the firefight and the Taliban position – perhaps 100ft above ground in battle formation – to shake the Afghans down and give our guys the chance to move.

It had the desired effect, and with the troops now out of danger, we were released to head back to Kandahar, with fuel running low. But what had been a relatively uneventful day by the standards of that war took another unexpected turn. There was a new 'troops in contact' alert back in the Chora area, and once again we got the job. This time, it was some Australian Special Forces guys, who had been pinned down by mortar fire in open country surrounded by steep mountains.

The Kandahar command and control desk tasked us to liaise with a refuelling aircraft on the way. Although there were no reports of casualties, time was of the essence, and I was the first to plug into the US Air Force tanker, high above the desert. As I eased my refuelling probe into the basket, I was hand-jamming the details of the new target into the controller below the head-up display.

The Aussies were in 4x4 armoured vehicles. They had been ambushed on flat ground by a group of fighters in a gully at the base of the mountains, less than a mile from them. They were taking incoming fire, with nowhere to hide, and they wanted us to hit the Taliban to give them a chance of getting away. Even small-calibre incoming mortar rounds at close range can have quite a large kill radius, and being subject to random explosions was no fun, whether you were Aussie SAS or not.

What I was about to do was going to lead to the deaths of people on the ground, but I barely gave it a moment's thought. My sole objective was protecting our troops, and ensuring that whatever we did eliminated the threat they were facing, without harming them. First, I had to match up the Taliban position on the pod with what I could see through my binoculars, then destroy the mortar pad and the people using it.

The Aussies called for my 1,000-pounder, but I advised them against it. A better weapon was the 540lb airburst bomb, which detonated at 10 or 20 feet above the ground and was extremely effective against people clustered in a relatively confined space.

It was my wingman who would be prosecuting the attack,

while I guided it in. This was standard stuff, and once I had locked on with my laser pointer, he came in at 15,000ft with wings level, and I counted him down to the release point.

'Laser is firing,' I said, once I was sure of the target in the cross hairs.

'Good spot, in hot, heading north, five secs.'

'Cleared hot,' the Aussie whispered into his radio.

'Stores away,' my wingman said, as he released the weapon bang on track, setting it up to free-fall.

Watching from above, I expected to see a cloud of dust and debris rising from the impact after about 15 seconds. But I saw nothing, and my heart skipped a beat.

What the hell had happened to that bomb?

I scanned the ground on both sides of the canopy. Had it tumbled out of control and landed somewhere else? I had noticed a small grey smudge in the air below my Harrier, and felt a slight rumble immediately after the release. But it was only when I spoke again to our Aussie contact on the radio that we realised what had happened.

'We saw no splash,' I told him.

'Yeah, mate, no splash seen down here either,' he replied, as another muffled incoming mortar explosion registered in the background. 'But we did hear a loud bang up in the air.'

It could only be one thing – a premature detonation of a bomb that was supposed to arm itself away from the aeroplane, and then fly to the target. Instead, it had armed itself almost immediately after release, and its radar sensor must have thought it had detected the ground and acted accordingly.

The big danger in these situations was for the releasing

aircraft. We both knew it might have sustained impact damage from explosive fragments that could be enough to cause the fuselage to catch fire or start to disintegrate, what we termed 'self-frag'. We needed to know whether my wingman was going to have to eject, and quickly, but we also had to get a weapon on that target. The Aussies were still dealing with an imminent threat to life.

'OK, looks like we've had a prem det,' I told my wingman, trying to sound as unruffled as I could. 'I'm now going to attack, but I want you to fly the profile with me, so I can inspect your aircraft on the way in. To start with, we'll be heading away from the firefight so, if you do have to jump out, you won't land anywhere near it.' We never used the term 'eject' in the air, unless we meant for someone to actually do it.

'Copy that,' he said as calmly as he was able, but I could sense his momentary terror at the prospect of ejecting into enemy-held territory, and all that that entailed. 'I'm not seeing any warnings or cautions or any unusual indications,' he added, as we continued the circuit.

Then he went very quiet as I flew up underneath him, within about 30ft of his airframe, and had a good look at the fuselage, the wings, nozzles and remaining weapons. After dropping behind, I pulled up and rolled over the top and checked from above.

'I can't see anything – you're looking good. But if you need to head back now, that's not a problem . . .'

'No, Nath, I'm all good. If you've looked and there's nothing – I'm staying,' he replied, as we completed the circuit and I came in and delivered hell on earth to the Taliban with my laser-guided 1,000lb bomb.

We thought our eventful sortie was over at that point. But although the mortaring had stopped, the Australians were still being zapped, this time by single high-powered rounds – the work of that lone sniper. They reckoned he hadn't been with the others at the base of the mountain, but was a long way up. And he was good – regularly pinging the armoured sides of the vehicles with successive shots.

'He's located somewhere on the ridgeline,' the Australian soldier said. 'And he's making life very difficult for us.'

'OK, I'll see what we can find.'

With the sun starting to set, this was a tall order. We scoured the precipitous slopes overlooking the vehicles, trying to find one man amongst the rocks and boulders, who could be near the top, at the top, or halfway down. I've always been good at finding needles in haystacks, but this was a long shot.

I scanned the moonscape below me, sweeping the binoculars from side to side, and checking anything that looked even vaguely like a human being on the pod. I saw nothing. I peeled off and swung round in another orbit, with the sun behind me and came in again. To start with I saw nothing. But then I caught the flash of something glinting in the sunlight, a gun barrel, maybe, or perhaps a long-range sight . . .

I looked again, right at the top of what was a knife-edge of a ridge.

And there he was, scampering along, darting in and out of the boulders. I lost him for a second and then saw him again as he stopped, crouching on one knee preparing to fire again. Then he darted over the ridge and into a small gap in the rocks.

'I've got him visual,' I told the Aussies.

'I've got him,' I said to myself.

We hatched a plan of attack. There was no point in trying to bomb a single human being on a rocky ridgeline, where the explosion would be fragmented and even a slight deviation from the target could see the projectile miss and land way down the mountain. Rockets would be more effective. We knew that if they were accurately targeted, they could get right into the small shadowy dip in the profile where the sniper had holed up.

We also knew we didn't have much time before he moved again, and that he had chosen the more challenging side of the ridge on which to hide. He was facing away from the Aussies, which meant we were about to risk leaving our friends vulnerable to anything that overflew the ridge.

The key to executing this with as much control as possible would be a steep dive to ensure the weapons were going down, not across. It was going to be more than a little awkward.

We flew out and back and I set myself up on the same side as my wingman to lase the target. Everything was looking good as he tipped in. Then, at the last moment, I heard him say: 'Stand by, I'm resetting.'

'Damn,' I thought, 'damn, damn ... we're going to lose him, and the daylight.'

There was no time to discuss it cockpit-to-cockpit; he may have decided he was coming in at the wrong angle, or too fast, or his aircraft wasn't picking up my laser pointer. Either way, we only had one shot at this, so if it took a quick reset to save some lives, it was worth it. It certainly wasn't easy, and was something we'd never practised.

Then I lost sight of his Harrier, and worse, I was still on the wrong side of the mountain, when he called to say he was tipping in again. I needed full power to roar across to get into position, and this time I watched all 38 of his rockets pile in and obliterate the area where the sniper had been hiding.

'That's a Delta Hotel,' I reported as we pulled away. 'Are you still getting incoming?'

'Nah, mate,' came the instant reply from our friend down under. 'All good here. You must have got him. We're planning to extract. Cheers, guys.'

'No problem,' I replied, and told him that we would now head back to base.

So that was finally that. We had taken out people on two occasions that day to protect our own troops. Once back on the ground, I felt relieved – that we hadn't made any mistakes, had dealt with a serious weapons malfunction and had still delivered under pressure.

People often ask how we dealt with the psychological impact of killing someone from the comfort of our cockpits. I never took that responsibility lightly, but I never had an issue on that score either. When push comes to shove, the only thing on your mind is protecting your own people. When you are coming in to attack, that is all you can be focused on. Nothing else matters, and there is no dilemma. The time for that was years earlier, in training, when we had had the opportunity to join the few who walked away.

When other people are relying on you to stand up and do your job, you no longer have that luxury. You're not part of a massive enterprise in which one absentee will make no difference. If you are not there, as a single-seat, fast-jet combat pilot, it really does matter. So it's a case of 'This is what you have to do, so now you need to execute' and make that work in your head.

About 10 days after that sortie, the Australians were transiting through Kandahar and their sergeant came over to our building to deliver a letter of thanks from the government in Canberra for what we had done to help. I was flying at the time, but they told my commanding officer what had happened after we'd returned to base.

One of their personnel carriers, armoured like the others and with no windows, was full of junior sappers who had not been in radio contact with us, but only with their sergeant in the lead vehicle. As the sniper had homed in on his target, they regularly experienced the alarming impact of rounds hitting their armour plating. Every now and again they checked in with the sergeant on the radio, seeking reassurance that the situation was being dealt with.

Unbeknownst to them, once we had killed the Taliban fighter, the sergeant and his mates decided to have some fun at their expense. They picked up handfuls of rocks – small ones to start with, then progressively bigger – and started lobbing them at the sappers' vehicle.

'Christ, this is getting really bad,' they howled on the radio. 'He's getting more and more shots off at us ... and they're getting louder. We need more air, we need help!'

This went on for a few minutes, before the Aussies took pity on their fellow countrymen and yanked open the doors. You can imagine what the young guys must have thought when they realised what had happened. I am sure they found it hilarious – not. And I still wonder how they got their own back.

Life at Kandahar continued according to the rhythm of that long war, as I counted down the days to my next visit home. We were allowed regular phone calls back to friends and family using the MoD's Paradigm satellite service, and it was during one of those that I proposed to Lucy.

That it happened that way – with us thousands of miles apart – her back home in the house we shared at Oakham near Cottesmore, and me in the desert in southern Afghanistan, was all to do with her upcoming thirtieth birthday and the pact we had made at Dartmouth 10 years before.

In fact, we had never really lost touch, and Lucy was one of the first to send me a message after my accident – from Italy, where she was then studying. It meant everything to me, at a monumental moment in my life, and it was typical of her. Fiercely independent, loving and caring, she has always been my protector and my rock, looking out for my best interests in every division of the hazard spectrum.

I didn't go down on one knee in the portable cabin near our rancid quarters at Kandahar when I phoned her to pop the question, but Lucy accepted and we married at our local register office in Oakham, just before she turned 30. It was a small affair with a handful of family present, but we celebrated in style when I returned from Afghanistan for the last time. The going-away party, on the eve of my next posting in the USA, really pushed the envelope.

13

I am lying in bed next to Lucy, in the half-world between wakefulness and sleep. Infiltrating my subconscious is a tiny but persistent bright red light and I am fixing on it ...

In the deep recesses of my super-vigilant mind, it is whispering 'Sniper ... sniper ... sniper' at me.

I'm back in Afghanistan, I'm on the base. It's another hot, cloudless night in Kandahar and there is an enemy sharpshooter picking me out. I can see his infrared targeting light flickering as he moves in the distance, and I know he is going to kill me.

I know he is, and I can't do anything to stop him.

But this is suddenly not clear at all. This is my bedroom, at my home. This cannot be happening.

Of course ... there is a TV standby light in the bedroom; I know that. But I wouldn't normally be able to see it. So why can I, from here? This cannot be right.

The confusion festers, as I drift in and out of consciousness, 24 hours after getting back home on a brief R&R visit. Until, finally, I realise I have to get moving. I have to get away.

I roll over, tumble onto the floor and crawl from the bed to the wall, under the curtains and the open window. I lie there, curled up, protecting myself, and waiting for the crack of the shot that will end my life.

Then I feel Lucy's cool palm on my forehead. Awoken by the noise, she had turned on her light and come over to find me.

I never experienced disturbed sleep in my camp bed in Kandahar, where I might have expected it, but the juxtaposition of peacetime at home and war in Afghanistan was playing with my head. It was as if someone had picked up the fabric of my life and torn it, leaving me with two realities, one on top of the other, and I was struggling to work out which was which.

She held me. 'You're at home, you're safe, it's OK,' Lucy reassured me.

I checked the room. Yes, this was our home. In Oakham. In Rutland. Down the road from the frontline Harrier base at RAF Cottesmore, and it was the mirror that was fooling me. I was seeing the TV light reflected in the mirror. *That's* why I couldn't explain it ...

I took a deep breath and let the air escape slowly from my lungs.

'I'm sorry, just got a bit mixed up there,' I said and crawled back into bed.

This was the first, but it certainly wouldn't be my last, war-induced night terror. In truth, those R&R visits, which lasted 10 days in total but boiled down to no more than seven or eight at home after all the travelling, were real double-edged swords.

After two months of relentless combat flying over the deserts and the green zone of southern Afghanistan, all of us needed a break or we would burn out. They were supposed to be a time to relax, to sleep and to enjoy the simple pleasure of not being mortared at night by insurgents beyond the airfield perimeter. The idea was to retouch reality – home reality – because out there our world distorted massively, in an environment where we were constantly on alert, constantly preparing and then executing our next mission, and constantly steeling ourselves to get rid of the enemy on the battlefield.

In theory, this should have been a time to enjoy the company of loved ones and family and friends, go to the pub, or pop out for coffee. It was a reset, so that we would be able to return to Kandahar for the remainder of our tour, refreshed and rearmed with the same moral convictions that had powered us through the first two months.

But it wasn't easy to take my mind off the day job, because I didn't want to turn off my war-fighting brain. I knew I had to go back. And I was always worried that another switch might flick on instead – the one that would light up the hazard warning display with the message 'I don't want to go back.' Or 'why should I go back, if I have a choice?' Or, worst of all, 'I'm scared.'

But I knew I had no choice – I had to keep my shield up. I had to focus on maintaining the steel and armour I needed out there. I had to keep my brain partitioned, so that I could remain someone who could go out and kill, even though I was in the middle of peaceful, rural England. I also knew that 'normal' would never be the same; a fundamental part of me had changed forever – we can't undo or unsee war.

It was jarring at all levels. We were not engaged in a

struggle for national liberation or national survival, but a NATO conflict in a foreign and distant land which most people barely gave a second thought. From the moment we touched down at Brize Norton, after flying in via Al Udeid Air Base in Qatar, we were square pegs stumbling towards round holes. The car from Motor Transport at Cottesmore would be waiting to pick me up, and I would feel completely out of place as I emerged from the terminal in my full desert combat uniform, with the dust of Kandahar airfield still ingrained in my boots.

I remember stopping at a service station near Silverstone and getting out of the car and feeling weird, amongst all those strangers. None of them meant me any harm, which seemed odd, and none of them was carrying a weapon – no side-piece hanging off their right leg, and I was thinking, 'Where's their protection?' In America, I was to find out first hand how members of the public warmed to people in the armed services. They would approach you to thank you. But in the UK nobody would come over. You just got strange looks – like, what are you dressed up as? What fancy-dress party are you going to?

The upshot was that Lucy and I tended to keep ourselves to ourselves during my visits home. We socialised only with close family, other service families and pilots who were doing the same job as me. They knew what we were doing in Afghanistan; no explanation was required. Normally we would avoid getting serious, avoid discussing the progress of the war, or our tactics or anything else like that, and focus instead on the superficial stuff.

'How's it going out there?'

'Oh, you know, same old, same old ... poo-pond life carries on ...'

'Any new restaurants popped up on the boardwalk?'

'Well, yes, actually, now we've got a Subway, da-daa!'

'No way.'

'Oh yes, fresh lettuce and SubStacks – we've got it all.'

'Well, that's something to look forward to on my next tour ...'

Walking down Oakham high street was a mind-stretching experience. I would think of it as Sangin or Nad Ali, hotbeds of resistance activity in Helmand. Round the corner would be a Taliban unit, about to appear in their pick-ups and open fire with AKs and RPGs. An open window above a shop was a sniper's nest. On it went, an imagination out of control in the turbulent margins between peace and war.

Being at home would give all of us time to reflect. To think about what we were doing and the requirement to deliver violence to the battlefield, but I never regretted anything that I had done. I built a wall around it. I never thought about what my weapons did to people. Even when I bombed them and saw them crawling away, I didn't think about it; I would just think about how I was going to stop them crawling away. However bad it was on the ground, my reflex – my self-preservation tactic – was to compare it with the accident and what happened to Jak. I would say to myself, 'I've seen worse,' and shut it out.

Sometimes at Kandahar, troops would come through on R&R breaks and show us photos of the places we had bombed. I would see big craters, something I would never get access to in training, and something I could never get to grips with through binoculars from 15,000ft. So I got an idea what high-energy explosive does. I never saw bodies in the images of my target areas, but it wasn't hard to imagine what they could have looked like, especially when they showed me what happened in IED detonations under armoured vehicles, and to our soldiers on foot patrol.

I never regretted anything because I had – and still have – a clear answer to the simple question: what would have happened if I had not delivered that weapon at that place at that time? The answer was that our own troops would have faced the possibility of being killed or injured, and I would have shirked my responsibility to intervene and help them. Not delivering bombs and rockets could have led to deaths and injuries among our own forces, and I couldn't live with that.

I made a point of going to every ramp ceremony for the fallen in Kandahar. These were poignant and desperately sad occasions, when the coffins of soldiers killed on the battlefield would be carried up the ramp of a C-17 Globemaster, wrapped in the Union Jack.

I knew I was one of the lucky ones, being based at an airfield and flying in and out of the combat zone in an air-conditioned cockpit, thousands of feet above the action. These were the guys who manned the checkpoints, defended the forward operating bases and led the foot patrols. And sometimes the coffins would contain the remains of soldiers who had died in firefights and ambushes in which I had tried to intervene. So I had no regrets about what I was doing – in fact, I would do what I did 10 times over, given a second chance.

If one night terror wasn't enough during my R&R, there

was always the odd extra challenge thrown in. Midway through my second tour I had been settling in back at home as best I could, when a Harrier passed over our roof at about 700ft. The Pegasus engine was at full power, with the landing gear down, flaps and nozzles all the way down, in a recipe for maximum decibels. It must have been about midnight, on an evening warm enough for us to have thrown open the windows, when Lucy and I were fast asleep.

Needless to say, the whole house shook, and it sent me rolling out of bed for the second time that week. I had no idea where I was in the world. But I knew which squadron was flying that week and, once I'd come to my senses, it didn't take long to ID the pilot. My mate Simon Rawlins had decided it was time for him to personally welcome me home, and that a surprise wake-up call was what I needed most.

Given the wind direction, Scranners could have flown in high and gone straight to the Cottesmore runway. But he had requested an instrument landing as a practice exercise instead, then plotted his approach with the centreline straight over our house, and come in super-slow, on a three-degree glide slope.

In case I hadn't worked it out, Scranners thoughtfully texted me when he landed. 'Hope you're having a good night's sleep . . .'

The next day we met in the Admiral Hornblower, our local watering hole on the high street.

'Hilarious, that was, Scranbag,' I said. 'You flew so low, Lucy thought it was an earthquake. You're such a knob . . .'

'Yeah,' he beamed. 'I got as low as I legally could.'

A few days later, after saying goodbye to Lucy and doing

my best to reassure her that I would be coming home in a few weeks, I was back in the car on my way to Brize Norton, thinking again about finishing the tour.

As the lush English countryside swept by, I prepared to face the desert and Kandahar once again.

14

The Harrier ground attack role in Afghanistan was about inflicting violence on the Taliban, and that violence – bombs and rockets – was almost always delivered in response to a crisis on the battlefield, when Coalition troops needed urgent assistance.

The normal way that would happen is that a pilot would scramble or be diverted to a given position where troops had called for help. Having reached the target area, the forward air controller on the ground would provide what we called a 'talk-on'.

This would give the pilot all the relevant detail: the lie of the land, pointing out specific features – a treeline, a compound, a line of ditches, an orchard – that would help identify exactly where friendlies were, and not-so-friendlies. All of this was critical information that would aid accurate targeting and avoid so-called 'blue-on-blue' attacks on our own people.

That talk-on was a heavily jargonised exchange, dominated by codewords to maintain battlefield order and security, and by acronyms to describe various actions and situations to help save time. It would lead to discussion or instruction on what weapons to release – usually given as a request from the guy on the ground – and then agreement to attack from the pilot, assuming they were happy that this would fall within their rules of engagement.

These encounters with forward air controllers were often fraught affairs, with soldiers trying to communicate while in grave danger, and with every second counting when, for example, a compound or a position was in danger of being overrun. In the cockpit of my fighter jet, circling high above, I often had to try and help them stay calm and focus on the information I needed, despite the noise of men shouting – or screaming – in the background, along with the constant chatter of small-arms fire or RPG impacts.

But sometimes situations developed when almost all of the procedures and training that had helped us prepare for these critical interactions went out the window. For me this was never more so than one afternoon, high in the Helmand Valley, south of Kajaki, when I had split from my wingman and diverted to a position where a small detachment of Dutch Special Forces was operating.

As I arrived on target and switched to the relevant frequency, my radio sprang to life, but not with the measured tones of a trained professional.

Instead I heard the terrified voice of a lone young man, screaming for help, fearing for his life.

Although he was on our frequency, it sounded as if he was calling to his mates on the ground; I could tell that he had no idea whatsoever about the language or procedures he was supposed to use when talking to a pilot.

'Help me, help me,' he screamed. 'I'm here – help me. Any pilots? The Taliban are coming – they are going to kill me . . . help. There isn't much time. Pilots!'

It turned out that this was a young squaddie, probably no more than 18 or 19 years old, attached as a radio operator to a Dutch Special Forces patrol. That meant he carried the radio and knew how to operate it, but had no training in interaction with aircraft.

He and his forward air controller had climbed onto a ridge where they could benefit from a good signal and a clear view of the Kajaki Valley, at the cost of being cut off from the rest of their team. Which meant that this youngster was left all alone after they were spotted by Taliban fighters approaching from below, who shot and killed the forward air controller with a single round to his head.

At this point, the kid got on to his radio and let rip.

My first thought, as my Harrier came within his earshot, was to try to get him to calm down enough to give me some useful information.

'OK, mate, I can hear you're in a bad situation,' I said. 'But I am going to need answers to some simple questions. I will get you home safely. I know you're really scared – I would be in the same situation – but you've got to help me to get you out of this.'

'Yes, I understand you.'

His English was heavily accented.

'But, please, you have to be quick. We don't have much time.'

This was not just a pilot talking to troops on the ground – it felt more like taking on the role of a Samaritan, or a buddy coming to help someone in serious psychological distress. I was trying to persuade him to stay calm, but I knew it was asking a lot from someone so young, who not only lacked the specialised training required to operate with aircraft, but had also just witnessed his mate being killed; if we didn't get this right he was going to be next.

Every time he transmitted, I could hear shooting on the hillside below him as I set about trying to work out where he was.

I needed him to listen to me.

'OK,' I said. 'Stop speaking.'

'OK, OK,' he replied.

'Now, the first thing I need you to do is pull out your compass and tell me from which direction the Taliban are coming.'

He gave me a compass direction, but again started shouting that there wasn't enough time to do this.

'I can see them coming up – they're getting closer . . .'

'Right, listen . . .' I tried to sound a bit more like someone giving him an order. 'I need you to tell me, have you got anything on you that can give me your GPS position?'

'No, no . . . I don't have that.'

Rarely had I felt the separation of the cockpit from the battlefield more acutely. There I was, circling at 15,000ft, in an orbit based on a vague idea of where this guy might be, with his abject fear filling my cockpit. I was already thinking, 'I can't lose him.'

'OK, let's try this. Have you got anything that you can see near you that might help me find you?'

'Yeah, I'm on the side of a mountain.'

'Good. Use your compass again if you need to, and tell me if there are any mountains to the south of you?'

There was a long pause, when I started to wonder if he'd

been hit, and this was going to end with two of our guys killed in action and nothing good coming out of it.

'No,' he said eventually. 'There are no mountains south of me that are near.'

I looked down on a peak that rose steeply above the plains leading down to a tributary of the Helmand River. I was pretty sure I knew roughly where he was, but I needed confirmation, and it was taking precious seconds.

'Have you got any shadows near you?' I asked him.

'Shadows? Yes. They're behind me.'

That meant he was on the south-facing side of that mountain. Now I needed to pinpoint him exactly.

I got back on the radio. 'Do the Taliban know where you are?'

'Yes, they fuckin' do,' he shot back.

So I knew nothing would be lost if I asked him to identify his whereabouts.

'Have you got a mirror, or anything that might help me see where you are?'

'I've got a smoke grenade.'

'Excellent. Let's use it. But make sure you throw it away from you.'

All of this had taken two precious minutes. Seconds later, I spotted the grey column rising from the ridgeline of the mountain that I had picked out as his most likely location. I was only about three-quarters of a mile from him.

'OK, I've got your position. Well done, mate. Just hang in there.' More rounds crackled in the background. 'I now need to know where the enemy are.'

'They're down there, below me.'

That wasn't helping. At 15,000ft I needed a better grip on what was going on. The last thing I wanted to do was attack too close and injure or kill this guy. And I needed a good fix on the Taliban if I was going to stop them.

'OK, I've got one option here and it's going to be really quick,' I told him. 'I am going to come down low. I know where you are. I am hopefully going to come between you and them, so I can see where you are and where they are. I will need you to tell me that I am coming in towards you, so I know I'm on the right track. Then I will pull up and immediately come in and attack them. But I will need you to get your head down.'

'OK, OK . . .' He was trying to suppress his growing panic. 'They're coming and they are getting closer.'

'How long have we got?'

'Two minutes,' he said. 'Maybe less.'

One thing that gave me an edge was that the enemy could hear my jet overflying them, and they were soon going to hear it coming in low. They were going to get the message that I could turn their world upside down at any moment. Maybe that alone would deter them from pressing home their attack.

I rolled and dropped the nose and came up towards the smoke from below, lining up parallel to the ground as I did so. As I reached the final part of the climb and approached the ridgeline, I saw three or four Taliban in shalwar kameez with AK-47 assault rifles, ducking and diving among the rocks, a few hundred metres from where the smoke grenade was still smouldering.

'You're right on target,' I heard the Dutch soldier shouting in my ear.

I pulled up. This was more or less unprecedented; I was going to release weapons on the enemy, with no formal targeting information from a forward air controller. We called this 'emergency close air support'. Time was of the essence, and either I did this, or a young guy, who deserved better, was going to get killed or captured.

I selected my airburst and told him once again to get his head down. I banked and came in for the kill. This time I was higher, with wings level, to give the weapon the necessary flying time to arm itself. I knew I probably had no more than one go at this. I needed to deliver it right on top of where I had seen the Taliban hiding.

I came hammering in again and watched the target as I pulled away. The hillside lit up for a second with an orange flash, and a big white cloud rose from the detonation point, which was wreathed in rolling brown dust.

I heard nothing for a minute and then got on the radio to check the young Dutchman was still with us.

'Are you OK?'

'Yes, sir,' he replied in a stunned whisper.

'All good?'

'Yes.'

I waited a little longer. 'Are you still receiving incoming fire?'

He was not, but he didn't know if the Taliban fighters were dead.

'OK,' I said, 'You need to establish yourself at a new position. I've just received re-tasking orders to the south of here, but I've requested follow-on fast air support for you; it should be inbound within the next five minutes.'

'Understood, and thank you.'

He sounded as though he was regaining his composure. In fact, I'd been directed to rejoin my wingman, who was now in another fight where Coalition forces were under pressure. I'd made a prioritised call to the Combined Air Operations Centre for back-up, and passed the young Dutchman over to a B1 bomber operated by the US Air Force.

I never found out how the rescue mission progressed, but he was eventually picked up and lived to fight another day. I never met him – the high tempo of operations and their vastly dispersed area didn't allow for face-to-face formalities and cordial meetings – but the young Dutch soldier left a lasting impact on me.

That sortie underlined why I was there – to help our people, who were putting their lives on the line every day in an attempt to bring the Taliban insurgency to an end.

15

It began as one of those forgettable days in NATO's war against the Taliban. My wingman and I took off from Kandahar and were sent from one minor scrap on the ground to another, all the time gradually travelling north and east towards Kabul.

On each occasion a show of force was all that was required, with me flying overwatch at altitude while my wingman dropped down to do the business. After a series of these interventions we were in the vicinity of Kabul and the big air base at Bagram – the only other Coalition airfield that we used in Afghanistan.

At this point my wingman decided he would have to turn back for the deserts of the south and Kandahar, while I – with more fuel on board – was re-tasked to head even further northeast, to territory I had never ventured into before. The flat, arid lands of southern Afghanistan were a long way behind me as I overflew the increasingly spectacular mountainous terrain north of Kabul.

Isolated hills jutted from flat ground, but, as I soared above the provinces of Kapiza and Laghman and into western Nuristan, the landscape became ever more wooded and rugged. By the time I reached Badakshan, Afghanistan's most northeasterly province, I was looking down on the snow-capped peaks of the Hindu Kush and some of the most spectacular scenery I have seen from the cockpit of a fighter jet.

The war in Helmand was fought almost entirely in the close-knit confines of the green zone on either side of the river; up here it was a different world and a much bigger canvas. You just had to look at that wild and unforgiving landscape to understand how difficult war-fighting conditions were for Coalition forces, in a terrain that could not be better suited to classic insurgency tactics.

The waypoint position or kill-box that I had been given by the Combined Air Operations Centre in Qatar was taking me into one of the most inaccessible and mysterious regions of Afghanistan. I was gradually turning onto an east-northeast heading into the Wakhan Corridor, a narrow series of valleys carved out by agreement between the British and the Russians in the late nineteenth century, to act as a buffer between the two great empires, and a region largely untouched by the wars of the last 40 years.

This remote area, bordered by Tajikistan to the north, Pakistan to the south and with a short stretch of frontier with China at its easternmost end, was breathtakingly beautiful on that bright winter's day. Brilliant white clouds and a deep-blue sky showed off the snow-capped peaks at their very best. The mountains rose steeply on each side of the flat valley floor, thousands of feet above sea level, creating the illusion of flying through a vast natural trench. At an altitude of 18,000ft, I experienced the unnerving feeling of flying below the ridges to my right and left, knowing that my

Harrier was vulnerable to attack by anyone with a Stinger surface-to-air missile.

I was well aware that I was venturing into a delicate geopolitical region with hostile – or, at least, inquisitive – powers on all sides. As I flew on towards my rendezvous point, my cockpit buzzed with electronic warfare sensors, pinging one after another, warning me that unidentified radar stations were watching me.

The electronic map in the cockpit was also telling me that I had little lateral room for manoeuvre, overflying a strip of land just 11 miles wide at its narrowest and 220 miles long, and I needed to try and keep inside a five-mile buffer zone guarding the frontiers. We were well versed in the rules relating to the Pakistani border – we were permitted to chase and kill insurgents heading across it to regroup – but I had no briefings to call on when it came to Tajikistan and China, and the last thing I wanted was to create an international incident.

The other thing on my mind was fuel, as I continued heading away from the centre of Coalition air operations. The rule book suggested we fly tactically at high speed, smashing around the sky so that we had enough manoeuvrability to be able to take evasive action when targeted by ground-to-air missiles. But like some of my fellow pilots, I always tried to fly in the most fuel-efficient way, to give me maximum range and maximum time on target.

On this occasion, however, even my most conservative approach was not going to stop me running out, and I warned the air operations centre that I would need a rendezvous with a tanker straight after I had completed my mission. It all added to a feeling of urgency; I needed to smartly execute my allotted task – whatever it might be – and get back out again.

I tuned in to the designated frequency and used the call-sign for the mission. 'We are US spec-ops,' came a calm and authoritative American voice in response, on a scratchy wavelength that kept falling in and out as the terrain played havoc with the signal. 'We have eyes on a cave compound on the southern side of the Corridor. We are troops in contact with that target.'

'Roger,' I said, knowing that the use of the phrase 'troops in contact' meant I was free to attack, on the basis that whoever was in that hideaway was presenting an imminent threat to Coalition troops on the ground.

He then gave me its latitude and longitude position and said they believed it housed a high-value target.

'Yes, copy that, and copy HVT,' I replied without thinking anything of it.

We talked through what weapons to use, and then he added: 'By the way, this is *the* HVT.'

'Roger,' I replied nonchalantly.

So that's why I was up here in the land of the Wakhi tribesmen, high above the Pamir River, at the limit of my fuel reserves, talking to a US Special Forces guy, callsign Ghost. Now it all made sense. There were many HVTs in this war, but only one that they could have in mind as *the* HVT. I was back on Bin Laden duty.

I always tried to stay level in the cockpit, regardless of what was going on below me, but I couldn't help feeling a pulse of excitement. I knew I had another chance to get the world's most wanted terrorist, whose deadly attack on the

World Trade Centre had sparked the invasion of Afghanistan in the first place. And what a setting to hide in – the middle of nowhere, with no roads, no settlements as far as I could see, and peaks rising on all sides to over 20,000ft.

'I can't get this wrong – there is no way you can mess this up,' I thought as I identified the mountainside the American forward air controller was talking about, and then picked up the laser spot he was using to lead me onto the target. I had no idea of the US soldiers' location, or how many of them there were, but I imagined a small insertion force of, say, four men on a secret reconnaissance or kill-or-capture mission. Either way, this was the moment they revealed their hand, and I didn't want to let them down.

I had a full weapons load, and we decided to try and deliver an impact-detonated 540-pounder to the entrance to the cave. This was at the snowline, about 9,000ft up from the valley floor, with stretches of exposed rock below it and a heavily wooded area above. It was a seriously impressive set-up straight out of a James Bond movie, not just a hollow in the hillside that someone was camping in, but an elaborate and properly fortified entrance with concrete retaining walls and roof timbers.

Checking it out with the binoculars, I wondered how anyone had managed to build it with no roads or even rough tracks visible in the vicinity. I guessed it might have been an old Soviet-era emplacement built during the occupation of Afghanistan during the 1980s, when the Wakhan Corridor was sealed off from the rest of the country and was said to be bristling with Soviet listening posts and monitoring stations.

On my first run, I came in at level flight. The 540 was not

a precision weapon but a dumb bomb, and it was always going to be hard to direct it precisely at the cave entrance. I had to release it early enough to allow up to 10 seconds to elapse before impact, so the fuse could initiate, which meant there was no way I could dive towards the target.

As I rolled away I watched the detonation produce a big cloud of flying rock and dust to the left of the entrance, which then started drifting down the valley. I had seen no movement in the area, but I knew immediately that this was not going to cut it. I needed to get inside that cave, and my focus on trying to achieve that, and what I did next, nearly cost me my life.

This time I was going to use my rockets, all 38 of them. Rolling the Harrier onto its back and dropping the nose as I pulled through into a 30-degree dive, I lined up on the cave entrance. I was treating this like a 'danger close' mission, when we drop weapons in close proximity to friendly forces at moments of extreme peril, and getting in low and tight is the order of the day.

At that stage the main danger in my mind was the possibility of being 'self-fragged' when the rockets exploded, but I was determined to go as close as I dared, so I was prepared to push the envelope. The normal air safety distance to release these weapons is around 7,000ft from the target, but I drove it down to the minimum, and held in for around 3,000ft, before I pressed the release button.

The moment they'd gone I started to pull up, but at that altitude, in thin mountain air, and still carrying one 540-pounder, the jet struggled to get a grip.

I would normally expect to pull 4 or 5G in this situation

and get a good dig in, as I heaved the nose up and away from the approaching hillside. But this time, as I planted the throttle as far forward as it would go and pulled the stick back as much as I dared, I could feel the airframe start to shake. The trees on that mountainside were coming closer as the aircraft drifted and gained height like a drunk on a staircase.

In that predicament the key is not to ask too much of the airframe. You need to fly on the edge of stalling, with the wings subject to a gentle vibration that tells you that you are flying at the most effective angle. Go too far, and that becomes a big, shuddering rattle and the plane will start to fall out of the sky. It is difficult to get this right when your vision is occupied by foliage connected to trees coming ever closer and a ridgeline that looks too high to overfly. Every fibre in your body is telling you to pull harder, but you cannot do that, and we all know stories of pilots, from the Dambusters onwards, who never made it, trying to pull up after delivering weapons on target.

I pushed the aircraft as hard as I dared, the engine roaring in protest, and thought for a few moments I was going to have to eject for the second time in my career. I had overcooked this, and not taken into account that the recovery phase after the dive was going to be at the limit of the Harrier's performance spectrum.

I flashed through the reality of punching out of the plane right there, high up on the sidewall of the Wakhan Corridor. This would not be like landing on an airfield in Cambridgeshire. I would be coming down on a remote mountainside in the remotest part of Afghanistan – probably too high for helicopter extraction – and almost on top of the compound I had been bombing. The nearest friendly troops would probably be thousands of feet below me, and I would be bouncing around in trees or on snow and rock, none of which was an inviting prospect.

I had to pull this off. I watched the dark green carpet of trees come closer. 'I am not going to make this,' I thought as the taste of panic rose in my throat. I inched the stick back further and watched the firs fill my canopy. There was a moment when it was in the lap of the gods. Then the Harrier seemed to respond just when I needed it to, and soon it was doing enough, as the tops of the trees flashed past at what felt like no more than a whisker below me.

Whoa! ... that was close ...

I barely had a moment to get my bearings and set the jet up on a west-southwest heading to get me to the fuel tanker as soon as possible, when the radio sprang to life.

'That's a Delta Hotel,' the American voice told me.

'Copy that ...' I was still catching my breath. 'I'm low on fuel and am returning to base, exiting to the west at 18,000ft.'

I never heard from them again, but I wasn't going to go back and give them a hug. I needed to find that tanker as soon as possible.

Ten minutes later, and down to my last few hundred pounds of fuel, I rendezvoused with a US Air Force KC10 over the peaks of Badakshan.

Normally when I was desperate for fuel, I'd position my Harrier behind where the hose would reach out on the flight line. This time I did something slightly different: I squeezed up next to the outboard end of the port wing and waited for the basket to deploy. Why? I will never know, but I'm glad I did.

The hose snaked out of the refuelling pod and I was about to reposition my jet in line and behind it to plug in, when the entire apparatus – hose, basket and fittings – disconnected from the tanker, whipped past me and crashed into the forest thousands of feet below. Had it collided with my Harrier, the sheer weight of it, and the speed at which it was travelling, would have caused catastrophic damage. I didn't want to think about it impacting the canopy or going down the engine.

'Are you guys aware you have lost your hose?' I asked, stunned by what I had witnessed.

'Yeah, yeah,' came the laconic reply from the American pilot, callsign Whistler, sounding as if this was perfectly routine. 'We lost that one, we'll try the next one.'

A few minutes later another one appeared from the starboard wing refuelling pod. 'We're good to go on the right,' he said, and I plugged in in the usual way.

But I was only able to take a fraction of the fuel I needed to cover the more than 480 miles back to Kandahar. They were either running out or something had gone seriously wrong with their systems, leaving me with no choice but to disconnect and work out whether I had enough to get me home.

It had been a long and exhausting day and the last thing I wanted to do was divert to Bagram. I needed to get back to Kandahar, to catch my flight home for 10 days of R&R. I was going to do everything possible to make that happen.

It was time to start the endless game of mental arithmetic in the cockpit, as I plotted my speed against distance and fuel consumption. All the way back, as the mountains became hills and the deep river valleys gave way to plains and then dry desert, I checked and rechecked that I had enough. I ended up completing the last 50 miles at max range airspeed – 230 knots – and landed with much less than was considered the bare minimum in the tank.

As soon as I got in, I checked in with the intelligence officer for my confidential debrief and he admitted they were surprised that Qatar had seen fit to send me so far north, and alone.

'We plotted it on the computer and were amazed at how far you'd gone,' he said. 'And you've been gone a long, long time.'

That sortie led to a discussion among Coalition air planners, who decided that, in future, Harriers from Kandahar should have the option of handing over to Bagram-based aircraft if they were being drawn too far north.

Naturally, the intelligence officer was interested in everything I could tell him about the cave, its location, what I had seen of it and whether I had seen anybody trying to defend it or escape from it – which I had not. I gave him as much as I could, and then dashed off to get my bags and head for the military passenger terminal for the flight home.

The military being the military, you were supposed to check in four hours before departure. I got there one hour before scheduled take-off, and came to a screeching halt in front of the RAF movements desk.

'Lieutenant Gray,' I announced. 'Checking in.'

'Well, let's see. You're three hours late, sir,' came the robotic reply from the desk supervisor.

'Yeah, I know,' I said. 'I'm very sorry about that, but I've been up country, fighting the enemy.'

He smiled. 'We all have our excuses, sir. But I am afraid you'll have to go on the standby list, and we'll just have to hope there'll be space for you on board.'

I sat there thinking through the last few action-packed hours of the day. I had nearly piled my jet into a mountain, dodged a rogue fuel hose in mid-air and endured an agonising flight back, with my fuel calculations telling me that it was going to be touch and go to land safely at Kandahar. I knew, before I landed, that I hadn't killed Osama bin Laden. That news would have travelled like wildfire and it would take American Special Forces another three and a half years to achieve that feat.

But I did make the flight, and we did take off, and this time I could relax and get my head down. Someone else was on the flight deck.

16

'Hey, Nath?'

'Yep?'

'Will you step outside for a minute, please?'

'No problem.'

It was the senior supervising pilot at Kandahar, and he looked a little edgy.

'This is not ideal,' he began, as we stood in the cool air of the desert night.

'There's no millilux,' he added, referring to the nonexistent light levels from the moon.

It was late in the evening and, together with my lead pilot, we had been going through the flight brief and preparation for what would be my first night mission in Afghanistan.

This was the beginning of my third and final tour during the NATO war and it was the moment when the risk level suddenly shot up. For the next three months I would be operating only at night – in our parlance, I was becoming a 'night player' in a game of high stakes, when the danger of killing yourself by flying into the ground was ever-present.

You were only assigned this role if you had already proven your worth as an experienced daytime ground attack pilot, because night flying involved all the same risks, plus the additional ones that came with operating in the dark. It was way over on the wrong side of the hazard spectrum, and involved some of the most challenging and dangerous sorties we did.

We used to say there was only one thing in a war zone that had 'a PK (probability of kill ratio) of 1', and that was the ground. In Afghanistan there was always a possibility of being shot down by Taliban small-arms fire, or someone using a ground-to-air missile, but a far bigger risk was flying into a hillside, when your only aid in the cockpit was your night vision goggles.

In training – in the Tucano or Hawk – we would practise night flying, but what we did then and what we were required to do in Afghanistan were two quite different things. Cruising along, wings level, at altitude over a gently snoring English landscape was one thing; coming in at treetop level in a show of force over unknown terrain, in the pitch black in a war zone was something else.

Because we were ground attack assets, our role was all about sudden interventions that often required the aircraft pointing at, and accelerating towards, the ground to deliver rockets, for example. And it was the ground that we couldn't see. Your aircraft could tell you the whereabouts of the target you were supposed to be striking – at, say, 3,000ft above sea level – but it could not tell you if there was a 10,000ft mountain rearing up right next door to it.

Looking down through the Perspex of the canopy, you had to try and assess all of that – and any other dangers – like trees, buildings or whip aerials. But it was never easy, especially in a pre-industrial society where there were no car headlights, street lights, courtyard lights and so on. Instead, some settlements and compounds had generators producing isolated light spots, and shepherds often lit fires to keep them warm on the hillsides. But on a clear night, the effect could be confusing because the land looked exactly like the starscape above it.

Our night-vision goggles were vital – effectively light-intensifying devices which picked up the light from the moon, except on those occasions when there wasn't one . . .

'It's almost zero,' the senior pilot was saying, as I scanned the sky above us, seeing only stars beyond the light pollution from the airfield. Just my luck, I thought, to start my new deployment on a night when the moon had gone AWOL.

'So your goggles are going to be worthless on this one, Nath,' he continued. 'You've never flown in these kinds of conditions out here before, and this is a mission where you're actually going to launch and support a strike on a high-value target, but I am happy to send you, given your experience.'

It was clear that he was more nervous than I was about this baptism of fire. But we all had to start these night tours somewhere, and there was every possibility, despite what he had just said, that this mission might involve little more than turning up on station and then being stood down and returning to base.

'So listen,' he went on, 'I need you to take it steady. Take it careful, take your time, don't get cornered, and think everything through twice before you act. Don't just dive in like you would in daytime – this is a very different ball game.'

He stopped for a second. 'OK, happy?' he asked.

'Yes, and thanks,' I told him, and I meant it.

I had got the message, and I took it to heart. I was going to be playing second fiddle as wingman to a pilot who was also our weapons instructor, so he was massively experienced. Although the lack of moonlight was going to make things a bit more tricky, I felt confident I could do what was required of me.

On this mission we were supporting US Special Forces, which brought its own challenges. If we were working with our own guys, they would have come over to our briefing room to give us a full run-down on where we were going and what we were supposed to be doing when we got there. With our American friends, we got none of that; it would be a case of turning up at the pre-arranged rendezvous and waiting for orders.

We launched just before midnight, following the same safety protocols as during the day, with one jet taking off half a minute ahead of the other, departing on different headings and pumping out flares to minimise the risk of being hit by ground fire. As I started to climb, and the runway lights and the ones from the terminal buildings faded, my cockpit was enveloped in blackness.

I flicked my night-vision goggles – which were attached to my helmet – down over my eyes. All I saw was a different shade of black – more like a greeny black – as the goggles searched in vain for light sources to fix on and magnify. I could see tiny electrical impulses flashing across them – a process we called scintillation, as they hunted for spots of brightness – but to no effect. As the senior pilot had advised, on this night, this bit of kit was almost worthless.

After a short flight, we were handed over to our mission

controller and we heard a distant and disembodied voice on the pre-arranged frequency, like an American-made robot, talking to us from outer space. As so often was the case, we had no idea where this guy was. But it became clear there was no one on the ground on this mission.

Instead, the Americans were monitoring the outskirts of a small Afghan village via a Predator drone, circling at 20,000ft. The voice we could hear might have been talking to us from Creech Air Force Base in Nevada, from where drones were controlled, or possibly from Kandahar. It made no difference.

We were given the target position and then came the start of the brief. 'We need you to hold off, 20 miles, 15,000 feet, and keep the noise down,' said the voice. 'We are overhead the target now and are observing an enemy rendezvous point.'

Intelligence sources had tipped them off that a vehicle was due to arrive outside the village carrying suicide vests for a group of bombers. They would be strapped up at the meeting point and would then disperse throughout the northern Helmand Valley, attacking NATO forward operating bases and perhaps civilian targets too. The assumption was that some would move into the town on foot, others would head off in the Jeep, while yet more might lie low until daylight and then move by bicycle or on small motorbikes.

It quickly became obvious that this was going to be a time-sensitive mission because the vehicle – some kind of open-backed Jeep – had already arrived. I was relieved that there was no one on the ground observing this at close quarters, because that ensured I could not be involved in one kind of disaster on my first night trip – a 'blue-on-blue' attack on friendlies.

But the adrenalin was starting to flow because, contrary to our expectations, we realised that we were the only two air assets on station. Whatever else may have been there – perhaps a US Air Force AC130 gunship or an A10 Warthog – had now gone, either to attend another incident or to refuel. So this was going to be down to us.

We waited, orbiting and trying to preserve fuel in case this proved not to be our only mission on that sortie.

'We've got eyes on the target,' came the update. 'Two enemy suppliers are now outside the vehicle and we've got up to 20 enemy bombers around the vehicle, waiting to be fitted up. So here's the game plan . . .'

The American mission controller requested one 1,000lb impact bomb to be dropped on the vehicle and the people swarming round it, which was parked on flat, open ground with no buildings nearby. I knew that that would be a task for my formation leader, because he was carrying the heavy bomb, while I had two 540s and 38 rockets.

Then came my bit. This involved killing any individuals who survived the initial explosion before they could escape, fully strapped up in their explosive vests. They may be wounded, they may not be, but we would usually regard them as still carrying an imminent threat to life. This was especially so in this case, because they were all carrying bombs that were irreversibly armed and could be detonated at any moment.

'We should expect runners,' the American was saying, 'so we need number two to come in with rockets and take them out and then we will reassess. Timing is critical. We need the 1,000-pounder and then 30 seconds later – or an absolute maximum of 60 seconds later – we need the rockets.'

I exhaled at length, blowing my cheeks out, as I took it all in. While my formation leader would be able to overfly the target wings level, and simply drop his weapon on cue, I was going to have to dive into the darkness with the nose of my Harrier pointing at it. I would have to score a direct hit, and do so within a tightly governed time frame, to ensure this mission was successful. We couldn't allow even one of those 20 bombers to survive.

I thought back to what the supervisor had told me on the ground. Take your time, don't get cornered. Now here I was, an hour later, about to attack, with the clock ticking, diving over a town with unknown topography all around it and with no margin for error.

'Roger, standby,' we told the Americans, as we broke off to have a quick chat between ourselves on how we were going to do this, a night attack with a sequencing that we had never trained for. We decided to go for a two- to three-mile lateral separation, which, at an airspeed of .7 Mach, or seven miles a minute (nearly 470 knots), should produce the right timing separation – first the impact bomb, then the rockets.

The waiting continued as the bombers were prepared, during what they all must have accepted were the last few hours of their lives, standing around in the darkness on the outskirts of that village and hearing enemy aircraft in the sky above them.

For us to launch a strike, and for them to be a legitimate target under our rules of engagement, they had to represent a clear and present danger. That meant they all had to have their vests on. At that point our 'kill-chain' was 'connected' and we could be released to head in.

Word came through that they were all now suited up. It was go time. We got our final orders and read them back to confirm.

'I'm happy. You're cleared hot to come inbound now,' came the voice in our ears.

'OK, roger. Turning inbound now,' replied my leader, a man who exuded professional calm in the most stressful situations.

I waited until I saw a two-mile separation from his Harrier and then turned in behind him. Through my goggles I could just make out his infrared lights, which were invisible to the naked eye and, importantly, to the enemy on the ground.

Nothing's easy in this work, but with a GPS laser-guided bomb and the Predator lasing the target for him, this was a relatively straightforward drop for my leader. I heard him count down to release.

'Stores,' he said as the bomb detached and began its journey to destroy the Jeep and as many of the people around it as possible. 'Time to impact, 18 seconds.'

Then it all went very quiet as time slowed in the heat of the moment.

'Splash,' said the leader eventually, as the bomb arrived at its destination, and then the controller came on and confirmed it was on the money. It was all very detached and procedural.

By that time I was already tipping in, inverting my upgraded GR9 Harrier and starting to come down, fighting the nagging anxiety that I was a fraction too early. I was certainly not late.

Then I heard the American describing the situation he had predicted and that I was there to deal with.

'We've got runners,' he said, for the first time using a slightly accelerated delivery, underlining that time was now of the essence. 'Runners are heading east. We've got eight to 10 of them, moving towards the village.'

At this point I could just make out a few brighter spots in the blackness marking the edge of the village, but my main focus was on trying to find the infrared flashing light, through my goggles and my head-up display, that the Predator was using to track the runners. As I came out of the roll, I called in.

'Tally target,' I said. 'I'm in hot.'

'You're clear hot and you've got to get them on this run,' came the response. 'They are about 200 metres from entering the village.'

So there were no other options now. I had to press home this attack. If I aborted, for whatever reason, it would be too late to have a second go. The bombers would have disappeared.

Instead of being on an easy 30-degree dive slope, I found myself dipping down at 45 degrees, as I adjusted my angle of approach to find the targeting light. Not only that, my Harrier was travelling a lot faster than I wanted it to.

'There it is' – I'd got it. The little light that was critical to this tightly choreographed manoeuvre was flashing away through my head-up display.

I pulled the throttle all the way back, but the aircraft was still accelerating, as I watched my rangefinder and placed my round aiming circle, with the 'death-dot' in its centre, directly over the flashing light, ready to fire.

I glanced at my speed and it was still rattling up towards 500 knots. I was now at a precipitous angle of almost 50 degrees, pointing straight at the ground, an angle that was way outside our normal training parameters.

In those few seconds, images of suicide bombers det-onating their backpacks at our checkpoints or in village markets flashed through my mind. I had to commit, whatever the speed and angle. I went to idle and deployed the air brake to try and slow the aircraft as it started to vibrate. At the same time I was conscious I had no idea what I was flying into, or what I might encounter once I pulled up. Both of these things were in the lap of the gods.

I watched the rangefinder and the countdown dial, and at 7,000ft slant range from the target – about 6,000ft above the ground – I pressed the pickle button and felt the aircraft judder as the rockets were released. My goggles, which were giving me next to nothing, suddenly exploded in a blizzard of bright green, as the rocket motors lit up the blackness ahead.

I snapped back on the stick and pumped out some flares. The fuselage protested as we went into the climb with the audible cockpit altitude warning – set at 5,000ft – reminding me that I needed to get away from the hard stuff. 'Whoop! Whoop! Whoop! – altitude, altitude, altitude,' it barked. Slowly the goggles reverted back to their scintillation of nothingness, and I was able to see the head-up display again, having had to rely on my standby gauges during the visual shock following the attack.

As I reached 10,000ft, where I felt confident I was clear of all possible hard deck obstacles, it all went quiet and serene again. The attacks seemed to have gone to plan. I hoped we'd done the business. I had seen nothing on the ground, no people, no vehicles, no movement – only a few lights tracing the outline of the village and the moving Predator infrared spot, so I had no idea what I had achieved.

'That's a Delta Hotel; all enemy neutralised,' said the American voice, confirming that I had delivered on target and in time to ensure the rockets covered the entire area where the bombers were moving. None of them had escaped. I had done all I could do, for now.

I reflected once more on the advice I had been given at the start of the sortie, as I levelled off and heard the American thanking us and releasing us to head for home. Of course, I'd been hoping I wouldn't be involved in any high-tariff stuff on my first night mission, but when the call comes, you have no choice but to respond. I had to get in on target on time, and ended up carrying out a synchronised attack in an area of unknown terrain, 50 knots faster and at a 10-degree steeper angle than I had ever practised, even in daylight. But you can't think of all the pitfalls, you have to get on with it.

I was relieved that it had come off, and I felt that on this sortie we had made a real difference. Often in a firefight we would come in and make a decisive intervention that could save the lives of Coalition soldiers. But on this occasion we had prevented a slew of deaths and injuries that was hard to quantify. The individuals with the vests were intent on wreaking as much havoc as possible, and I thought again about the squaddies manning checkpoints, who had to face the danger of suicide attacks every day. They were some of the bravest people in this war, and I hoped we had done something that night to make their chances of survival that little bit greater.

After landing and checking the spare jets to make sure they were ready to go, we debriefed with the intelligence officer at 3am and then went back on standby, ready for the next call to action. When I bumped into our supervising pilot, he winked at me.

'Followed my advice, did you, Nath?'

'To the letter,' I said, with a straight face.

With the completion of my third tour – my four months of night flying – my contribution to the war in Afghanistan came to an end. At that stage – late 2008 – the intensity of the NATO Coalition effort was increasing to match the growing Taliban insurgency, and there was no sign that our campaign was doomed to fail.

But we all know what happened in NATO's Afghan war, and how it ended, following President Joe Biden's decision to withdraw all US forces in 2021, which prompted their allies – including Britain – to follow suit. It was a disastrous decision, and it led to a complete Taliban victory and the start of another dark age in Afghanistan.

Looking back, I sometimes wish the generals who commanded us out there spent more time doing what we did – flying across that vast, rugged land at an altitude that was high enough to appreciate how big and beautiful it is. Jumping into a helicopter to nip down from Kabul to Helmand was not quite the same.

I say this because every time I launched on a mission, and I did that more than 140 times during deployments between 2006 and 2008, I was struck, without fail, by the same thought. There we were, bombing and fighting in one village, in one tiny valley, while over the next ridge was another valley with scores of villages that we had barely touched. And beyond that was another, and another . . . and then another province, another stretch of desert and a mountain range, none of which we'd come close to.

Confronting that reality, it was almost inevitable that you would start to think we were devoting ourselves to a crazy idea – a plan to subdue Afghanistan by force if necessary. There is an important distinction to make here: I never for one minute felt disillusioned about my job – supporting the guys on the ground – and I always tried to carry it out to the best of my ability. But that did not mean I could dismiss the growing feeling that, overall, we had an impossible task.

During my first tour, I genuinely felt I was making a difference with everything I did, and came back inspired by our work, even as the Taliban upped their military campaign and Coalition casualties mounted. But, by my second tour – after a gap of eight months at home – I started to notice how little progress we had made. We seemed to have got bogged down in an endless game of cat and mouse as the war and the rituals of the war repeated itself.

A big focus for us on my first tour, for example, was operations around the key Helmand Valley district of Nowzad, where I flew on numerous occasions. During one sortie, I was asked by troops on the ground to bomb a particular building on the edge of a village. It had an excellent field of vision over the surrounding countryside, and a sniper was using it to target our forces in the area. I came in and destroyed it, along with the sniper.

A year later, with different troops on the ground, who had no idea what had gone on before, I was called in again to the same grid reference. Once again I was told there was an enemy sniper, and he was in a building that gave him a perfect position from which to hunt our troops on the ground. I checked my maps and grabbed the binoculars. Sure enough, it was the same place, albeit rebuilt and reoccupied, and now I was going to bomb it all over again.

The implications of that were hard to ignore. How could we be making progress if we were stuck on the same treadmill? Bombing the same places, in the same valleys, while trying to gain control of the same villages? I know it's easy to judge with hindsight, but our mistake was to get involved in what became, for the Taliban, a war of national liberation, whereas, from the beginning, our focus should have been on hearts and minds. In a country the size, and with the complex tribal texture, of Afghanistan, force was never going to work. The only way was to get everyone on board with us and gain their trust.

And that's why I feel so angry about the way Biden followed Donald Trump's lead in the dying days of the latter's presidency, and simply walked away from a country that our soldiers had given their lives for. We had looked the Afghans in the eye and assured them that they were safe with us; we would protect them and would do so for as long as it took, and then we reneged on that. Some say we should have committed to at least 30 years, to ensure that guarantee was delivered. In my book, it should have been an indefinite mission, to irreversibly place Afghanistan on a new footing.

The way the Biden decision worked itself out underlined how weak Britain's role was. We originally went in alongside the Americans, as part of Operation Enduring Freedom, because they decided it was what they were going to do in the wake of 9/11. When they decided they'd had enough 20 years later, they simply pulled the plug, and we had no choice but to follow suit, along with all the other members in the NATO Coalition. We had no capacity to remain independently.

The decision to walk away and to abandon the Afghans to their fate may be the American way, but it certainly damaged American power and undoubtedly damaged Britain's credibility. As a small nation living up to a big past, we rely on our word – that we will do what we say we will do – and our undignified exit from Afghanistan underlined that our word meant nothing. I believe it will take generations for the damage to that credibility to be restored, so that other oppressed peoples in other war-torn nations will believe us if we tell them we are there for the long haul.

Among the men and women I served with in Helmand, there was no walking away, no talk of defeat. We did all that we could to win every battle, every firefight and every debate, when it came to hearts and minds. We had the commitment, the training, the kit, the intelligence, the aggression and the compassion to achieve our goals. But in the end, whether we won or lost was down to what, in my view, were misguided political decisions, not our competence as a military force.

In America, later in my career, I often got the impression from veterans of the Afghan war that they believed they had accomplished their mission, and they did not talk of a defeat. In Britain we are more realistic, more honest. One or two of my friends in the Royal Marines paid a heavy price for their service in Helmand, returning with severe and life-changing injuries, and I completely understand if, in their darkest moments, they feel that their sacrifice meant nothing.

This is what I saw from my garden in Stoke-on-Trent – the Space Shuttle on the back of a NASA 747 – and it set my heart on a life in aviation.

The first time I got my hands on the controls of an aeroplane of any kind during a trip with my parents to the museum at RAF Cosford.

Basic fast jet training at RAF Linton-on-Ouse in the mighty Tucano.

Canopy drama pilot honoured

Faulty blade blamed for Harrier tragedy

Final seconds

How *Navy News* reported Jak London's remarkable recovery of his Harrier after its canopy shattered at 40,000ft in December 1998.

Article from the local press reporting on the inquest into Jak's death. It heard how a tiny nick in a fan blade led to the engine of our Harrier T8 exploding shortly after take-off.

RAF Wittering – the taxiway where the accident happened is parallel to the main runway and to the right of it. The field where I landed after ejecting, top right, is ploughed in this shot, as it was on the day of the accident.

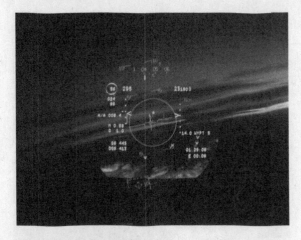

Sunrise over Helmand as seen through the head-up display on the Harrier GR7 after a night mission in NATO's war.

The fertile Green Zone northwest of Kandahar, where so many of the engagements I took part in were based.

In the aircraft sun-shelter at Kandahar, wearing combat flying kit, ready for action in a Harrier GR7 with bombs and rockets loaded. Note the binoculars wedged in the side of the canopy – one of the most important bits of kit we carried.

In North Carolina during my time with the US Marine Corps, alongside my loyal rescue pup, Scout.

The US Naval Test Pilot School at Pax River in Maryland, where I went from flying one plane at a time, to quite a few in succession.

The MiG 15 on the flight line at Pax River – it was a lot more fun to fly than it looks.

Test pilot: inspecting the enormous rear nozzle of the F35 as I prepare for another mission with the Integrated Test Force.

With the moon keeping watch, flying the F35 on test with an F18 'chase' plane alongside.

'Scrabble', aka Andy Neofytou, my friend and fellow Harrier pilot who was first on the scene after my accident at Wittering.

Gary 'Gazza' Langrish after a mission over Bosnia – I couldn't have asked for a better mentor.

Simon 'Scranbag' Rawlins, instructing in the rear seat of a Harrier T10 – one of the most naturally gifted pilots I knew in the Navy.

Soaring above the western Atlantic, with HMS *Queen Elizabeth* and her escort HMS *Monmouth* below me, as I prepared for the first landing of an F35 on the new carrier.

Unchained for a dusk launch from HMS *Queen Elizabeth* – we relied on the flight desk officers and their old-fashioned flag signals.

The distinctive silhouette of the F35, with its 'toilet door' open and rear nozzle down, coming in for a vertical landing on the white line running down the centre of the carrier's flight deck.

The old and the new. The Sea Harrier FA2 looks – and was – from a totally different era to the F35 5th Gen stealth fighter.
I was lucky enough to fly them both.

With Scrabble and Scranbag, at the base of the ski jump at RAF Wittering, to mark the twentieth anniversary of my accident in December 2022.

With Lucy – I couldn't have done any of this without her.

17

'Mac, did you see that?'

I was on the hot mic to my co-pilot, Tom MacGregor. We were at 22,000ft, flying through the blackness of a Texan night, somewhere between Austin and Houston.

'Yeah, that was weird,' he said from the seat behind me.

'What *was* it?'

'I don't know ... shall we check in with Houston?'

'Yeah, but don't say what you saw.'

'Yeah, roger that.'

'Houston control,' I said, and gave them our callsign, 'has somebody just passed directly underneath us?'

'Negative,' came the clipped response. 'There is no traffic in your area.'

Well, that was even weirder. Both Mac and I had seen a sudden flash of bright light in the cockpit of our two-seater US Marine Corps Harrier TAV-8B. We were midway through a long delivery back to our east coast base at Cherry Point in North Carolina, after attending a weapons training course at the west coast Marine Corps Air Station Yuma in Arizona.

The light had appeared from nowhere. It had started in front of us and seemed to go almost through the cockpit. It then backed off and sat in the distance, before coming towards the cockpit again, and passing underneath the jet and disappearing. The whole performance took a matter of seconds and happened at a speed and with an irregularity of trajectory that could not be explained by normal aviation.

We both knew that this was something very odd – with a capital 'O'. We'd been buzzed by an unidentified flying object – and knew it was best to keep it between us. The last thing either of us wanted was to be put down as weirdos fantasising about spacecraft from distant galaxies. That was a route to an appointment with the squadron doctor, and being grounded.

But the fact was both of us had seen it, and we struggled for an explanation. We wondered whether it could have been a laser shining up from the ground? Except that we were over flat, open Texas farmland. Or perhaps it was some kind of spotlight – the sort you get from big stadiums during night games? But again there was nothing down there to support that explanation.

'It was the strangest thing I've ever seen,' said Mac, who later became a test pilot on the new F35 fighter, as we continued our approach to NASA Ellington Airport in Houston.

I've no idea what it was that we saw, but when it comes to the wider universe, I am prepared to accept that there could be other life out there. If we are capable of landing a spacecraft on the moon and sending unmanned vehicles to Mars, it strikes me as naïve to assume there is nothing more advanced elsewhere in the cosmos.

That encounter, which we never reported – even after the fact – came midway through my three-year secondment to the US Marine Corps, which started a month after I had finished my last tour in Afghanistan. It was the reactivation of an old exchange programme, between the Royal Navy and the Marine Corps, that originated during our Sea Harrier days. The idea was to share best practice and bolster the much-vaunted special relationship.

As a lieutenant commander I had the equivalent rank of major, and I took over as operations officer of VMA-542, a night attack squadron, which operated 14 of the 60 Harriers based at Cherry Point. My commanding officer, Lieutenant Colonel T. J. Dunne, had been on the Sea Harrier exchange some eight years previously, so he knew me and Jak and all the rest of the crew at Yeovilton.

I was taking over from a Harrier weapons instructor – Captain Rob Miller, whose callsign was 'Dusty' – whom I had met in Kandahar, when he and a group of Marine Corps pilots had come through at the start of their first posting. We had talked through the tactical experience we had gained, and given them copies of all our maps, marked up with targeting and location information. This gave me a good background from which to take up my new post.

I had managed to avoid flying of any kind on 5 December, but I was defenceless in the face of the squadron of bureaucrats at the British embassy in Washington, DC responsible for the logistics of my arrival. When I called to ask if there was any way my transatlantic flight could be moved forward by a day – or delayed by 24 hours – the powers-that-be made it clear that was out of the question. I was to arrive on the following Friday, spend the weekend acclimatising and then check in with the embassy, before beginning my posting on the Monday.

So on Friday, 5 December 2008, we took off on board a Virgin Atlantic flight to Washington, enjoying a complimentary glass of champagne in economy, organised for us by some of my old mates from Yeovilton who were now flying for Mr Branson. To start with, Lucy and I stayed in a hotel in the quaint town of New Bern, next door to the air station at Cherry Point, and then moved into the well-appointed home of a colonel who was being posted elsewhere.

We were in the swamp on the edge of the Deep South, right on the coast of the stunning Outer Banks. This was Marine Corps territory, in the Bible Belt, and it came as quite a shock. Coming from a family of avid TV watchers, I felt I had a good understanding of American culture, from staples like *The Wonder Years*, *Cheers* and *The Dukes of Hazzard*, but life in this part of the States was very different to how I'd imagined it.

Whenever there were decisions to be made, they'd often be prefaced by the question, what would Jesus do? When our unfailingly generous new neighbours popped round to say hello, it was also to invite us to join their church 'family'. This was a little outside my frame of reference, to put it mildly.

The Marine Corps pilots saw themselves as Marines first and pilots second. They regarded their Harriers, as I did, not so much as jet fighters, but as weapons with which to assist their buddies on the ground, and they were all cut from the same cloth. Infused with a rigid and extreme patriotism, they were super-committed, determinedly optimistic and usually religious.

In the Fleet Air Arm and RAF, our culture was highly professional, but we were realists. In my first couple of weeks in the US, I was chatting to some of the pilots I had met with Dusty in Kandahar, and we compared notes on what we had done. I was saying how tough it could be to drop bombs on rural communities in Helmand, with the ever-present danger of collateral damage.

'You'd be naïve to think that innocent lives were not lost in that conflict,' I said.

But the Americans were having none of it.

'I can tell you, Nath,' said one, 'that my bombs only hurt and killed the enemy. Period.'

And that was that. This was the American high-five culture in uniform, fired by righteous zeal.

I turned up at Cherry Point with my three combat tours under my belt and, together with my other qualifications outside the cockpit, I sensed the Marines saw me as one their own. I was more than just a single-seat fast-jet pilot. But they were well disposed to British Harrier pilots in any case. They regarded us as some of the best in the world. They were in awe of the low-level training we did, alongside manoeuvres like dipping the nose when in the hover. We did it routinely, as a kind of mechanical bow, but it could go so horribly wrong that they were banned from even attempting it.

The biggest problem I had in my first few weeks in the new job was making myself understood. They say Britain and the US are two nations separated by a common language. That was never more true than in the cockpit of a Harrier, sitting on the taxiway at Cherry Point, trying to communicate with the controllers in the massive tower at the base.

I would request permission to move onto the runway and be met by silence. I would repeat my request, and still get no reply. Eventually another pilot in my squadron would chip in and repeat what I had said and the tower would immediately come back to acknowledge me.

It was exasperating.

'I'm sorry,' I told them, 'I don't understand why you don't understand what I just said.'

They ignored me, probably because they didn't understand that either. After the first week, I went to see them, and they seemed perfectly polite and helpful, but the problem never fully went away. Some British pilots in the US learnt to Americanise their accents. But not me; I found it impossible to pull off a credible version of their Southern drawl.

During my time with the Marines I dealt with the typical workload of an officer in charge of operations. My first full-on crisis came early in my posting, when one of the brightest young pilots in the squadron, with a glittering career ahead of him, made the sort of mistake on the range that would normally have got him fired.

He was doing a weapons exercise with live ammunition during a three-week stint for our unit based at the Naval Air Facility at El Centro in southern California. Somehow he mistook one small hill in the desert for another and ended up firing a volley of rockets at a group of Marine Special Operations Command ground controllers, who were running the exercise. He was incredibly lucky that no one was killed or injured.

I viewed this as an uncharacteristic and remarkable error that would never happen again, by one of the most gifted pilots in the squadron. I argued strongly that he should not be sacked or removed to non-flying duties, which would have wrecked his career, and that we should hold off informing the general until he'd had another go at the same exercise.

The next morning the young pilot did exactly that and it all went off without a hitch. When we did 'fess up to the general he was not pleased, but accepted our point of view. My feeling is that many of our successes in life are built on past failures, so why not give people a second chance? The young pilot went on to become a weapons instructor on Harriers, and then became an F35 instructor. Eight years later he was the supervising officer when I executed my first vertical landing in an F35.

Other challenges included a transatlantic visit by the carrier HMS *Ark Royal* to the US Navy port at nearby Norfolk, Virginia. The old Invincible Class was bereft of fighters in the last months of her Royal Navy service life, but her crew were keen to stay current. We detached 12 Marine Corps Harriers to the carrier, along with 150 Marines, for a couple of weeks on a joint exercise. *Capella Strike* was a complex project that I was heavily involved in and, as a linchpin between the Americans and the Royal Navy, I got it in the ear from my own people when the pressure came on.

It did so in the form of a disagreement about a relatively routine hydraulic leak that developed in the undercarriage of one of our visiting Harriers. This meant the plane could no longer take off using the carrier's ski-jump, because its undercarriage would have collapsed under the stress. It seemed the only way to remove it at the end of the exercise was to crane it off in dock.

But I looked at it, assessed the risks, and decided the plane could leave under its own steam, if we brought the carrier close to the coast. The Harrier could execute a vertical take-off, but with the ground lock on the undercarriage deployed, so the gear would be stuck where it was throughout the short flight back to Cherry Point. It could then land vertically on the airfield.

I convinced the captain that this would be safe. But the senior hierarchy of the Royal Navy air engineering department were sceptical, and found it difficult to accept that someone of my rank, and a pilot rather than an engineer of all people, could sign off on something so inherently risky. They were furious; this was their decision, not mine. I found myself telling them in no uncertain terms that, although I was a Royal Navy officer, I was making the decision on behalf of the Marine Corps and the president of the United States.

After all the teacup rattling and wine-induced chest poking, the Harrier, resplendent with bright-yellow stripes on its tail fin – the symbol of the Flying Tigers, as the jets in VMA-542 squadron were known – took off vertically from *Ark Royal* and was delivered back home for repairs without incident.

My stint at Cherry Point afforded me plenty of flying hours all over the States, as we conducted exercises out west, and returned much as we were when Mac and I encountered that strange phenomenon in Texas. Coming back from the Mountain Home US Air Force base in Idaho – where pilots from the German Luftwaffe were conducting weapons exercises against a range of aircraft, our Harriers included – I survived my worst-ever landing in a Harrier.

A group of four of us, in fingertip formation, were on the delivery flight back to North Carolina. Soon after we took off we were notified by air traffic control of an unusually powerful and extensive thunderstorm system that was running the length of the Rockies. With the danger of lightning strikes and the possibility of flying into high-energy, super-cooled hailstorms that could punch holes in the carbon-fibre fuselage of a Harrier, we had no choice but to head further and further south, as we searched for a gap in the system.

We found one right down on the Mexican border, and then headed for a refuelling stop at New Orleans. It was on the approach to the naval air station in the city that I discovered that the demister function in my cockpit, which kept the canopy conditioned and ensured that I could see out, had broken. I was coming down from the cold upper atmosphere into the intense, early-evening humidity of Louisiana and I couldn't see a thing.

Ahead of me, the three other Harriers were landing one after the other, at 10-second intervals, and I couldn't see any of them. I was reduced to pulling off one of my flying gloves and wafting it around with one hand towards the forward end of the canopy, in a largely futile bid to clear sections of Perspex. I came in on the instruments, relying on fleeting glimpses of the ground, as I deployed the air brake and reduced speed to lower the landing gear.

This was not ideal in all sorts of ways, but just when I thought it couldn't get worse, number one in our formation warned us that the airfield had rigged arrestor cables across the runway. Our Harriers couldn't land on tensioned cables. They would have torn off the outrigger wheels and probably irreparably damaged the main undercarriage too.

Calling on my night-flying experience in Afghanistan, I used the forward-looking infrared imaging system, based on a sensor in the nose, and watched the display on the screen, glove still in hand, as I brought the Harrier down. I was focusing on trying to make sure I was a safe distance behind the jets ahead, and lined up correctly. But I was also watching like a hawk for the tell-tale line across the runway. At 50ft I spotted the cable and powered up to ensure I was well past it when my wheels hit the ground. I slammed on the brakes and steered to the right, shooting past the three other Harriers, before coming to a stop at the end of the runway.

I opened the canopy to catch my breath, after my experience in the fast-jet hurt locker. But the demister issue was still making it hard to see where I was going. To get off at the correct taxiway, I had to make my ejection seat safe, unstrap and stand up on the cockpit floor for a few seconds at a time. I got somewhere close to the dispersal area, but could not see the ground marshal directing me in. Eventually I decided enough was enough, stopped where I was and shut it all down. As I climbed out of the cockpit, the sun was setting at the beginning of a perfectly clear night. I was exhausted and heard myself thinking: 'Too close for comfort. I can't keep doing this.'

The final part of my Marine Corps secondment was overshadowed by the sudden and unexpected decision by the British government to scrap all our remaining GR7 and GR9 Harriers, and get rid of our carriers. This bolt from the blue occurred on the morning of 19 October 2010, with the publication of the Strategic Defence and Security Review (SDSR). The axing of the Harriers was part of a series of measures to try and reduce a huge black hole in the defence budget, and pay for the new Queen Elizabeth Class carriers and the F35s.

Like everyone else in the Harrier world, I had been warned to keep an eye on the details, but none of us were expecting to see our most capable, war-proven ground support aircraft immediately and unceremoniously chopped. We expected the RAF to lose one or two of its Tornado squadrons, whilst the Harriers would continue in service on the Invincible Class carriers until the F35s and the new ships came into service.

I was watching the announcement in the House of Commons on *Sky News* and got the shock of my life. Rarely do political decisions affect anyone instantaneously, but this one was like a whirlwind. It brought new meaning to the notion of having the rug pulled from under your feet. On the one hand, I was suddenly facing a very uncertain future back home as a Harrier pilot, with no jets to fly. On the other, my US hosts were seriously pissed off. By that stage I had become an instructor and moved to one of the training squadrons at Cherry Point – VMAT-203. Among my charges were two young British pilots who were about to finish their conversion to the Harrier as part of a similar exchange programme to the one that I was on.

Later that same day, the CO called me in and he did not mince his words.

'I have a message from the commandant of the Marine Corps in the Pentagon,' he said curtly. 'You and your pilots here are to cease flying immediately. You're grounded.'

'What?' I was completely taken aback. 'For how long?'

'Indefinitely. You are to tell your students that they must leave the air base, go back to their homes, not travel anywhere in this country, and exit the US within 14 days, when their visas will be withdrawn.'

I stood before him, speechless and seething. So that's how special the Special Relationship is, I thought.

I was furious on behalf of my students, who were on the brink of going to the frontline as Harrier pilots, and who were now being told that their careers were over, through no fault of their own, before they'd even started. At the same time, they were being treated like illegal immigrants by their hosts in the Marine Corps.

In the following few days, the row over their treatment boiled over as I confronted the general at the base. Having thrown them out of Cherry Point on the day the SDSR was published, Washington then decided that their 14-day period of grace, before they were to leave the country, should be cut to seven. Lieutenant General Jon Davis, a clean-cut, no-nonsense Marine aviator who was in charge of the Second Marine Aircraft Wing, summoned them to his office to let them know in person.

I was outraged. In my view the US military had divested itself of all responsibility and control over our pilots three days earlier. If anyone was going to tell them to go home, it would be me, not them. After a stand-up row with my CO, I drove over to confront the reception committee at the general's office.

'Look, Nath, you need to calm down,' said his second-in-command. 'We need to talk about this.'

'No. You have no right to tell these British naval officers what to do,' I said through clenched teeth. 'If you are not going to do it cordially, and you're going to just kick the guys out, then you'll have no part in this. I will speak to my officers, and I will inform them of your decision to send them home. You have no control in this situation any more – I don't care what rank you are.'

I was angry, but they were annoyed as well, not least because David Cameron's government had also – in its wisdom – made an equally controversial decision to switch from buying the F35B version to the 'C'. The 'B' is the STOVL variant, which the Marine Corps were championing, while the 'C' was the naval carrier version that required arrestor wires and a catapult to land and take off. Two years later, this decision would be reversed. But at the time it left the Marine Corps feeling exposed as the sole customers for the F35B, an aircraft very much on probation, beset with cost issues and regarded as technically very risky.

I was heavily invested in the 'B' programme, because part of my job involved being the Marine Corps F35 representative at Cherry Point. Together with my opposite numbers elsewhere in the US, we had been in the process of designing a new training squadron for when the jets came on line. It was going to be split down the middle, 50–50, with British and American officers and British and American pilots, and a rotating command. But now it was 'in the trash', as they put it that day.

The 2i/c disappeared for a moment and returned with General Davis alongside him. To give the latter his due, he was very civil, and could tell I was not a happy camper.

'Lieutenant Commander Gray, I know you're angry,' Davis said. 'I'm angry too. But I'm being told by the deputy commandant for aviation of the Marine Corps that this is what I must do. So I am literally going to pass the message on to your pilots. I will tell them thank you, you've done brilliantly, that this is nothing to do with you, but I've got to send you home.'

They arrived a couple of hours later. After the general had delivered the bad news, I told them to take two weeks' leave, ignore the visa issues, have a holiday and then go home. Neither of them stayed in the Fleet Air Arm; one joined the Royal Canadian Air Force, who had set about recruiting our Harrier pilots following the announcement, and the other joined Cathay Pacific.

I took a week off to cool down and think about my future. The charms of Cherry Point and being part of the US military were wearing somewhat thin. When I returned to duty, my plan was to head home as soon as possible, but General Davis had other ideas. He summoned me back to his office.

'We, as the Marine Corps, have gleaned a lot of information off of you, over the last two years, but equally we have invested a lot of time and effort into you too,' he said. 'So based on that, it would be against our interests to let you go early, because you are doing a job for us, training our people, and the Royal Navy is paying your salary. We have spoken to your admirals back home, and the British embassy, and we are happy to continue this posting for another year, on the condition that what you do here is teach our Marines how to fly Harriers.'

He poked me in the chest and told me to shave my beard because, he said, it looked scruffy. And with that I was dismissed.

We stayed on for most of the following year, but the spell was broken and we wanted to get out as soon as we could. Back home there was considerable fanfare as the Harriers were put through their last flights, with tributes to the plane in the media, but I was still flying them long after all other British pilots had stopped.

In the meantime, I had begun protracted negotiations with Portsmouth to sort out my next job. Although I was an experienced combat pilot, I had no transferable qualifications for life after the Royal Navy, so I decided the best thing would be to become an RAF-qualified flying instructor, a skill that was recognised worldwide. There was a job going, back on the old Tucano, as a basic fast-jet flying instructor at RAF Linton-on-Ouse in Yorkshire; I went for it and managed to get it.

Once it was confirmed, I was able to go to the Marine Corps and show them my posting orders. My time at Cherry Point was finally over. My last Harrier sortie was a routine maintenance test flight. I landed vertically, but not before turning towards the squadron and dipping the nose, and then doing the same towards the general's office. It was my small gesture of rebellion.

As I taxied in, I could feel my right leg shaking a little – it was a physical reminder that this was the end of an era for me. Although the AV-8B I was then flying was a world away from the old Sea Harrier in which Jak and I had crashed, I had been flying that fantastic, challenging, temperamental and bewitching aircraft solidly for nine years. I knew I would always look back on it with affection, even if it had changed my life forever – and not in a good way – that morning at Wittering.

Like many of my colleagues in the Harrier world, my dismay over the SDSR was not just a selfish response to seeing my career prospects suddenly take a downward turn. We knew the Harrier was still a critical part of the UK defence capability, as a close air support and ground attack fighter that gave us the all-important carrier strike threat. Getting rid of it seemed remarkably short-sighted, and it led to a period when we had neither carriers, nor jets to fly from them.

What grated most was that the decision to scrap the Harrier fleet and sell them off on the cheap to the Marine Corps for spares, it seemed to me to be the result of self-interested empire-building by senior officers, especially in the RAF. When confronted with the need to cut costs, the air marshals didn't scrap any of their Tornado squadrons, presumably because that would have reduced their total manpower more dramatically than getting rid of the single-seat Harrier. It troubled me that they may have ended up going for what was best for them, not what was best for the nation.

At Cherry Point, I experienced the downdraft and it was unnerving. I felt betrayed from both sides of the pond by the decision to chop the plane I was flying and teaching while, at the same time, being shunned by the upper echelons of the organisation I had been working with for two years. I had become a political pawn and the experience would forever colour my view of our fabled old transatlantic alliance.

The last thing I expected was that, within 18 months, Lucy and I would be contemplating coming back to the States – albeit to a different location. We would do so with a completely different mindset and with a new challenge ahead, one which would give me the opportunity to heal my fractured relationship with one of our closest allies.

18

I couldn't know it at the time, but my journey from Harrier pilot to F35 test pilot began almost as soon as I started my new job, learning to be a flight instructor at RAF Linton-on-Ouse.

This would be a three-year posting when I would learn to teach students on the Tucano, using the tried-and-tested techniques of the RAF Central Flying School at Cranwell. Along the way, I would be acquiring a qualification that would stand me in good stead, whether I stayed in the Royal Navy or not.

I have to admit that after the Harrier, in all its various forms, going back to the single-prop Tucano was a bit of a shocker, and there was certainly no thrill, or much enjoyment, in the flying aspect of my new role. But I enjoyed learning how to teach young pilots how to get the best performance out of them, and found the mentoring side of it very rewarding.

Perhaps most importantly, we had turned up in Yorkshire feeling wrung out after our stint at Cherry Point and by the politics that surrounded my last months there. We were determined that we were going to settle down and appreciate some stability.

However, I was aware that there were people in the Navy

hierarchy who were scratching their heads about what I was doing up there. While I saw it as a stepping stone, and a chance to slow down for a while, they seemed impatient to move me on as soon as possible.

This was underlined at the end of our first week at Linton, when the name of my appointer from Navy command lit up my phone as we were out walking our dog, Scout, on the station football pitch behind our new married quarters. I shut my eyes for a second to prepare for the curveball that might be coming my way.

'Hi, Nath, how's it going up there? Must be great to be back in Blighty.'

'Yeah, you're not wrong there ... we're just—'

'Look, something's come up, a really exciting opportunity, and we want you to consider it.'

'Hmm ... really?'

'Yes, the French Admiralty and ourselves have chosen you for a new exchange programme on the Super Étendard. This is going to be a high-profile job where you will gain unique experience with one of our key European allies.'

'Hang on, we've only just got here. We haven't even finished unpack—'

'No, I understand that of course, but this really is a great opportunity and you will be based in northern France and, as I say, the admirals have said they'd like you to fill the role.'

I have always gripped exciting opportunities whenever they arise, but on this occasion it didn't feel right. Even the subtle linguistic nuances from my time at Cherry Point reminded me that I've always been a slow learner when it comes to foreign languages, and I reckoned the Super Étendard was an ugly fighter which was already on its way out.

I stuck to my guns and said a polite but firm 'non' to our old friends across the Channel, and to a programme that was part of Whitehall's attempts to bridge the gap, during the years when we had no carrier strike capability of our own. I was digging in at Linton and that was it.

I had to reconvert back onto the Tucano during my first weeks there, alongside a newly promoted commander who, to start with, I thought had come to take over at the base. But it turned out that Mark 'Sparky' MacLeod had just been appointed commanding officer of Empire Test Pilots' School (ETPS) at Boscombe Down in Wiltshire – an establishment with a worldwide reputation for excellence – and he needed to learn to fly the Tucano too.

He explained that before he could start his new job, he was required to convert on most of the aircraft the school used and, after the Tucano, it would be the helicopters, which were his speciality. As a pilot who had spent my entire career flying only one plane at a time – and for most of the last decade just the Harrier – I was intrigued. It seemed amazing to me that you might go from being a specialist to flying a whole host of different aircraft at a moment's notice.

'You qualify on all of them and you just fly whichever you have to for the course,' said Sparky.

His approach to the Tucano was completely different to mine. He was short-cutting it, and focusing on the key elements. He read through the flight reference cards, looked at the emergency drills and the operating limitations, memorised the bits in bold type, but not all the checks like you would do if the Tucano was your sole focus. By the end of the first day he had been through the whole book; the next day he was up and flying, and within a week or two he was gone.

During those few days I was lucky enough to spend time chatting to him in the crew room. Sparky was the first person to explain a test pilot's role to me, and he planted a seed. He talked about the interface between designers, engineers and pilots, and the idea of a pilot as an engineer who bridges the gap, so that each side understands the other's needs. It sounded fascinating and, along the way, I mentioned to him that I had studied aerospace engineering at university.

'Well, that's absolutely perfect for a job like this,' he remarked. 'It's just unfortunate that we don't have any fast jets for your cadre to go and test. It's all rotary wing in the Navy at the moment.'

But he also said that one of his challenges, as the new CO at ETPS, was to re-establish a test pilot position in the Navy. 'We're going to have the F35 at some point in the next five or 10 years, so we do need it, but it has to be funded and it must be a properly set-out programme. One issue is that the allocation of places on the test pilot courses is controlled by the RAF, and they don't necessarily want one of our lot invading their patch . . .'

He told me about the daunting two-day selection procedure for ETPS and what was involved in getting through. He also mentioned that they might be looking for new candidates, and that I should keep an eye on the DINS – the Defence Instructions and Notices. These were administrative messages sent out by the MoD, where new jobs were routinely advertised.

That was advice I cheerfully ignored. I could never be bothered to plough through all that boring MoD stuff and, in the back of my mind, I thought I didn't have a chance anyway. My old mate imposter syndrome made sure of that. I'd be found out, I thought; I wouldn't have the credibility, the experience or the intellect to be a test pilot. Time to get back to my day job.

About six months later, I was required to attend a course at the Defence Academy at Shrivenham in Wiltshire, where I joined a wide range of military pilots and civilian flying supervisors for a week-long affair, to refresh us on all aspects of flight safety. No Harrier pilots, of course, but there were Typhoon pilots, Tornado pilots, Hercules pilots and helicopter pilots – and at quite a senior level.

Among them were two test pilot instructors working for QinetiQ, the defence contractor that runs ETPS. One was ex-Navy, the other an ex-RAF pilot who had tested the X35 in the States – an early prototype of the F35. He was also a former Harrier pilot. During one of our early breaks from class, Justin Paines introduced himself, and then aimed me at his QinetiQ colleague, Paul Edwards, as we made our way to the officers' mess that evening. They seemed intent on finding out what I was up to.

'How are you finding Linton?' Paines ventured.

'Well, it's OK – you know, flying the Tucano ... but I'm enjoying the teaching side ...'

'Actually,' he said, 'we chatted to Sparky about you. He's getting on really well in his new role and he remembers you from when he was up at Linton a few months back. He mentioned you have an engineering degree ...'

'Yes, that's right, aerospace engineering at Manchester . . .'

'And you've been on operations, I gather?'

'Oh yeah, I've been to Afghanistan a few times.'

'How did you find that?'

'Not always easy, but mostly interesting,' I said rather blankly. 'I'm glad I don't have to go back.'

An articulate and thoughtful individual, who was massively on top of his brief, Paines then started drilling down to more technical issues. He wanted to know about the armour-piercing rockets that we carried on the GR7 and their aiming system.

'It was good,' I said, 'but it would have been better if there was some sort of feedback, something like a laser target finder.'

He smiled. 'Yes, I know what you mean . . . and what did you make of the braking system on the Harrier?'

'Well, it was alright but, of course, we kept popping tyres and you couldn't brake over a certain speed because of it.'

'D'you think that's because the wheel brakes weren't very good?'

'Maybe, I'm not sure . . .'

Paines was warming to his theme. 'Well, think a bit harder, Nath,' he pressed me. 'Could it be that the wheel brakes were actually too good, and that's why they were clamping on the disc and popping the tyres?'

'That's interesting,' I replied, 'and possibly very true – we might need a better anti-skid system instead, to stop it doing that.'

'Exactly,' he said. 'Now, talk to me about anti-skid systems . . .'

And on it went, as we made our way to where the drinks and snacks were being served outside the mess. When we got there, Edwards mentioned that they were surprised that, with my background and experience, I had not applied for the new Royal Navy test pilot position.

'Oh, I didn't realise there was one,' I said, only then remembering what Sparky had said about the DINs.

'Yeah, the DIN went out about four or five months ago and there's been quite a lot of interest,' he said. 'We had loads of applicants, and they got whittled down to a few, and we had them all in for interviews last week.'

'Oh, great,' I said, feeling suddenly deflated and fearing I had well and truly missed this boat. 'Who was it, who got it?'

He paused and looked me steadily in the eye. 'Nobody, Nathan. None of the applicants came up to the required standards.'

I guessed the Navy hierarchy had been desperate to select someone, but the greybeards at ETPS were not prepared to lower their high standards, no matter how much pressure they were under.

I took a slug of beer and swallowed hard. Now I was beginning to understand what this might be all about. The more I thought about it – and my mind was whizzing at the speed of sound – being a test pilot could be the dream job for me, and the fact that the F35 was coming along made it all the more enticing.

Paines concluded our discussion by saying that if I was interested, I should give Sparky a call, and he gave me his number. Lucy and I didn't want to move, and I needed to know whether she was happy for yet more upheaval in our life, but I didn't need a second invitation. I called him straight away.

Sparky seemed to be waiting to hear from me. He revealed that he too had been surprised my file was not one of those on his desk when he was sifting through applicants for the next course a few months earlier, especially after the conversations we'd had at Linton. He invited me to pop over to see him that evening.

I jumped in the car and drove the hour or so south to Boscombe Down, calling Lucy and telling her what I was up to on the way. I was escorted onto the base, where I found Sparky waiting for me in his office. His was the only light still on at eight in the evening.

He made me a cup of tea and we sat and chatted for nearly three hours. He talked me through the whole gamut – what the job involved, the 20-hour days, the endless technical studying and what my chances were. He emphasised that, though I would be a late applicant, no corners would be cut. And he talked about the difficult 'political' background, including the role that the RAF would play in a chicken-and-egg situation. There was no job to go to, which meant there was no point in qualifying, but then again, unless someone *did* qualify, a job would never materialise.

He invited me to think slices of Swiss cheese. Positioned correctly, it would be possible to align the holes so that I could travel through them. 'There is no Royal Navy test pilot job, but that post will exist at some point,' he said. 'There has to be a Royal Navy test pilot for the F35 – who else could do the first landing on board one of our new carriers? But in order to get onto the F35, the Americans will have to accept you, which will probably mean going to the US Navy Test Pilot School and, in order to do that, you will have to qualify for ETPS.'

I was buzzing when I left him. After completing the course at Shrivenham, I went home to discuss it with Lucy. After much soul-searching, we decided to sleep on it. Which meant lying in bed with the light off and our eyes wide open. We both knew this was a great opportunity, but we were still battered and bruised from our US tour and neither of us wanted to up sticks any time soon.

Lucy switched the light on and broke the silence. 'Would you regret it if you didn't go for it?' she asked. This was not the first time in our life together that she had asked that question. 'If the answer is yes, then you've got to go for it,' she added.

And that was it. I called Sparky the following morning.

I knew this was going to be a long shot. I'd missed the selection process, and, more than that, I had missed the long period of preparation most pilots undergo before they even set foot at Boscombe Down. Sparky, meanwhile, worked hard on a bespoke application plan, and managed to get everything in place for me to attend a two-day board in only three weeks' time.

It felt overwhelming; I had to learn huge amounts of ground school stuff – all the theory and practice of flying. I had to reacquaint myself with A-level maths up to graduate level, and I had to fully grasp the professional and political aspects of applying for this sort of high-profile job and demonstrate commitment to the role.

During those three weeks I went back to Boscombe, where I

met the students and instructors. I visited RAF Coningsby and spoke to the pilots in the Typhoon and Tornado test squadrons, and the engineers at the weapons test unit. I also bought a copy of the Letts revision guide to A-level maths and physics and went back to studying my imaginary numbers, double integers, differentiation and logarithms. That was hard . . .

My second visit to Boscombe Down will always be etched in my memory because it was there that I met the chief ground school instructor, a certain Alan Mattock, who was obviously a bit of a legend at ETPS.

He occupied a very long office and, after knocking on the door, I walked in all bright and cheerful.

'Hi, I'm Nath Gray, I—'

'The chair . . .' he said, indicating one near the door about 20 metres from his desk, not the one right in front of him. That seemed a bit off. But I went and got it and carried it to his desk and sat down opposite him.

'Hi, I'm Nath Gray and I am a bit . . .'

'I know who you are,' he said brusquely. 'And I know you're late.'

The subtext was already clear. I had not applied as part of the advertised process, I was not going to get any special treatment, and they were certainly not going to take any short cuts on my behalf. Mattock's message was, essentially: 'I am here to destroy you. Prove to me that I won't be able to do that.'

'So I've got just three weeks – in fact, two and a half now,' I said, still unbowed. 'And I was wondering if you could help me by telling me where I should focus my effort for the interviews.'

Mattock leant across to his bookshelves and picked up

the first of nine volumes of something catchily titled AP3456. This was the RAF Central Flying School's manual of flying and it was *the* authority on aerodynamics. Line the individual volumes up together, and the spine was several inches thick.

'You need to read this,' he said.

'OK,' I replied breezily, 'and which bits should I focus on?'

He placed his hands on top of the book and looked up at me over his glasses. 'All of it,' he said, indicating the other volumes on the shelf.

So that was it. I left feeling deflated and knowing, not for the first time, that I had what seemed like an impossible mountain to climb and the daunting prospect of a fortnight's cramming ahead.

When it was time to travel back down for selection, I didn't think I had a chance. I realised immediately that appearing before boards that had been specially brought together just for me was a big disadvantage. I would not be surrounded by other candidates, discussing what questions they had been asked, or by candidates who had tried and failed before, and who might share the odd tip. I was going in solo, and cold.

The first part was a two-hour written maths and physics exam. Then it was the academic interview in front of the head of academics at ETPS, the head of fixed wing training, the chief flying instructor and the head of aero systems engineering. It was another two-hour session, and they provided paper and pencils, graph paper and a whiteboard to help me illustrate my answers. No chance of bluffing my way through this one, I thought.

They started by asking me to identify various planes from pictures and models on the walls and on the shelves of the windowless conference room. Then we talked about the chines on the Lockheed SR71 Blackbird long-distance reconnaissance aircraft, and how they contribute to aerodynamic efficiency. We discussed the stability characteristics of the Harrier, and then things got more theoretical and more difficult. I was answering less and fumbling more.

At one point, I attempted to respond to a question by drawing a graph on the whiteboard. 'If you are flying a constant calibrated airspeed in a climb to altitude, what is the relationship between equivalent airspeed, true airspeed and Mach number?'

Not sure I quite got that one right . . . in fact, I now know I didn't.

Then it was on to inertial navigation . . .

I thought I had probably bombed in this interview but, in my defence, I reminded myself that there was often no definitively right answer to any of their questions. They were more interested in the way I presented myself, and whether I had sufficient depth of knowledge and experience to draw on, and how I used that in my answers, than whether I got everything absolutely right.

After wolfing a sandwich from the Spar, it was back for the professional interview in front of the head of QinetiQ, the head of ETPS in the familiar form of Sparky, and the RAF's chief test pilot. This encounter veered from motivational – why I wanted to train to do this job when there wasn't necessarily a role available – to technical stuff, like how I would design a test programme to fit a Tucano with rockets. My answer was to take little, incremental baby steps – one thing at a time, and test each one in turn, starting with the rockets, then a pylon to mount them on, then the joining electrics and so on. They seemed to like that.

Then it got quite heavy, with the RAF guy bearing down on the funding issues, like the question of who was going to foot the £1.5 million bill for my training – at which point Sparky jumped in and pointed out that there was a contract and a memorandum in place to say the Fleet Air Arm would have a test pilot.

I fought my corner but tiptoed diplomatically with my answers. I even heard myself point out that my ambition to be a test pilot should not be seen as a land grab by a Navy aviator at the expense of the RAF. It was like no other interview I had ever attended, and by the end I was drained by the turbulence in the room. One positive was that the guy from QinetiQ seemed happy. 'Well done,' he said, as I made my way out. 'Good effort.'

I spent the night at the base, and went to see Sparky the next morning to find out how I had done. It turned out my maths and physics papers were flawless – this was an area that many of the earlier candidates had struggled with – my academic interview was not as good as they had hoped, but was considered OK, while my professional interview had been excellent.

'So, Nath, I have spoken to Navy command,' said Sparky, enjoying this moment as much as I was, '. . . to the chief test pilot and the appointer, and I've got a letter here from your station commander at Linton, who supports the whole thing. And I am very pleased to say that you have passed test pilot selection.'

I sat there in a state of disbelief. Somehow I'd found my

way through the cheese slices. I couldn't wait to tell Lucy, with whom I'd shared all my doubts about my performance on the phone overnight. Now it was time for us to start a new adventure.

And so, after 18 months at Linton-on-Ouse, we packed up again and headed to Boscombe Down, where I began studying test pilot ground school, flight test techniques and report writing. This would be a preamble to test pilot school proper that gave me an opportunity to continue to catch up.

In the meantime, the Navy plucked me away for a short posting at RNAS Culdrose in Cornwall, where I filled an administrative role as deputy fixed wing force commander. When I got back to Wiltshire, I got the posting I had been waiting for.

All British student test pilots attend one of the 'big four' schools – either ETPS at Boscombe, EPNER, the French equivalent at Istres-Le Tubé Air Base near Marseilles, the US Air Force Test Pilot School at Edwards Air Force Base in southern California, or the US Naval Test Pilot School at Patuxent River in Maryland.

'Pax River' was the best fit and the posting of my dreams, because it offered a direct route to the F35. And that's where Sparky had secured a place for me. We were going back to the United States, but this was going to feel very different to Cherry Point. It was an exciting new beginning, and a new chapter in my flying career, as we flew together across the Atlantic to be guests of our close ally once more.

I will never forget driving down Three Notch Road, in St Mary's County in Maryland, and through the gates of my new base for the first time. It was early July 2014 and there in front of me were vast twin hangars, with the words 'United States Naval Test Pilot School' emblazoned on them in big blue capital letters.

In truth, I was experiencing a mix of excitement and terror. This was imposter syndrome on steroids. I saw the amazing range of aircraft sitting on the flightline and, as I reported for duty for the first time, I wondered how I was going to hold my own.

19

They knew how to put you in your place at the US Naval Test Pilot School. Each year two classes of 'students' would arrive, to start their respective courses six months apart and a lot of them did so in alpha-male, chest-beating, *Top Gun* movie mode.

'Oh yeah, I've done four tours in Afghanistan, and I've flown this and that; I was top on this course and I'm an instructor in this and that discipline . . .'

I was treated to the full range of macho, testosterone-filled bravado for which US fighter pilots in particular are famous.

But then the staff arrived and everyone gradually came back down to earth.

'Right, Class 148, welcome,' the senior instructor greeted us after we had been ushered downstairs to the classroom, where we were to spend hundreds of hours over the next 12 months.

We had got there by walking through the lobby, another intimidating experience when you do it for the first time. In addition to the imposing, life-sized bronze statue of a test pilot – a work called *Reflection* by the American sculptor Rodney Carroll – that dominated the hallway, the place was full of plaques and cabinets celebrating star graduates. Many of them were astronauts with NASA, the legendary John Glenn among them.

If you were feeling nervous, wondering whether you were up to it, this made things worse.

'You are now the junior class,' the instructor continued. 'Class 147 is the senior course, and you are subordinate to them and they are subordinate to the staff here.'

He paused as we waited for him to set out the challenge that lay before us – one that involved not only flying multiple aircraft in a constantly changing routine, but intense academic study, punctuated by exams.

'You all want to be test pilots,' he said. 'You've all been interviewed and had your CVs and everything reviewed. But this is where the hard work begins, and this is where you prove that you're worthy to test the most advanced aircraft systems in the world.'

He talked about test pilot culture. 'Your role is to make the most hazardous and risky activity appear dull and mundane, and to be the gate guardian, ensuring you only allow aircraft to pass your scrutiny that are fit for purpose and safe.'

He made a big point about ethics and honesty. 'The success or failure of multimillion-dollar programmes – a trillion-dollar programme, in the case of the F35 – will rest on test pilot opinion. A company's survival or demise can pivot on what you say. No matter the pressure or the monetary reward, it's your role to speak the truth – truth data is the only commodity with value in the test pilot world, and one day it will be your responsibility to call someone's baby ugly.'

He paused and moved to the front of the stage.

'From now on you are all students again,' he said slowly

and firmly. 'It's time to forget about your seniority and rank. We want you to use your knowledge, but don't think you know anything. All of you know one airplane – you are about to fly more than 20, fixed and rotary wing, in the course of the next year, so you are starting from scratch. So clear your minds and let's get to it.'

It was a simple and straightforward introductory message, but to make sure we had all understood it, the CO marched in and rammed it home. This guy was a strict disciplinarian from the US Army – the position was rotated between the US Navy, the US Marine Corps and US Army – and he seemed to have a genuine dislike of students, especially new arrivals.

After he had stared at us for a few seconds in deathly silence, we got both barrels from the immaculately turned-out Lieutenant Colonel Felix Griffin.

'Right,' he said, 'you think you're all great. Well, listen up. I'm here to tell you, you're not. You don't know *anything* about test flying, test evaluation or reporting. You are here to learn, so pin your ears back, be a student, don't answer back and work hard.'

He told us to follow his version of the five Ps. In the British military we all knew the time-honoured rule that 'prior preparation prevents piss-poor performance'. Griffin's less catchy version started with – inevitably – 'perfection'. Then came 'proportional ego', 'positive attitude', 'positional excellence' and finally 'patch value' – a reference to the requirement to respect the traditions and status of the institution that we had now joined, and whose crest adorned our flying suits.

And it was not hard to feel that history, seeing all the photos of the classes that had passed out before us, and looking out at a flight line that included some iconic aircraft. These ranged from the T38 Talon jet trainer, to the towering and spectacular F18 multirole fighter, the Calspan Lear jet, the T6 Texan, the Blackhawk helicopter, various gliders and other jets, and two of the oldest planes in the US naval inventory, the prop-driven Otter and Beaver.

Everywhere you looked, you got the sense that you were merely the latest naïve and ambitious undergraduates of an institution that traced its history back to 1945, and which had already produced more than 100 astronauts. It had also churned out more test pilots, flight officers and engineers than all the other three major international flight test schools combined.

Griffin's little party piece concluded with him telling us another pearl of homespun wisdom, namely that 'humble preparation leads to confident execution'. Then, as he was about to leave, he spotted me.

'That beard,' he thundered . . .

I still had my naval beard that I had worn throughout my flying career at home, in Afghanistan and even with the Marine Corps at Cherry Point.

'That beard,' he repeated menacingly, 'will be off by tomorrow – it is not part of the regulations.'

And then he walked out.

'Brilliant,' I thought. 'I've been singled out on day one.' There were 40 of us in the room, almost all Americans, but the group also included one pilot each from Sweden, France, Italy, Singapore and Norway. And he'd chosen me . . .

In case I had any doubts about the seriousness of Griffin's order, the senior instructor came over and reiterated the command. The explanation given was that facial hair could affect the seal of an oxygen mask to the face, something that had never happened to me.

'The CO will not compromise on safety, so it has to go, Lieutenant Commander Gray,' he said. The beard was gone by the following day (to return by graduation day, a year later), despite my objections that wearing one was my right under Queen's Regulations.

After the introduction, we were shown upstairs to the open plan office where we would be based for our academic work – the hard grind of learning and exams that continued throughout the course, alongside the flying. The walls were piled high with stacks of printer paper which, our instructors informed us, would only last the first few months – they were right about that – and a countdown clock hung over the door. It showed 336 days to go.

The room was divided into small cubicles, and mine was No. 15.

I walked in and sat down. In front of me was a laptop, two screens, a mouse and two imposing piles of books. On one side were theory texts – works on mathematics, thermodynamics, aerodynamics, systems engineering and electronics. On the other were aircrew manuals and flight reference cards for all the different aircraft types we were going to fly.

That cubicle was going to be my home for the next year, as I settled into a routine which comprised ridiculously long working hours, no days off at the weekends and almost no time for family. All around me were classmates with brilliant flying careers behind them and master's qualifications in subjects like astrophysics, or what amounted to rocket science. And many of them were younger than me – I was then 38 – because the American system pushed pilots through much quicker than the Fleet Air Arm or the RAF. It all felt massively daunting and, once again, I could sense the draining insecurity of imposter syndrome. Was I really going to be up to this?

The routine at Pax River was based around mornings devoted to academic work, from 7.30 to 12.30, and flying in the afternoons. The first three weeks consisted of nothing but ground school theory – testing us on everything from calculus to the technical details of each aircraft type we would fly. The aim was to prove that we were ready and worthy to move forward.

The flying aspect was built around three elements – planning, executing and reporting. At any point on the course, you would be preparing for your next flight – setting out your test objectives and methodology – flying the test itself, or analysing data and writing up the test report. This could run to anywhere between 50 and 100 pages of technical analysis and opinion.

The objective in the cockpit was not merely to learn to fly a range of different aircraft – shuffling them constantly in the process – but carrying out flight test exercises that we might execute if the plane was a prototype. It would be as if we were one of the first pilots to evaluate its characteristics, systems and design, or its suitability for various mission tasks.

Every time we took to the air, we were focused not just on safely flying a strange aircraft, but often on manually taking down data to use for our reporting. I would take notes, but also voice all of my observations and assessments on my hot mic, using a tape recorder carried in an arm pocket and a mic taped in my helmet earpiece.

Apart from data collection, we would also use portable instruments in the cockpit, like handheld force gauges to measure stick force, while the student engineers would use tape measures and stopwatches to measure deflection during a timed manoeuvre. The old rule, about not having loose items in a cockpit, went out the door, and you had to be careful. It was easy to lose focus on the flying side, as we concentrated on capturing all the technical information we needed for our reports.

It was often a difficult balance to strike because test flying – if it is to be useful and used as evidence – has to be pinpoint accurate, with a tolerance of plus or minus one knot in airspeed for example, or variations of altitude of no more than, say, 50ft. And we learnt to fly peculiar, out-of-envelope trajectories, to tease performance limitations from aircraft in flying exercises that operational pilots would never attempt. It was our welcome to the full hazard spectrum, which describes everything from routine flying to the most extreme aviation imaginable.

The school gave us no access to the work of previous graduates, so each pilot had to start from scratch on every plane and every exercise. There were no rights and wrongs with a lot of this work. One day a particular aircraft might perform efficiently under the given conditions, and a report would reflect that. On another, it could be the complete opposite and our report would focus on its shortcomings and all the tests we carried out to demonstrate those.

Early on in our course, one of my classmates made the career-ending mistake of 'borrowing' from the work of a previous graduate in an exercise report. When this was discovered, the CO hit the roof and – though now conspicuously beardless – I seemed to be in his sights once again.

Both classes, 148 and the senior group, 147, plus all the instructors, were ordered to assemble in the main conference room. Lieutenant Colonel Griffin burst in and read the riot act as the offending pilot, who was chopped from the course, sat in a chair in front of us like a sacrificial lamb.

'We will not tolerate plagiarism of any kind at this school,' roared Griffin. 'At this institution you do your *own work* at all times, and anyone caught doing otherwise will pay the price. It takes a lifetime to build credibility, and an instant to lose it. Be truth-based or nothing!'

He ranted and raged, even throwing a textbook across the stage at one point, and finally reached the end of another bravura performance.

'Do I make myself clear?' he shouted.

We all nodded in assent.

Then he spotted me . . .

'And you,' he said, 'yes, you,' he added, pointing at me. 'You can wipe that smile off your face.'

I looked around. But no one near me was smiling. I looked back and he still had me in his sights, nostrils flared . . .

'Are you speaking to me?' I replied, astonished that I had been picked out again.

'Yes, I am, Lieutenant Commander Gray. And if you think this is funny, you will be the next student marched out of here . . .'

I said nothing but glared back, feeling by turns humiliated and angry, as Griffin continued.

When he had finished, he pointed at me: 'I want to see you in my office immediately after this session is over,' he bellowed. And that was it.

Even the instructing staff seemed bemused that I had been chosen for this treatment. But, as ordered, I went and stood outside Griffin's office, and waited for 20 minutes like a naughty schoolboy for him to admit me.

'Lieutenant Commander Gray?' he said quietly as I walked in.

'Yes, sir?'

'Look, I needed someone to make an example of out there, and I knew you could take it,' he said, by way of explanation. 'You're seasoned and you know the deal.

'I find it helps to get the point across, in large groups, to have an individual to focus on – so apologies if that was a bit of a shock. It's nothing personal.'

'Right,' I said, trying not to sound as astonished as I was.

'And by the way, I would be grateful if you didn't share this conversation with anyone else, it might spoil the effect.'

'Uh-huh . . .'

And with that I was dismissed.

Later Griffin was replaced by a calmer and more sympathetic individual, who did not need to regularly demonstrate that he was 'all-powerful', in the form of Lieutenant Colonel Timothy Davis of the US Marine Corps, with whom I got on well.

All of us had made it to Pax River because we had been outstanding pilots or flight engineers of individual planes that we would have got to know inside out – understanding the control system, the electrical system, the fuel system, the design quirks, the flying characteristics and all the little nuances and work-arounds that we would need to operate them in all conditions. At test pilot school, the approach was quite different – they trained us to learn only what we needed to know, not the full A–Z of any plane.

Whereas we would normally read and study the full aircrew manual over a matter of weeks, with reinforcing lessons, and then reread it once a year and sign to show we had done it, at the school that was just our night-time entertainment. We learnt to read the whole manual at pace, but focus only on the important bits. We quickly realised that most aircraft were quite similar, with small variations that made them unique.

In ordinary, non-test pilot flying, we rely heavily on our flight reference cards and our training is based on memorising all our checks, so we rarely have to consult the cards. We get into the cockpit and work from left to right, checking this and that, checking conditions, turning things on and off, as your hands whip around like a concert pianist's.

As a test pilot, we use the cards in the cockpit and follow what they tell us. Pre-flight, we focus on an aircraft's limitations and emergency immediate actions, the only part that we would have memorised. These might include what to do in the case of an engine fire, a take-off or landing emergency, and anything that might force us to eject.

We started at Pax River on an aircraft that was not our staple diet. Fixed wing and big wing pilots had to fly a helicopter and the rotary guys had to go fixed wing. For a fixed wing pilot, the many changing variables of a helicopter could be unnerving, with your feet and hands interconnected as you attempted to manipulate it. It could not have been more different from what I was used to – it felt like I was still on the earth, still breathing oxygen and still moving, but everything else was different.

We would fly with a fellow student in the back and an instructor alongside who would have to take the controls every now and again, which was always humiliating and sometimes soul-destroying, even if understandable. Halfway through we would land and the students would swap places. The idea was to embarrass us in front of our mates, expose us and reinstate the student–teacher relationship.

It was a daunting challenge, but perhaps less so for me than for some of my fellow students, because during my original Harrier conversion I had practised hover techniques in Gazelle and Squirrel helicopters. At Pax River, I flew a Lakota Eurocopter, and although I managed it fairly proficiently, the underlying message from the pilot's point of view was clear: you know very little about aviation – you know a lot about your tiny specialist area, but now you have to be able to fly and test anything.

The flight line set-up at Pax River was unique. I would put on my 'flight gear' with my parachute harness, helmet and G-pants for the plane I was due to fly that day. I would have with me the relevant flight reference cards, which I would have studied the night before, and flight test cards that I would have prepared. I would head out through the door and make my way to the aircraft that had been assigned to me for that day. It might be the little single-prop Otter, with its tail sitting on the tarmac, the Soviet-era MiG 15, or it could be the F18 Super Hornet – the essence of a modern 'war-bird', towering above everything else in grey steel and with orange US Naval Test Pilot School markings.

Among the jets we spent most time in was the two-seat T38 Talon – a mainstay of the US Air Force, NASA and the school, which had been used to train thousands of military pilots and was the American version of our Hawk trainer. The big difference with the Hawk was that the twin-engined Talon, complete with afterburner, could go supersonic. With its super-thin delta wing, it was an aircraft I treated with the utmost respect because its stall margin was tiny.

A fast lander with very small flaps, even a momentary loss of speed – read concentration – on approach could see it fall out of the sky. We were all aware that the school had lost two pilots in a crash on landing 14 years before. The T38 looked like it would be fun to fly but I never saw it that way – it had upgraded and excellent avionics, but the aerodynamics of something that should be overpowered, whereas in reality it was quite the opposite.

It was in the T38 Talon that I did some of the most extreme flying on the course during a week-long stint at the US Air Force Test Pilot School at Edwards Air Force Base in California, where Chuck Yeager broke the speed of sound. NASA used the T38 to keep astronauts current on the Space Shuttle's unusual flight profile after re-entry, and we got the chance to practise this. With no engines, the Shuttle was basically a giant glider, and we copied its approach by climbing to 25,000ft over the top of Edwards and then flew a descending spiral in a super-fast glide, at 350 knots.

This was way over the speed the T38 was normally cleared

to do with the landing gear down, but we had special dispensation because it was a NASA training exercise. We would turn finals high in the profile and come down on a steep trajectory, then use special Shuttle approach markers on the lake bed below to judge when to flare in stages, in time to touch down right at the start of the runway. This would give the Shuttle time to slow down and stop with the aid of a chute.

While I flew most hours in the Talon, my favourite plane at Pax River was the F18. Twice the size of the T38, it carried twice the fuel with twin engines that were more than twice as powerful. With all the infrastructure of its weapons-carrying capability, its radar system and the cooling it required, it needed to be a far bigger airframe. You felt this when you walked out to it, because by the time you got close you couldn't see the cockpit. Every time I touched one and began my pre-flight walk-around, I would have to pinch myself – a lad from Stoke-on-Trent preparing for another sortie in one of the most capable fast jets ever put together, and the star of the show in the second *Top Gun* movie.

Flying the F18 was a weird experience for me – and inherent in it was one of the dangers of being a test pilot – because, like the Harrier AV8B, it was a Boeing aircraft. That meant there were quite a few switches and dials in the cockpit that looked familiar. But they were in different places to the Harrier, and sometimes did different things, so it was easy to revert to 'muscle memory' and make a mistake.

The big differences between the two planes were the afterburner and the performance of the F18 when pulling G. In the Harrier you would always pull to a certain point – say, 4 or 5G – and then ease the aircraft to 6 or 7, depending on what speed you were flying. The key was keeping the flow attached over the aircraft's wings, to stop it spinning and departing. With the F18, by contrast, the airframe was designed to tolerate what they called 'binary flying'.

This meant you could snap it straight to 7G without any graduation. The aircraft could cope with just about anything. In the pilot's seat it was an awesome sensation, but flying in the back – as I did on occasion – was awful. The sudden changes in pitch and angle of attack would induce serious nausea and you'd be thinking, 'Why can't you just ease it round gently for once?'

While the Harrier was subsonic, with a maximum speed of around 570–80 knots, the F18 could go all the way to Mach 1.8 – around 1,100 knots. The initial thrust sensation in a Harrier during take-off remained in a class of its own, snapping your head back in a violent motion as you slammed to full power. But once the F18 got going, it built steadily and then it kept on going until, after about 150 knots, it was off and away.

Like the T38, its twin engines meant you had two throttles. You started with one, then the other, and then they joined together. To go into afterburner, you pushed forward to a false gate and then pushed forward again. At the back of the plane, the nozzles on the engine exhausts, which had narrowed to increase thrust, dilated again and, with the extra fuel injection, you felt the plane lurch forward, pushing you back in your seat as the power came on. Then the nozzle indicators in the cockpit swung open and the numbers in the head-up display just kept going up.

You needed the afterburner to go supersonic, to propel

you through the Mach-drag induced by breaking the speed of sound. You might be at full power, going at 600 knots. Then the afterburner would force you through from .98 to Mach 1 – an extra 20 knots – and suddenly release you, to accelerate all the way up to Mach 1.8

If the F18 was high-octane flying, some of the other aircraft were anything but. At the opposite end of the performance spectrum, the Beaver and Otter were both hard work, with tail wheels that I found tricky, being used to jets with tricycle undercarriage arrangements. While modern jets would start at the push of a button, these two required you to prime the fuel system, pull chokes, press down on the throttle and all sorts of little tweaks to get them going in a big cloud of billowing black smoke. The secret was to catch the piston firings with the throttle, and not let them conk out once started.

But these vintage airframes were there for a reason – to remind us where it all began, and that we had to master everything and anything. They may have been old and slow, but they were also potentially dangerous to modern pilots because of their lack of augmentation, which gave them undesirable control characteristics you wouldn't find in today's aircraft.

The larger Otter was the easier of the two. The Beaver was a lot more twitchy on the ground, something that was underlined when one of my fellow students tapped the brakes at the wrong moment on landing, and dug the prop into the runway, writing off the historic rotary engine. He took a week off after this little 'mishap' – as the Americans would term all accidents, whether fatal or minor – and completed the course.

We flew the 'flying classroom' – a Lear jet where we would sit side by side with an instructor with an array of sticks and controls that could radically alter the flying characteristics of the plane at will. Another unusual option was the SAAB S340M – a small passenger aircraft fitted with an elongated nose into which radar for an F16 fighter had been installed. We would sit in the back, in a simulated cockpit, testing the radar, electronic pods and avionics, as might happen during the development phase, before a prototype with radar had been produced.

Every now and again, visiting aircraft would arrive at Pax River and we would fly those. Among them, in my time, was the North American B25 Mitchell – a Second World War-era bomber with a gun turret which afforded me a glorious view of the ocean, as we flew over Chesapeake Bay on a beautiful autumn afternoon. Another interesting addition was the HU16 Grumman Albatross flying boat. I landed one of those on the Colorado River near the Hoover Dam, where I went for a swim, before taking off again and returning it to an airfield outside Las Vegas.

Some weeks before the graduation dinner as the course reached its final, defining stages, I phoned the naval attaché at the British embassy in Washington, and we discussed my chances of passing. The F35 was very much in my thoughts and in my sight, given that the jet's Integrated Test Force was part based at Pax River, alongside operations at Edwards.

'You promised me this would be the path into the F35,' I told him. 'How can there not be a place for a Royal Navy test pilot, with the ship trials for the jets only a few years away?'

I told him I was standing talking to him on the phone outside the Test Pilot School, and I was looking at an F35 taking off next to the ski jump on the airfield. 'It's there, across the road, the F35 test unit . . . that's got to be the next step, hasn't it?' I said.

'OK, Nath,' he replied, 'I hear you. Leave it with me. The RAF is saying there's only one position, and they're not giving it up, but I'll speak to Whitehall.'

A week later he called back. A place had been secured for me on the test unit at Pax River – the first for a Fleet Air Arm pilot.

'But please keep up the good work,' he implored, 'and please make sure you graduate – failing to do so would be very embarrassing after we've taken this to secretary of state level.'

That upped the ante a bit . . .

The final part of the course was a dissertation. I had to spend two weeks planning a test programme to assess my chosen aircraft. That included presenting a safety case for the plane, all the hazards associated with it and how those could be mitigated on the spectrum. Then I flew my test week and afterwards began 10 days of intense work to prepare my report.

I had requested the F15 Strike Eagle, the US Air Force multirole fighter, for dissertation and, in a decision that was unprecedented for a foreign student, was granted my wish. If the F18 was a big beast, the F15 was even bigger. Much as I loved the F18, with the possible exception of the F35 the F15 was the most versatile fighter I ever flew – and the fastest, capable of hitting Mach 2, or 1,300 knots.

Despite being the size of a tennis court, it was a superbly manoeuvrable air-to-air combat fighter and equally capable in a ground attack role, with an expansive weapons suite.

However, there was one important aspect where the F18 won through. If you pushed it too far, the F15 could kill you, whereas the F18 was a carefree handler. If you put the F15 into a true vertical climb and then let it fall backwards out of the sky, with its vapour trial wreathing the cockpit on both sides, you might end up in big trouble as you tried to recover the aircraft. The F18, by contrast, would sort itself out without a second thought.

I flew out of Eglin Air Force base in Florida for my F15 tests. Thunderstorm activity heavily curtailed my time in the air, so that my five carefully planned sorties were cut to two intense outings lasting about four hours in total. My focus was on evaluating the jet in the strike fighter role, both air-to-air and ground attack. This involved flying dogfight manoeuvres against an imaginary opponent and then simulating attacks on ground targets, using oil rigs in the Gulf of Mexico.

Then it was back for the final push on the written work, as the aptly named 'divorce course' drew to a close. Indeed, it was mentally and physically draining not just for us students but for our families too – everybody was pushed to the limit by the course.

I had no idea how I'd done. I was convinced there were people who were better than me in each of the disciplines that we had mastered, and my goal was simply to make the grade as a test pilot. Like all my classmates, my aim had been to finish 'second', the place everyone except the top dog could lay claim to.

Before the gongs for best dissertation and top student were handed out at the dinner, each one of the 40 of us in

Class 148 was called up on stage to receive our graduation certificates from the CO, Lieutenant Colonel Davis. He was accompanied by Lieutenant Colonel Kevin 'Buzz' Erker, the CO of VX-23 – the US Navy Strike Fighter Test Unit, whose responsibilities included the F35. I made my way up as my name was read out, once again proudly sporting my British naval officer's beard that Lieutenant Colonel Griffin had so aggressively objected to.

The Americans love shiny stuff that you can put on display and, as I thrust my hand out to shake Erker's, I realised he was holding a commemorative coin. Lucy spotted the look of surprise on my face as I realised what was happening when my hand settled in his around the coin.

When I returned to my seat I examined what Erker had given me. On one side the words 'Strike Aircraft Test' and 'VX-23' were picked out in black, with gold naval wings. On the other, it had 'Salty Dogs' – the unit's callsign – and 'VX-23', with a jet depicted flying through a red symbol for a lightning strike.

At that moment it became real. I knew I was on my way to the plane I had been thinking about for the past three years. Whoever won the awards for best dissertation and best overall student, I already had something to celebrate. As the dessert course drew to a close, it was time to find out who'd won the dissertation. When she heard my name being announced, Lucy burst into tears, proud and overwhelmed at the end of what had been a tough 12 months for both of us. It was a blur for me, and when I sat back down with the award, I could barely believe what had happened.

Then came the big one – best overall student – so I

knew I could relax. I'd never thought I was the best in my class – far from it. There was a whole host of supremely talented individuals on my course whom I considered better than me in every one of the disciplines. I was taking in the atmosphere and enjoying a beer when, for the third time that night, my name was read out. I reckoned Lucy must have been the only person in the room who didn't think it was a mistake.

I'd become the first British pilot to graduate top of class at the US Naval Test Pilot School, and with best final project. I had no illusions about the garlands, though. Someone had to win and, somehow, that was me, despite the fact that I didn't think I was anywhere near the top of my game. But I hoped they would make my passage to F35 test pilot – the real prize – a lot more secure.

The senior hierarchy of the Senior Service were delighted to have the top graduate at Pax River among their ranks, and Vice Admiral Keith Blount, who was assistant chief of the Naval Staff and boss of the Fleet Air Arm, sought me out during a visit to Washington. He was kind enough to write beforehand of his delight that a Royal Navy pilot had taken a 'clean sweep' of all the prizes, and said he had shared news of my success with Captain Eric Winkle Brown, then in his mid-90s. He was the legendary Navy test pilot who flew 487 types of aircraft, more than anyone else in history.

Coming top also opened doors to a career at NASA, firstly as a research pilot and then, potentially, as an astronaut, which the recruiters at the US space agency were keen for me to pursue. But that would have required changing from British to American citizenship, which I was not prepared to contemplate. You can take the boy out of Stoke, but I'd always known you can't take Stoke out of the boy ...

And in any case, my sights were firmly set on the F35 and the role of test pilot of NATO's brand-new stealth fighter, something that had captured my imagination ever since I had first discussed the possibility with Sparky MacLeod back at Boscombe Down three years earlier.

20

Layers of security protected the Integrated Test Force at Pax River – the unit across the base from the Test Pilot School – and within those layers were more barriers and checks, barring the way into the hangar where the F35 Lightning IIs were kept.

Inside were the planes we called 'flight sciences' – current production representative aircraft, packed full of specialist flight instrumentation. In one caged corner, behind a black rubber curtain, was one of the most highly developed F35s in existence, a B-variant with all the top secret modifications and latest tweaks.

I had seen F35s taking off and landing during my year at that US Navy base in Maryland, and we had been given the chance to 'fly' the jet's simulator as part of our training, so I had an idea about what the Joint Strike Fighter was like.

But I had never been near the product of what has been described as 'the US Department of Defense's most expensive ever weapons programme', let alone touched one. And I don't mind admitting I was pinching myself as I came across this supersonic, 5th Gen, stealthy gladiator for the first time.

This was an aeroplane, a machine, a beast even, and it was unlike anything I had ever encountered. My first impression, close up, was of a huge, real-life Transformer, hunched and ready to pounce. You could imagine it flipping and crunching, and turning itself into something even scarier.

Up close, there was an intensity about the form, shape, smell and mood of the F35; it was a manmade instrument of aerial warfare that was so high-tech and out of this world, it seemed to have taken on its own personality.

A successor of and the intended replacement for the Harrier, F16, F18 and A10 Thunderbolt all rolled into one, the F35 is big and it's solid. But comparisons with 3rd or 4th Gen aircraft only underline the gulf in concept, design and execution between them.

When you walk around an F18 or a Harrier, you can see how it is put together, that it is an engine surrounded by metal and you can see the bolts and rivets. You know there is a radar in the nose and a computer or two somewhere in the fuselage, and that the wings are fuel tanks. You know that the sum total of its parts creates a highly capable jet fighter.

With the F35 all you see is form and texture. There are no visible pins, no hinges, no rivets, bolts, panels, exhausts or cooling vents. All of that stuff is designed and hidden within the structure. Instead, there is a transformative being – one solid mass of lethality. That's because this aeroplane is a system of systems, the ultimate attempt to integrate and fuse together all the desirable properties and functions of a state-of-the-art multirole fighter. These include its stealth and supersonic performance characteristics, its fused sensors, weapons armament and delivery systems, its short take-off and vertical landing capability, and its unrivalled ability to process information and data.

'Can I touch it?' I asked the maintainer who was showing me around.

'Yeah,' he replied, looking at me slightly strangely. 'You can touch it, alright.'

I had approached the aircraft from the rear, and the first thing I saw was the huge and cavernous exhaust where the incredible power of the F35 is expelled in a high-decibel roar. I looked in at the enormous engine before moving round and running my hand along the flap, on the trailing edge of the delta wing.

That was when I got the strange sensation of touching skin – not sheet metal, but skin. It was the F35's radar-absorbent stealth coating system, created out of a multilayer rubbery composite material, which is 'baked' into the air-frame, and it felt unlike anything else. And I could smell the plane too – similar to what you experience when climbing into a brand-new car for the first time. This $300 million test aircraft had only flown for a couple of hours and the tyres still had bobbly bits on them from the moulds, which had yet to be worn off through use.

Like the F15, the wing is high, and I walked underneath it as I came round to the big intakes on either side of the cockpit. My frame of reference here were the two semi-circular intakes on the Harrier, with their delicate fan blades lined up inside them. On the F35 there was an angular chasm, and then nothing; it was like one big aeronautical visual illusion.

All the aircraft I had ever flown required you to be in the cockpit and to switch it on to see into the plane's brain. Not so with the F35. I turned round to see the maintainers wheeling up a big trolley bristling with wires, antennas, computer screens and boxes of tricks, and with a massive umbilical cord, which they plugged into the side of the fuselage. Within a few seconds, the screens came to life, displaying a world of information about the heart and brain of the beast, while it sat there without making a sound.

It was time to look into the cockpit.

You need steps to climb aboard most fighters. The F35 had its own lightweight ladder incorporated into the fuselage, which emerged at the press of a button from an almost invisible panel. The last thing anyone wanted was for a rusty set of steps to come clattering into the side of the plane, given that even a small chip in its skin would compromise its invisibility to radar. Inside one of the steps was the button to release the canopy, which opened forward with a quiet buzzing sound.

Looking in from the top of the steps, the cockpit was black, completely dead. There seemed to be almost nothing to it: a stick, a throttle and a big blank screen. Again, this was quite different to any other plane I had flown, and I could immediately tell that this was a space that had been designed with the pilot in mind, giving him or her a super-simple 'human–machine interface', with excellent visibility and physical room.

As I eased into the seat, it all felt so clean and sanitised. I instinctively ran my fingers around the one familiar item, the yellow and black striped loop for the ejection seat, set in the centre between my knees. This activated a Martin-Baker 'zero-zero' that could save your life with the plane at a standstill on the ground. With this variant, the seat included an 'auto mode' which would automatically fire the pilot out in the event of an engine failure during a hover manoeuvre. It also incorporated a stabilising system, so that if a pilot ejected at an angle – something I knew a little about – it would correct the trajectory to ensure the seat went out vertically.

In order to access the plane's systems, the pilot had to input a classified security pin – a lengthy sequence of letters and numerals that you were required to learn by heart. Writing it down anywhere was a court martial offence. Like an old high street cashpoint, if you failed to get it right it would shut itself down. This was a highly embarrassing situation at the start of any test mission, typically supported by teams of engineers, NASA telemetry and an orbiting airborne tanker which, together, would cost the programme around $150,000 per hour.

'Are you happy for me to energise the aircraft?' asked the maintainer on the ground.

'Go for it,' I replied.

He pressed a button and the aircraft came alive, starting to hum, as the screens lit up in front of me. With other aircraft, you would hear each individual component starting up – a fan, a cooling system or an avionics package. Even though every cubic centimetre of the F35's fuselage was crammed with sensors and systems all feeding information to the pilot, it happened in one go. That's because every system was fully integrated and harmonised with everything else, and together this gives the F35 pilot unprecedented 'situational awareness' in any domain or dimension, whether it be air, land, sea, space or cyber.

The cockpit is built around a big, touch-screen computer display. This can be divided and subdivided in almost any way to show an infinite variety of information about the air-craft's systems, its flying characteristics, its engine operation, fuel state, radar, navigation, weapons systems and targeting information. The throttle is on the left-hand side, while the stick is on the right – not in the middle. This was something the F35 had in common with the F16 and it always used to throw me.

The F35 can be flown in many modes, and the throttle and stick do different things, depending on the mode. That said, the jet is also subject to what is called unified control law, so that the throttle always controls forward and aft acceleration, while the stick always governs vertical acceleration and roll, no matter whether you are travelling conventionally or in STOVL mode. The sophistication of the controls available on the throttle and stick amazed me when I first tried them out, with 12 buttons on the throttle and 10 on the stick, each with a different texture, shape, functional movement and tactile feedback.

The plane can be flown manually, automatically or by voice command, and is packed with automated features that blur the boundaries between pilot control and the machine taking over – a function not just of immense computer pro-cessing power but clever programming too. The F35 would take control, for instance, if a pilot were to fly straight towards the ground. This might happen either because of an over-committed target attack – known as 'target fixation' – or perhaps because the execution of high-G flying manoeuvres has left him or her unconscious, in 'G-lock'. At that point, at the last moment, the plane would make a correction by pulling away, saving the pilot and itself in the process.

The extent to which the F35 has assumed control in some areas is no better illustrated than in the way the B-variant converts from conventional flight into STOVL capability. On the left-hand side of the cockpit there is a small, innocuous-looking button, just above the landing gear lever, which is second only in its power to the red weapons-release button on the right-hand side of the stick. The STOVL button activates the transformation from one mode to the other. In the Sea Harrier this always presented the pilot with a unique challenge, demanding simultaneous and manual control of the nozzles and throttle in a fine balancing act in the hover. On the F35, you press the button and the plane does the rest.

It starts with the opening of the upper lift fan door, known as the 'toilet seat'. This is followed by a deafening noise immediately behind your head as the clutch engages into the main engine and the lift-fan spools up. Nozzles then open in the wings that provide stability and roll control. They are assisted by the main engine exhaust, tilted downwards at the back, using the three-bearing swivel nozzle. This remarkable piece of engineering and design moves the thrust left and right, and forwards and backwards, as required.

As a former Harrier pilot, it was difficult to get used to the idea of pressing a button and watching it all happen. Muscle memory in those situations is a powerful instinct and I almost needed to sit on my hands to stifle the urge to interfere.

I climbed out of the aircraft. It was time to return to earth. But it was not long after that first introduction that I made my maiden flight in an F35, which came after 11 90-minute sessions in the simulator. Unlike any other plane I had flown, there was no two-seater training version to go up in with an instructor first time round, so this was going to be a solo trip.

Apart from the simulator sessions, I had prepared by carrying out intensive practice to familiarise myself with the functions of the main computer screen in the cockpit. I had been provided with a powerful laptop, along with a throttle and a stick, that came together in a large hardened suitcase that we were allowed to take home with us. I spent hours and hours getting used to the commands and display options so that it became second nature, whether using touch-screen technology, buttons and knobs or by voice command.

My first flight was not from Pax River, where all the air-craft were committed to the test programme, but from the Marine Corps Air Station Beaufort in South Carolina. Known as 'Fighter Town East', this was home to four F18 fighter-attack squadrons and one US Marine Corps F35 training squadron. It was an eight-hour drive from Pax River, a journey that gave me plenty of time to prepare for what was coming, running through emergency actions and limita-tions . . . and my pincode.

That apart, I wasn't nervous about the procedural aspects of flying the plane, although time would tell if the simulator and real-world experience matched each other. My main concern was using my bespoke F35 prototype helmet for the first time.

The day of the flight – 15 November 2016 – dawned over-cast and all other flying from Beaufort was cancelled. But as a newly qualified test pilot, I felt confident about my ability to deal with flying in cloud on my first outing in the 'flying computer', even though I would not be F35 instrument-rated.

'It's just a bit of cloud, you're as experienced as me; let's get on with it,' said one of the two senior instructors detailed to supervise me.

Connected to me on the radio, the other instructor stood by the aeroplane on the flight line as I settled in, while his colleague was getting ready to fly alongside me in a second F35, in the role of chase.

It was pincode time and I managed it without difficulty as I closed the canopy. At that moment the cockpit became a safe, with me locked inside it – a top secret place in which the aircraft could display its bag of classified capabilities and lethal tools. No external electronics, including smart watches and mobile phones, were allowed in the cockpit, such was the extent of the secrecy surrounding the jet and the test programme. Knowing that would be the case, I used my old mechanical Breitling watch for all my F35 flights.

It was time to initiate the auxiliary power unit, or Integrated Power Package as we termed it. This is the plane's starting system, which is more powerful than most aircraft engines and delivers electrical power to the engine and the emergency systems. I could hear its roars and screams all too clearly, despite the noise-reduction system in my helmet.

Then all the electronics came on together, and I started to hear the chimes of the F35 command and control system for the first time, with a 'Bing!' to signify that one system was now working and a 'Bong!' for another. These carefully curated sounds were telling me that I was almost ready to fly one of the most advanced warplanes ever built.

Like your computer at home, the F35 hates an impatient pilot who doesn't wait for the systems to fully initiate and tries to push ahead with commands while it is still warming up. The trick is to sit quietly for a few minutes until the jet decides it is ready. Unlike older legacy aircraft, this flying machine was designed to have a short pre-flight checklist with minimal pilot input. Basically, it does it all for you. You simply watch all the relevant information come up on the display and make adjustments to suit your requirements.

The engine came to life at the press of a button, and built to a deafening crescendo. It was the simplest plane to start of any I had flown. Normally in a jet at this point you would be timing the moment to open the throttle, monitoring fuel flow, the rate of rpm and indicators like the exhaust temperature, but again, the F35 does all that for you. Once it reaches idling speed, the engine page on the screen goes green and the plane treats you to another reassuring 'Bong!', which means everything is fine and good to go.

Then came the moment of truth – time to turn on the Head Mounted Display (HMD). Whereas other jet fighters used a head-up display fixed on the glareshield, with a projection that you looked at, the F35 shows you the information by reflecting the projection onto your iris and pupil. It means that a version of the information it is displaying from the plane's multiple sensors is always in view wherever you look. The HMD requires the pilot to wear a highly sophisticated and expensive helmet, with photocromic visors at the front and a computer system built into the back of it. The whole thing is then plugged into the aircraft via a large data cord.

In the weeks leading up to the first flight, I had been for a two-day helmet fitting because, in order to work accurately, the projection onto your eye has to be pinpoint accurate. This requires the $300,000 helmet to fit precisely to your head, with everything measured by laser scan. The scan data is then sent to the UK, where a custom styrofoam cap is created to fit inside it.

Now I was about to find out whether the fitting, using the 'pupilometer', had been within the tiny tolerances that the HMD could cope with. It wasn't. I immediately realised that something had gone wrong with the alignment. There were two projections, one onto each iris, and after I toggled through them for a few minutes, I realised that the left eye was about alright, but the right eye was clearly not level with the horizon. When I tried to look through both, things weren't right at all.

'All set?' I heard the instructor in the chase F35 ask.

'Just having a few problems with my HMD,' I said.

This was a flight I was determined to complete, and having to cancel it now would be more than annoying, it would be expensive too. I knew that the optics on the helmet would have to be reset, and that would take at least a day, and it might be much longer before I got another chance to make my first flight in an F35.

'Have you tried turning it off and back on?' he was asking, as I continued fiddling and finally decided to turn the troublesome right eye-tilted projection off altogether.

That left me with only the left side, which I reckoned was two or three degrees out of kilter. But I considered the dangers and worked out how I could compensate for them. I went through the whole matrix of hazard risk analysis until I had moved it down the spectrum in my mind to a point where I was content, even if this was my maiden flight in the world's most advanced fighter aircraft.

'Are you happy?' the instructor inquired, using the time-honoured phrase that all pilots recognise, that can cover a multitude of small decisions about an aircraft and its systems, leading up to one big conclusion about your personal safety.

'Yes, I'm happy,' I replied. 'Ready to taxi . . .'

The moment the chocks were taken out, the F35 wanted to go. I released the brakes, heard another 'Bong!' and was careful not to ride them, which could lead to overheating and harm their performance in an emergency. As we taxied out to the runway, I was leading the instructor in the chase plane, again not something you would normally find yourself doing on your first flight in any legacy fighter.

This was going to be an afterburner launch, and we set up in staggered formation on the runway.

It was time to fly the F35 at last . . .

Given the extraordinary forces exerted on the pilot by the old Sea Harrier, you might expect its successor to be even more impactful in the cockpit during take-off. But not so.

As I slammed to full power, pushing the throttle forward and then forward again through a false gate to ignite the afterburner, I didn't feel I was being violently thrown back in the seat. Instead there was a firm, progressive push against my chest – not unlike the F18 – as we gathered speed.

While the C-variant, with its massive wings, just wants to go flying and lifts off on its own, this one, with its smaller delta wing, only does what you tell it to. And you have to tell it you want to go flying, by forcefully pulling the stick back to bring the nose up. Otherwise the plane will sit there, quite happily going faster than a Formula 1 car, straight off the end of the runway. So at 150–60 knots the nose came up, and things started to change rapidly.

It was almost like the F35 was talking back to me: 'Oh, I get it ... so you want to go flying, do you?'

It launched itself into the realm for which it had been designed and built by the boffins at Lockheed Martin, at a cost of hundreds of billions of dollars. Nothing was slowing it down. It was where it wanted to be, in a three-dimensional world influenced only by its own aerodynamics. And it wanted to shift, so much so that I had to quickly retract the undercarriage before I went past the speed – around 300 knots – where I might break it.

As it came up, I felt a gentle thud.

Then the plane kept on going, and going, and going ...

I came out of afterburner, as the jet accelerated under full 'dry' power, and at 10,000ft pulled the nose up to intercept 400 knots and continue the climb to 25,000ft. It was time to turn out over the Atlantic Ocean to start some exercises and handling practice.

My first impression, which was always important in any new plane, was that this was exactly like the simulator, and the more I flew it, the more that became apparent. This plane did precisely what it was designed to do at any speed, at any attitude of flight. We have talked about carefree handling in the context of the F18, and this too qualified under that rarefied category. In the F35 you could do almost anything knowing that, even if you over-reached yourself, the jet's automated safety systems would look after you.

This felt serene, almost effortless, and with the hugely effective active noise-reduction system in the cockpit there was very little sense of speed. It was too easy to miss an acceleration of 200 knots while doing something else. So I had to be watchful. It added up to a plane that was simple to fly – a vital quality for frontline pilots, giving them more time and capacity to focus on the demanding task of learning how to fight it. It may not be the most exciting fighter plane to scream around the sky in, because of its highly advanced control laws and aerodynamic efficiency, but it was no less effective for that.

In manoeuvres, the F35 felt like it had been more elegantly put together than the F18. It was still a binary-type flier – you could switch from one attitude of flight to another almost instantaneously – but those transitions felt like they had been blended or softened. It was as if it was saying, 'OK, you want to roll left? I'll ease you into it,' whereas the F18 flips from one side to the other, flinging you around in the cockpit.

This was an intuitive aircraft to fly, with fine response to small stick adjustments that seemed to interpret what I was intending even before I had thought them through. And each time, however demanding I was, it would do what I asked of it – there were no weird bobbles or meanders, but that didn't mean no feedback at all. In a tight turn, pulling high G, the aircraft would tell you the wings were working hard, and it was under stress, with the fuselage shaking like any other fast jet, but you knew it was never going to stall on you.

Much has been written about the F35's performance in air-to-air combat. My own view is that it would compete with anything in a dogfight, if it had to. But the reality is that this plane is unlikely ever to be in that situation because, before its opponent ever gets within visual range, it will have been shot down thanks to the F35's stealth characteristics, superb radar and weapons capability.

One aspect that was enormously impressive was the sheer grunt of the single engine and afterburner that allowed me to push through the sound barrier without a thought. It was more powerful than the F18. But it is easy to forget that the F18 has two engines, which means the single F35 engine – the Pratt & Whitney F135 – is more than twice as potent.

When you fly behind an F18 – when carrying out a mid-flight inspection after a weapons drop or during aerial refuelling – you hear the steady rumble of what sounds like a soft-tempered aircraft. When you do the same with an F35, you hear and feel a roar. You get behind it and the noise is like nothing you will ever hear in aviation, with that massive rear nozzle, which is capable of producing 43,000lb of thrust, pounding and contorting the air behind it, and it doesn't care who knows.

The trickiest part of my first flight was the landing because the pilot makes all the decisions and flight control inputs in that phase, not the plane, and I had to compensate for my dodgy HMD set-up. With murky low cloud over the airfield, I had to perform an instrument approach and lead my instructor in, off my starboard wing. I knew that the HMD was not going to correlate with the outside world, so I deliberately set myself up on a glidepath that looked, on my display, like I was going to end up in the field short of the runway. As I came in, I continually cross-checked, comparing what I was seeing on the HMD in my left eye with what I could see of the ground below me with my right.

My correction turned out to be spot-on as the wheels

touched down a fraction after the runway threshold. Then my focus was on the aero brake technique that the F35B demands in order to slow down sufficiently after touchdown. As with the F15 and T38 Talon, this involves landing on the rear wheels and holding the nose up, almost as if you're doing a wheelie down the runway. This creates added air resistance before you ease the nose down and apply the brakes. You have to be careful you don't overdo it, because you can easily scratch the plane's tail on the ground if you do.

The F35 had earned a controversial reputation in the US during its development phase, largely because of cost overruns. Undaunted, the US Defense Department, alongside Lockheed Martin, the UK and other partner nations, had set out to produce a multirole fighter that was best in class. And although there was still much work to do to improve and optimise the plane's myriad onboard systems, I would argue they had achieved that hands down.

The Joint Strike Fighter is a world-beater. It is a hugely capable aircraft that has proved easy to fly and has been successfully used in real-world operations. It is lethal to enemies but, importantly, is safe to friendlies, with only one pilot lost in over 500,000 hours of flying for the entire fleet by April 2022.

21

In the military, they used to say that if you were not the new guy every two or three years, then you were doing something wrong and your career was heading downhill.

My move across the air base from the US Naval Test Pilot School at Pax River to the Integrated Test Force (ITF) meant only a small adjustment in my journey to work, but it was back to square one in almost every other respect.

I had graduated as top student at the school, but I quickly discovered that it counted for nothing as I arrived at the test pilot office at the ITF for the first time in December 2015.

This was the heart of the F35 test flight operation on the shores of Chesapeake Bay that had started six years earlier. By April 2018 it had conducted more than 9,000 sorties, accumulating over 17,000 flying hours and executing more than 65,000 test points.

In that room were 10 of the best test pilots on the planet. They included a pilot who had tested and expanded the envelope of the F16, and who was a former president of the society of experimental test pilots – effectively the president of all the world's test pilots. There was a pilot with experience spanning back to the X35 – the F35 prototype – and one who had done some of the first flights in the Sea Harrier.

In addition to the Americans, I was alongside two Brits, Squadron Leader Andy Edgell of the RAF, and the hugely experienced former Fleet Air Arm and now BAE Systems test pilot Pete 'Wizzer' Wilson.

The fact that my desk wasn't in the test pilot office, but the corridor outside, demonstrated how far I was down the pecking order. I guessed that all new guys to the ITF went through this ritual and the idea was to bring you down to size. You might think you were top dog – I had just been promoted to commander – but even newcomers who had already flown the F35 were regarded as juniors. Not until you had flown your first *test* mission – until you had legally flown the world's most advanced multirole 5th Gen fighter outside the parameters that it was cleared to operate to – would you have made the grade.

The desk in the hallway also brought home to me that while I had learnt how to be a test pilot on the other side of the airfield, I had no idea what it took to actually *be* one, and what the day-to-day business of this remarkable operation involved. It would be 11 months before I made my first conversion flight onto an F35 and 13 months until my first developmental test flight.

To start with, I never went near an aeroplane. I spent several months reading into the various testing programmes, completing security checks and being instructed in and grilled about what we could and couldn't say, and what we could and couldn't do. I was slowly getting to grips with a top secret flight-testing operation that was regarded as the most comprehensive and rigorous in history. It was costing millions of dollars every week, and was under constant scrutiny by the US government, amid continuing concern about budgets and the performance of a jet that was attracting, at that time, what we all regarded as undue bad press. All in all, it meant the ITF had to be watertight in every way.

We all found it intensely frustrating to read ill-informed criticisms of a plane that was still in development in all three variants and was yet to reach its full potential. These were brickbats that we couldn't legally respond to, even though every one of us, pilots and flight test engineers alike, regarded the new fighter as a rock star.

That shared confidence was tangible and exciting. We felt we were helping to develop the right product and it's worth remembering that this was a discerning group – pilots who had flown F18s, F15s, F16s, F22s and A10s. You might hear people say, if they could pick and choose, they might prefer this attribute of the F16 or that from the F15, but no one doubted the F35 was a world-beater.

We knew that once the main work of the ITF was completed, this jet would go to the frontline in its fully augmented form, not just with US and British forces but with the programme's other partners around the world, and then people would see what it could do. That's when the world would start to understand what the F35 was all about.

In those first few weeks and months, I learnt more about test pilot culture, especially the idea that, as military pilots embedded in a civilian team, we were 'gate guardians'. My job would be to report on any capability or technical feature on the jet. I knew that if it got past me, it would go to the fleet, where my mates would take it to war. I also knew that if something was to go wrong with a component or system

I had said was satisfactory, I would be held to account for that decision for the rest of my life.

I reported to a variety of people, not least the admiral of the Fleet Air Arm and the chief of the Air Staff in the UK, plus a series of senior officers in the US overseeing the F35 programme. But, closer to home, my boss at the ITF, and indeed mentor, was the American Lockheed Martin chief test pilot for the F35, Dan Levin, who ran the test pilot office.

Quiet, pragmatic and forceful when he needed to be, he had flown F16s and A10s with the US Air Force. Among his core principles was the requirement that we should tell the truth at all times. If something wasn't good enough, we had to say so without fear of the consequences. Given that he was an employee of the corporation that designed and built the F35, this was a strong and potentially problematic position for him to take, but he never wavered. There was never any pressure from Dan to soften criticism or doctor conclusions, even if that meant the designers and engineers at Lockheed Martin had to go back to the drawing board.

The unit at Pax River was where the system development and demonstration phase of the testing programme was carried out. Operational testing was conducted at Edwards Air Force Base in southern California, the home of a slightly smaller cadre of test pilots. Our role was to assess air-worthiness and mission suitability – was the jet safe to operate with whatever modification was being introduced, or weapons system carried? Then the guys at Edwards would take that system and test it from end to end, to see whether or not it worked in anger.

I guess the big difference between test pilot school and

the ITF was the sheer scale of it. At the school you operated almost entirely on your own – I would receive a test brief; I would plan it, execute the flight required and write up my report. Now I was part of an enormous organisation. I was risking my life, often pushing this new aircraft to its limits, but I was only a tiny cog in a huge, $1.7 trillion machine, with hundreds of people overseeing, analysing, reporting and advising on my every move.

After the initial security vetting and introduction to the programme, my first task, several months in, was to head off to Naval Air Station Oceania at Virginia Beach, south of Pax River at the entrance to Chesapeake Bay. This was where I converted onto the F18. As the newcomer to the group, my role for the next few months would be to fly as chase plane pilot on F35 test missions, with a photographer in the rear seat, so everything could be monitored and recorded in real time, in the air. This often involved flying up close underneath the F35, to check on the condition, for example, of one of the weapons bays, or any other detail of the fuselage that might be exposed to extreme stress.

Although I had flown the F18 at test pilot school, it had always been with a qualified captain keeping an eye on me from the rear seat; now I had to learn it myself, and learn how to fly as a chase pilot. It would normally take six months to convert to the F18, but the ITF required me to complete the process in two weeks, with no instructor. It was a case of 'go read the book, and go flying'. I had to get reacquainted with the aircraft and log 10 hours in it, in short order, and then get back to Pax for my first chase missions.

In the build-up to my first F35 test mission in January

2017, I followed my maiden flight in the aircraft with two more familiarisation flights, accumulating around five hours altogether and plenty more in the simulator. Finally, the day had arrived when I would make my debut as a fully fledged ITF test pilot.

The eighteenth day of that month dawned clear and sunny over St. Mary's County on the Maryland coast, with no thunderstorms predicted. Everything looked set for what should have been a fairly routine 'weapons environment test'. I was in a confident mood; I was familiar with the airspace and with the radio calls at the Pax River base. But, as I was about to discover, things didn't always go to plan in the test pilot world.

Before I got anywhere near the jet that morning, I had to read and inwardly digest the test plan. This was an inch-thick brief, with all the 'mitigations' that had already been established on previous flights, to take the risk level of this task down the hazard spectrum. It had started in the 'high-risk' category, then made its way to merely 'dangerous', and finally to something that was regarded as 'acceptable'.

Prior to the flight, I had been to the simulator at Pax to conduct a full mission rehearsal with the whole test team present, including 30 or 40 engineers and scientists. For the first time I found myself sitting at the head of the table in the pre-flight briefings, helping to decide whether the mission should go ahead, and getting used to being at the helm of the process alongside the test director.

My task was to help establish the F35's capacity to deploy a laser-guided bomb. We needed to know whether it could carry the bomb, whether the aircraft was safe in all flight environments with the added weight – at different speeds and altitudes. Then we would focus on the bomb itself. Was it safe in its bay? Did it get too hot or too cold? Was it subject to excessive vibration in certain conditions that could lead to a catastrophic detonation?

We were in the process of monitoring all these elements on separate sorties, in planes bristling with sensors and cameras that were part of an extraordinary test and data-harvesting process. The scientists and engineers in the control room on the ground below us, at Pax and other locations, were capable of processing around 250,000 parameters from the jet, at a rate of 3 million samples per second. So nothing – not even the tiniest variations in performance, condition of the aircraft or the pilot – escaped their notice.

This phase involved loading a flight-tested and instrumented concrete dummy bomb and taking to the skies with the doors open on one of the weapons bays. We wanted to establish if that was safe in all scenarios and environments, accelerating in stages, up to the speed of sound. If the answer to all those questions was yes, we would see whether it disengaged properly from the aircraft, and fell away, and did not come back to hit the fuselage from underneath. Our goals were safe carriage and safe separation. Once we had achieved them, we'd be ready to hand over to Edwards, where they would test the weapon for real, dropping a live, laser-guided version on target from an F35 for the first time.

Dan would be keeping an eye on everything, flying chase in an F18, a reassuring presence on my first test mission.

Once I settled into the cockpit, I experienced, for the first time, the slightly weird and unnerving experience of being on an open hot mic to a test team, alongside my routine, press-to-transmit radio comms with the tower, and with Dan in the F18. Only test pilots fly with an orchestra-sized live audience listening in and monitoring everything you do. Most of them were based at Pax, but some were connecting in from remote locations like the Lockheed Martin aeronautics HQ at Fort Worth in Texas, or the Pentagon in Washington. To start with, hearing someone else on the line – in this case the test director, or 'Control', who had hundreds of other people feeding him information and data – took some getting used to.

I got the ball rolling rather awkwardly, as I prepared my F35B to start up.

'Er . . . hello?'

'Control,' came the instant and businesslike response. 'Radio check?'

'You're loud and clear,' I replied. 'How me?'

'Loud and clear.'

It was strange not having to press a button to activate a radio channel and instead having this open airway over which I had no control. A few minutes later I got my first lesson in how detailed the supervision of these flights could be.

'Test, Control . . .' The director in my ear again.

'Go ahead,' I replied.

'Can you stop tapping the pedals?'

'Sorry, what?'

'Can you please stop tapping the brake pedals?'

'Is that something I do?'

'According to the flight control engineers, they are seeing the pedals just slightly move every now and again.'

'Roger.'

I smiled inside my helmet and told my feet to behave themselves. I reckoned they'd probably been twitching throughout my career, in everything from a Chipmunk to an F16.

As I taxied out of the secure F35 compound, Dan was waiting for me on the taxiway while, in the deep-blue sky above us, a KC135 tanker aircraft was taking up position.

You could almost hear the dollars cascading into the 'spent' column that morning, as that vast team prepared to execute yet more test points, on the way to producing a battle-hardened aircraft with carefree handling. We wanted to hand on an aerial fighting platform that would give its pilots all the time they could ever need to utilise its formidable offensive capabilities to their maximum potential, and that came at a price in more ways than one.

The pressure to complete the system demonstration and development phase, so that the planes already in frontline service could operate with advanced capabilities, was immense. We all knew that any setback – or, God forbid, a major disaster – could set the programme back years or see it cancelled altogether, which made this process as high profile as the testing world could get.

Dan and I lined up together at the start of what should have been a three- or four-hour sortie. We both slammed to afterburner, with Dan following me as I broke free of the runway. From that moment on, he was always alongside, with perhaps a lateral separation of a quarter of a mile, keeping an eye on everything, while I concentrated on the myriad test tasks we had planned, and dealt with the constant stream of interactions with the test team. Situational awareness is a key attribute of any pilot, and Dan was there as an extra pair of eyes to ensure I didn't miss anything.

We climbed effortlessly to 20,000ft, where I carried out the 'roller-coaster' manoeuvre, enjoying getting to grips with this virtuoso flying machine again. We performed this routine exercise at the start of every test flight, to ensure that everything was working properly and the test instrumentation was correctly calibrated. It involved dipping down a few thousand feet, pushing forward to –1G, and then pulling up to 4G and levelling off. A full left roll followed, and then a full right one, to give the flight engineers the data they needed to approve the mission. Afterwards I flew for a few minutes with both weapons bay doors open, to make sure all was working as it should.

Again I got the thumbs up from the team on the ground. 'Everything is looking like it is functioning,' confirmed the test director. 'We are go for the test.'

Our first objective was to refuel, to top up the tanks after take-off, so that we could embark on an uninterrupted series of tests, without having to pause in the middle, when conditions might change. But it was as I was approaching the US Air Force Stratotanker, high over the glistening waters of the Atlantic, that this mission went abruptly off course before it had even begun.

In the blink of an eye, all my screens went blank and I started to hear warnings in the cockpit.

'Caution! Caution!'

I scanned the console, looking at the integrated warning display for the trigger.

'Caution! Caution!'

And there was the explanation: 'Gen 2.' My jet had experienced a failure in one of its two power generators.

The sudden audible and visual crisis came as a bit of a shock to the system. But I knew that this sort of thing was all part of the job, even if it was my first-ever test mission.

I eased away from the tanker and took stock. I knew I did not have a full generator failure because generator 1 was still operational. But I also knew that in this test aircraft some sub-systems would now be out of action, and it was going to be very unlikely that we could continue with the test. The issue for me was that I had no real idea about what was compromised and what was working normally.

Following my training protocols, I put the plane into what we called a 'minimise manoeuvre envelope', test aviation speak for a flight profile that placed the least stress possible on the fuselage, engine and all the control systems. This meant flying wings level, at 1G, and at less than 400 knots. The objective was to put myself in the safest place possible while I dealt with the problem or, at least, understood the nature of it.

'Control, are you still with me?'

'Yes, Test, we've got you – stand by . . .' The director's voice didn't betray even a hint of panic or, worse still, exaggerated calm. He was one very, very cool dude.

For the first time in my career I was experiencing what every modern-day test pilot knows only too well – that point in a mission when something has gone wrong and you don't know what it is, and the team on the ground don't tell you.

They're not necessarily keeping you in the dark deliberately, but running through their data to try to pinpoint the problem. It is a horrible feeling, not knowing, and sitting there for what seems like an age in silence, wondering if somebody down there has seen something they really don't like.

Later in my time at the ITF, I would sit with flight engineers during post-mission debriefs, and watch them pointing out various graphs and data streams they'd downloaded while I was in mid-air – charts that would have made the hair on the back of my neck stand up if I'd known about them at the time. 'Yeah, Nath, you should've seen this in real time – it was way off the charts . . .'

So you never knew.

'Control? Do we have an update?'

'Stand by.'

That dreaded command again. I waited another 30 seconds, during which it struck me that my wingman had said nothing since the failure.

'Chase? Are you with me?'

There was no reply from Dan.

'Chase?'

Again, nothing.

'Control, I've got a problem – are you able to call up Chase?'

'Yes, stand by.'

They called Dan and came back to me to tell me that one consequence of the generator outage was that my radio frequencies were now compromised, and I could no longer contact the F18.

'OK,' I said. 'Have you got any words of advice at this point?'

'We're returning to base. Stand by for gameplan.'

After another ice age – probably no more than 30 seconds, or perhaps a whole minute – I finally got my instructions. I was to descend gently towards the coast, and they would get back to me en route.

It's easy for your imagination to run wild. I began to think about the astronauts on Apollo 13 and how they must have felt when Houston did not give them the full picture of how perilous their situation was, as they prepared for re-entry in a stricken spacecraft. I could certainly understand what they must have been feeling all those years ago, as I eased the stick forward and put the jet on a westerly heading.

My training kicked in again as I prepared for any eventuality in the next 20 minutes. The engine was working fine and I still had full control of the aeroplane. What if my oxygen system goes? I could get myself down to less than 10,000ft and disconnect the hose and breathe normally. But what about my power-hungry landing gear? This was harder to think calmly about. Will it activate as normal? Is that what they're worried about? Are they looking at the connections and thinking, 'Uh-oh, he's never going to be able to land'?

I pointed the jet towards Washington, DC and Pax and continued my descent. As I did so, I waggled my wings to signal to Dan that I was in distress. He immediately flew up alongside, and I pointed to my ears and mouth and gave him a bouncing thumbs down, to convey that I could not talk to him, or hear him. In response he waggled his wings and moved ahead to take the lead, and I formatted on him. All of this was routine emergency procedure that we had pre-briefed, but it was also the product of 25 years of aviation experience, going back to my early days in the Tucano or the Hawk.

It was time to speak to the test director and try to find out what I was really dealing with.

'Control, Test. Have we got any landing implications here?'

'Negative,' came the response. There was a slight pause. Then: 'But you may have some flight control restrictions,' the director added. 'You may not have the full AOA [angle of attack] pitch control that you'd be used to, possibly affecting the flare and landing control.'

He was referring to the aero-flare technique on landing – effectively using the whole plane as its own air brake – that was a key component of slowing the F35 down. So now I knew I had to prepare for touching down heavy and faster than normal. I would have to let the speed wash off as much as possible before reaching the end of the runway, and then slam the brakes on with about 3,000ft of concrete still to go.

'Roger that.' I checked my seat straps and glanced at the ejection seat handle between my knees.

As we reached the coast, I informed the team that I was going to play with the frequencies to see if I could raise Dan, and eventually I found a channel that was clear and working.

'Chase, Test. Radio check.'

'Hey, you're loud and clear – you're back up!' I could tell by his more upbeat delivery that he was enjoying the excitement and the adrenaline rush of this emergency.

I explained to him that I only had comms with the test team and not with air traffic control, so I was unable to request landing clearance. It turned out that Dan had been thinking ahead. He'd already got us cleared on a direct track to Pax River, and he went through the protocol that would confirm that we both had clearance to land from the tower at the airfield.

We would both come in over the runway at 1,000ft, and if I saw him break right as normal, then I was cleared to land and should follow him. If he went round again, it meant we did not have clearance and I was to follow him on the circuit.

We came in, and I heard the roar as Dan broke to the right and saluted me as he pulled away. I counted 10 seconds and followed suit. Then I came back around and watched his tyres smoke black dust on touchdown, as I brought my F35 in. I started to flare as normal, but realised at that instant that, just as predicted, I no longer had the authority over the plane to execute it as I needed to.

Instead of coming up quite swiftly, as I pulled back on the stick, the nose took its time and, before I knew it, I was down on the back wheels moving quicker than I would have liked. I pushed forward on the stick to deflect the tail down, to give me a spoiler effect and dig the nose in, and sat there watching the runway disappearing beneath me, travelling as fast as a Formula 1 car. When I got to the point of no return, I had no choice but to ram the brakes on and bring the F35 to a juddering halt.

'Whoa! Got that done, even if a little faster than I expected,' I whispered to myself – a little message that the entire test team would have heard.

Dan was waiting for me at the end of the runway and I followed him back in, taking a few deep breaths as I cooled down.

'Just so you are aware, we are seeing the wheel brake

temperatures increase.' It was the test director warning me that the violent braking manoeuvre had overheated the landing gear.

'Roger.'

'Still increasing,' he added. 'We've called the fire trucks, just in case.' And sure enough, within a few seconds, two huge fire engines were rumbling across the airfield towards me.

Fans were brought out and attached to the wheels, to cool the gear down, before I was allowed back into the F35 compound. The danger in this situation was that the thermal valves on the wheels could blow, or the hubcap could explode, which could kill someone on the ground. It took about 10 minutes for the temperatures to start coming back to normal and I could bring the jet back in and release the emergency fire team.

At the debrief, I thanked Dan for supporting me on my first test mission, which had been more eventful than I had anticipated.

'That's what we are there for,' he said. 'You've been doing that for us in the F18 for the past five months, now it is our turn to do it for you.'

'Thanks, mate,' I said.

'And by the way, Nath,' he added, 'welcome to life as a test pilot. Never expect it to go to plan, because often it doesn't.'

I noticed that the test team's attitude to me changed at that point. Now I was being treated like a grown-up. I had been inducted by fire into the test world. I had operated outside the envelope. I had had an emergency and I'd dealt with it. Best of all, I hadn't crashed, and everyone was still alive.

*   *   *

I completed over 100 test missions on the B- and C-variants of the F35 over the next 18 months. There were probably as many again that were cancelled for technical reasons or adverse weather, which would leave me sitting on the flight line waiting for the thumbs up to go, plus around 50 chase missions in the F18.

I was involved in a variety of test projects, including serving as lead test pilot for the UK weapons-testing programme, and working on the STOVL capability that ensured the F35B was safe doing its vertical operations. I was also the lead test pilot for the cockpit – or 'pilot–vehicle interface' – when we tested everything from the general layout to the use of pee bags, checking whether a pilot could easily pee into one while flying. He could!

Almost all these flights went off without incident, but there were one or two that had to be aborted when things went wrong. The most dramatic came a few months after my first mission, when a vertical landing test went pear-shaped through no fault of the aircraft.

We had decamped for a month of special tests to Bogue Field in North Carolina, a relief landing ground next to my old Harrier base at Cherry Point. The team had built a series of four slightly sloping landing pads alongside the beach. They were made of strips of metal sheeting that the Marine Corps used on expeditionary operations.

We were using these 'mexipads' to test the aircraft's ability to land vertically on a sloping surface after a short take-off. That day I had very little fuel in my F35B, just enough to get airborne and come back down in STOVL mode. It meant I had few options if something went wrong – like a seagull getting sucked into the lift fan seconds after my plane had left the ground.

Not knowing the extent of any damage, I decided that the lowest-risk option was to remove the lift fan from the safety equation and convert to conventional flight, and use the small amount of fuel on board to get across to the main runway at Cherry Point. It was an instantaneous decision and it relied on me landing without delay.

As I approached the main runway at my old base, I got on to the tower.

'Lightning 62 is declaring an emergency, and I am going to be coming straight in to land,' I told them.

'OK,' came the reply. 'We've got four Harriers recovering and two aircraft currently approaching.'

This wasn't going to work for me. I needed to be on the ground, and quick. It was time to trigger a phrase that we had been told we could use only in dire emergencies.

'OK, Lightning 62 is a national asset,' I told them, making the effort to enunciate clearly. 'I need direct track for immediate landing.'

It had the desired effect because at that moment the waters miraculously parted and I was cleared to come in.

I never fully understood what 'national asset' meant, but it certainly made those guys sit up and pay attention. I imagined it was something to do with the sheer cost of the $300 million aircraft I was flying, its irreplaceability and its significance to the US defence effort. Not to mention the fact that no one wanted to see an F35, which was part of the ITF, crashing on approach to land because it had run out of fuel.

Those tests outside Cherry Point were useful not just to

demonstrate the F35's STOVL capability on sloping surfaces on land; they also gave us a useful read-across for what it would be like coming down on a carrier. And as the months went by at the ITF, myself and the other British pilots on the programme spent more and more of our time practising for the first flight trials of the F35 on the new Queen Elizabeth Class carrier.

We mocked up its landing deck on the ground at Pax River, mimicked the approach pattern we would fly and completed scores of practice landings, day and night, using highly augmented flight controls that were progressively downgraded. We also practised the ski-jump launch off a ramp that was built on the airfield and based on the launchpad that protruded from HMS *Queen Elizabeth*'s bow. The flight tests were accompanied by hundreds of similar exercises in the simulator at Pax River and at the new specialist F35B simulator that had been built by BAE Systems at Warton in Lancashire, to which we decamped for a week or two every three months.

I had known from the day I first arrived at the ITF that, in addition to my duties on the general test programme, the carrier trials would be my main objective. Before I joined, we already had our full allocation of two British test pilots on the team as a Tier 1 partner nation to the Americans – in the form of Pete Wilson and Andy Edgell. But the Admiralty, in talks with the Pentagon and with Lockheed Martin, had opened up my place alongside them, to ensure that a Fleet Air Arm pilot would be able to play a major part in the Queen Elizabeth Class trials, and execute the first landing.

As the summer months of 2018 ticked by, that date with

destiny drew ever closer, as the schedule for HMS *Queen Elizabeth*'s maiden transatlantic crossing was finalised. It would be off the eastern seaboard of the United States that we would finally bring Britain's new F35 fighters to the carrier for the first time and I knew that this would offer me arguably the pinnacle moment of my career.

22

I can trace the beginning of the build-up to my first F35 landing on HMS *Queen Elizabeth* right back to the time when I was instructing at Linton-on-Ouse seven years earlier, and Sparky MacLeod first spoke to me about being a test pilot.

From that moment, I knew the Royal Navy wanted its own test pilot in the hot seat for what promised to be a momentous event, marrying up the new carriers with their airborne fighting force.

The build-up for the UK and the Ministry of Defence went back many years before that, as the government reached the decision to retire the old Invincible Class carriers and replace them with the much bigger, and more capable, Queen Elizabeth Class. That massive procurement commitment to two identical ships was followed by the unexpected – and arguably ill-advised – decision to scrap the Harrier squadrons, which left Britain with no fast-jet capability from a carrier for eight long years.

It added up to turning this into a very high-profile mission, during which every setback would be pored over by the press, and when there was enormous pressure on everyone – on the ship and in the F35 test team – to get it right first time.

My role crystallised during my stint on the Integrated Test Force at Pax River as we approached embarkation. I was made officer-in-charge of the test team that would conduct the initial flight trials on the carrier, starting with the first landing and launch, and followed by three months of intensive additional trials.

My old travelling companion, imposter syndrome, made its presence felt yet again during the build-up to the first landing on the carrier on 25 September 2018. Throughout the training and endless planning, I never managed to shed the feeling that I would be summarily ejected from the programme by someone in authority after the penny had finally dropped.

'No, you're not doing this,' I would hear them whisper. 'In fact, why are you even here?' I was always waiting for that, right up until my last day.

And my last day in the Royal Navy was approaching fast. One of the long-term consequences of the accident that had killed Jak 16 years earlier was that I had promised myself I would no longer be flying fast jets by the time I was 43 – the age at which Jak had lost his life at RAF Wittering. I was determined it would not happen to me, and my way of avoiding it was to set my leaving date – effectively ending my career in the Fleet Air Arm – for February 2019, just ahead of my own forty-third birthday, in March that year.

That meant the first landing and launch, and the flight trials that followed, would be my last operational duties for the service, which made them all the more poignant. I had taken the decision to leave with the full support of Lucy and my family, but I had trouble holding my ground with the admirals, who were incredulous that their most experienced 5th Gen test pilot was telling them it was time to go.

In December 2017 – over a year before the first landing – I flew back to the UK to attend the official commissioning of HMS *Queen Elizabeth* at Portsmouth. It was during this visit that I sat down with the careers officers and revealed my plans. They assured me that the route to three-star admiral was a racing certainty, but adding more gold stripes on my cuffs had never been one of my priorities. I wanted to fly, not be tied to a desk. They offered all sorts of other induce-ments – a sabbatical among them, and even the chance to become an astronaut with the European Space Agency. But I resisted those too.

I knew I had lived a charmed life in the Navy, going from one glamour posting to the next. I had spent almost my entire time flying fast jets, from Sea Harriers to the GR9 in Afghanistan, and then a dazzling array of American airborne fighting machinery, ending up with the best of them all, the F35. During my few ground tours, I'd been lucky to have been welcomed by the most professional and deadly ground forces on the planet – the Commando Green Berets. And now, I was on course to hit the headlines as the first pilot to land on the new carrier, something that would be featured in a three-part BBC television documentary.

Along the way I had mostly avoided dull postings and desk jobs, and I knew the resentment among some within the Royal Navy was building. Despite what the admirals were telling me, I was odds-on for some dire jobs that would be designed to bring me back down to earth with a bump. I knew that two steps behind the people who would soon be shaking my hand to congratulate me on the first landing would be those intent on ensuring the next few years would be rather less exciting – it was going to be like stepping back into the lion's den.

So, the die was cast and I knew I had just over a year left to complete the task for which I had become a test pilot in the first place.

At the commissioning ceremony on the carrier, I got the first taste of how high profile this mission was going to be, after the initial formalities were completed. I was asked by a lady-in-waiting to the Queen to join an impromptu meet-and-greet line in the vast main hangar.

'She would like to meet you, Commander Gray,' said the lady-in-waiting.

On that day of pomp and ceremony, Her Majesty was in her element, and as she made her way towards me, I saw her eyes light up ... at the sight of two old boys ahead of me in the line. Soon the three of them were chatting away and the veterans were fishing out photos of the old HMS *Queen Elizabeth*, the great battleship that was scrapped in 1948, from their blazer pockets.

'It's so nice to talk to people of my own age group,' quipped the Queen, laughing with them as they reminisced about old times and how things had changed. Time was racing by, and the lady-in-waiting reappeared to give her boss the subtlest of nods. She had to move on and there was no time for her to chat to me. I wasn't remotely disappointed because it was plain to see how much she had enjoyed her encounter with the veterans. She looked at me, smiled, nodded and walked on.

However, the lady-in-waiting had not forgotten me and a few minutes later she came back.

'Commander Gray,' she said, 'Her Majesty is sorry she did not have a moment to speak to you, but she and the family, including Prince Philip' – who was not present that day – 'are looking forward to watching the first landing and hearing your news. So good luck. And,' she added with a broad smile, 'Her Majesty wants you to know: no pressure!'

I couldn't think of anything else to say but thank you as she headed back into the throng.

During that trip to the UK, I also carried out a couple of interesting visits which had been suggested by the team working on the BBC documentary about the first landings. The first was a trip to my old stomping ground at Yeovilton, where I went up in the rear seat of an open-cockpit Fairey Swordfish, the oldest aircraft in the Fleet Air Arm's history. A biplane torpedo bomber, it had played a critical role in the attack on the Italian fleet at Taranto in November 1940.

It was a balmy summer's day in Somerset and it was a great way to reconnect with the past and remind myself how far we had come – to the point where we were about to bring our newest carrier together with the most advanced multirole fighter jet ever built.

Making that connection even more real was the next stage of my journey, when I drove to the Cotswolds to meet the family of Edwin Dunning, the first naval aviator in the world to land an aircraft on a moving ship. It was as a result of what

Dunning did that the notion of flying planes at sea was born and he was the truest of test pilots. I met his nephew and his great-niece, and they showed me the letter from the Admiralty he received in appreciation of his feat on 2 August 1917, when he landed a Sopwith Pup biplane on HMS *Furious* at Scapa Flow for the first time.

What was interesting was that Dunning already had the sense that he was the 'gate guardian' for those who would follow him, the same philosophy we operated by at the ITF. After he had completed the first flight, he was determined to follow it up with more, to prove the concept he was pioneering. Just five days later he was killed when, on his third landing of the day, an updraught caught his plane, throwing it overboard. Dunning was knocked unconscious and drowned in his cockpit.

The family had dug out the letters from his commanding officer agreeing to his request to carry out further landings, and the one that said how sorry they were for his loss. They also showed me the hip flask that he was carrying on that fateful day off Orkney, which was scuffed and dented in the crash.

Those experiences only underlined how daunting our own mission was. It felt like a tidal wave was coming in to swamp us and we simply had to stick to our principles and prepare as thoroughly as we could. As I flew over the Atlantic on my way back to Pax River, I thought about the Queen watching on from afar. And she wouldn't be the only one. I'd also met Gavin Williamson, the then defence secretary, who said he would be there too, as he shook my hand and wished me luck, not to mention past and present admirals of the fleet and other senior officers.

So, as Her Majesty had so succinctly put it: no pressure . . .

In the months leading up to the landing, there was a pervasive feeling that it might not happen. That something would get in the way to delay it, or even stop it for good. Would we be ready? Would there be a setback in our own F35B testing programme? Would the carrier be ready? Would she be fit to make her first Atlantic crossing on time? And would all the elements come together in what would be a first in so many respects?

This was going to be the first time an F35 had landed on the carrier. It was the first time the specially commissioned deck would have been subject to the extreme heat and hugely destructive force of the F35's engine, which produced 40,000lb of thrust and could melt concrete. It would be the first time an F35 would be refuelled on board, the first time the deck marshals would have worked with the state-of-the-art jet on a pitching deck, and the first time the ITF test team would have operated from a Royal Navy carrier. In each of those categories, any number of things could go wrong and call a halt to the whole process before it had even begun.

My own biggest worry was not so much the aircraft, over which I had control and increasing confidence, but the ship. And not just the deck of the ship. What about the question of what would happen the first time we tried to hover alongside, and then slowly move across the gangway that runs down the side of the carrier, below the edge of the deck? That was full of kit that could be picked up, torn apart or thrown overboard.

We were not the only ones doing our homework. The ship's company was also intently focused on completing this mission successfully. They were planning – as they must – for every eventuality, including a crash landing, a fire on the deck or a plane going over the side. The deck marshals were going through intensive training to prepare for the landing and subsequent manoeuvres on the flight deck.

Twenty of them, accompanied by Jim Blackmore, the commander air who would oversee the landings from the FlyCo tower – the rear of the two superstructures on the carrier – flew to the States to spend a week with us, as they familiarised themselves with the jet.

On day one, as they stood on the flight line at Pax River, I started the jet in front of them and taxied round so they could appreciate what was involved, how noisy it was and how dangerous the rear exhaust could be. They needed to understand the look and feel of a stealth jet that would be the Royal Navy's first fixed wing aircraft on a ship for nearly a decade. For most of those young men and women, this was brand-new territory.

Finally, it was time for HMS *Queen Elizabeth* to set sail from Portsmouth and make her way across the pond, a voyage not without its moments of drama, with new equipment playing up and one engine going offline. After a short stop at Mayport in Florida, she steamed up the coast to the huge US naval port and dockyard at Norfolk in Virginia, just south of Pax River, at the entrance to Chesapeake Bay.

I took the opportunity to visit the ship at that point as

all our gear – test equipment, spare F35 engines, tools and ammunition for the jets – was being loaded on board, alongside the arrival of more than 100 members of the ITF, who would be spending the next three months on board.

The first thing that struck me was the sheer scale and size of this gleaming new seagoing military airport. She was slightly smaller than the rusting US Nimitz Class carriers moored elsewhere in the harbour, but she was still big and you got the sense that this was a significant statement on our part. We were back in the game, no longer a 'toy Navy' that critics had enjoyed making fun of, but one with what would soon be two world-class carriers, and with a deadly strike force of 5th Gen fighters on their decks.

At the commissioning ceremony, the flight deck had been cluttered with tents and marquees, so it was difficult to appreciate its size and scale. Now it was clear and it was huge, a vast expanse that stretched for more than 900ft from bow to stern, and 230ft from one side to the other. My only frame of reference in Royal Navy terms was the old Invincible Class and there was no comparison. It always felt on those carriers like you were landing on a very thin strip – which it was, especially with helicopters parked along the deck. This was like two or three Invincibles rolled into one. The landing spots would be the same size, but the real estate around them – dominated by the two towers – was massive.

An unusual feature of this embarked test programme was that it didn't start, like almost all other military aviation projects, with a take-off. It was the other way round as far as the ship and her crew were concerned. We would start by landing, and then attempt a launch. That meant I needed to have all my gear on board in advance. The other purpose of my visit was to find my way below decks to the cabin that would be my home for the next three months.

Over the years I had shared shipborne accommodation with 15 other men, or four, or two, but now I found myself on the head of departments' deck in a little quarter of my own at the aft end of the ship. This was luxury, and on that corridor we even had a steward.

I was opposite the ship's padre, who was busy with the pastoral care of the 1,500 souls on board, while on the other side of the bulkhead was an engine storage compartment. This was used most days as a practice area by the bagpiper with the Royal Marines Band.

With my kit stowed and meetings with the key members of the flight team completed, it was time to head back to Pax River to wait out the final couple of days before we flew the mission. Lucy had already returned to the UK, in anticipation of my departure from the Navy in the new year, so I was living in a cheap hotel outside the gates of the base.

It was hard to relax as the hours ticked slowly by. Most of my test team were on the ship, and we had already pre-briefed the flight before they left, so there was nothing to do but wait . . .

Actually, there was one thing. I redrafted my will.

23

It was one of those hazy days when the sky met the sea in one blurry mass of blue and white, so that from 15,000ft it was hard to see where one ended and the other began.

From that altitude, HMS *Queen Elizabeth*, Britain's newest £3 billion aircraft carrier, looked like a black dot. But as we got closer, I started to make out the distinctive twin superstructures, and then her Type 23 frigate escort, HMS *Monmouth*, steaming along on her port side.

The 65,000-tonne Royal Navy flagship was sailing about 10 miles off the American coast – close enough for us to get back to land if something went catastrophically wrong.

I knew the sense of expectation was building down there, along with the adrenaline and the nerves. Even as we took off that morning, the flight deck crew on the carrier were finishing off their latest 'FOD-walk', a line of sailors checking every inch of the deck to ensure there was nothing that could damage our aircraft.

The ship's company had been working towards this for almost as long as I had, and today they were proudly flying flag Foxtrot – a white square with a red diamond on it signifying shipborne fixed wing aircraft operations – for the first time on a British warship in nearly a decade.

I looked down and imagined coming in to land. I knew we couldn't have prepared more thoroughly for this most high profile of test points, and I was confident we could pull it off. The Americans had achieved it on their carriers several years earlier, so we weren't reinventing the wheel, but these were *our* pilots and this was *our* carrier and the variables were by no means the same.

We had launched 15 minutes earlier, at about 9am. That was later than planned because we were delayed by fog at Pax River, and then at the ship itself. Four aircraft had set out. First two F18s – one a tanker jet ready to orbit the carrier in case we needed to refuel; the other a chase plane with a photographer in the back seat, as was normal practice for all ITF test missions. Then it was the turn of the two F35s – with myself in a fully specced-up F35B test aircraft, and Andy Edgell in a more standard test version of the Lightning II.

The sea was calm, the breeze a gentle whisper that was perfect for our first landings, and everything was in order on all four aircraft. It was time to begin the choreographed plan that we had rehearsed so many times. The first move was for me to split from Andy and leave him sitting high with the tanker.

I broke away and, with the F18 chase aircraft on my wing, eased down to 1,000ft and flew my first pattern over the ship. At that point I was handing over from air traffic control on land to the control tower on the ship. But, not for the first time in my F35 career, I was to discover that gremlins had got into the all-important communications set-up that we relied on – and on this mission more than any other.

While I could hear the team in the FlyCo tower on HMS

Queen Elizabeth, led by Jim Blackmore, and they could hear me, I had not realised that my test team were struggling to pick me up on the hot mic. This was the critical channel which the test director used to update me on all the aircraft's technical data, and to clear each successive step in the flight. It was also the channel that I used to let them know what I was doing in the cockpit.

The problem was getting worse as I got closer to the aircraft carrier. They could hear me only intermittently – and it was not long before the test team realised there was something on board that was causing interference with their antennas and aerials, which had been set up especially for these trials.

The carrier is a highly secretive environment, sealed to all outside communications, and we were aware that marrying up our team with it in comms terms might be problematic. But a flyover of the ship by one of our F35s, while she was berthed at Norfolk a few days earlier, had convinced us that everything would be OK.

Now we knew that it wasn't.

I had dropped down to 600ft and had begun talking to the test team using the conventional push-button radio as I completed my first circuit. It meant I had to use a separate channel for the FlyCo tower, another one for the team and still one more for my chase aircraft. I had my hands full on a day when we wanted it to go as smoothly as possible. But that was the whole point, I reminded myself. Expect the unexpected and find a way round it.

The way round it was to be methodical, and work through each radio call. But I kept tripping myself up, saying out loud, as if on hot mic, what I wanted to do next, and then realising I would have to repeat myself with the radio switch depressed.

Now well into my second circuit, I checked with the test team if they were happy for me to lower the landing gear, and they replied in the affirmative – but did not also approve conversion to STOVL configuration. I took this as a sign that there was now uncertainty about whether this historic landing, or 'recovery' as we termed it, should go ahead. Perhaps we were going to have to retreat back to Pax with our tails between our legs.

I watched on my screen as the three green lights showed up to indicate the gear was down correctly, one for each wheel. The plane was working perfectly – it was the communications that were on the blink.

Then I asked for a 'go' to convert, and this time it was approved. I pressed the magic button and all the noises peculiar to this modern-day 'jump jet' started happening, as the F35 did its Transformer thing – wobbling and clunking, as various vents and the lift fan door opened, and the fan started spooling up to its high-pitch mechanical whir.

'Control,' I said, remembering the press-to-transmit button, 'conversion is complete.'

'A-firm,' came the reply. 'Showing good conversion. Stand by.'

I was on my third circuit – one more than we had planned – and beginning to wonder whether fuel might become an issue. We only ever had enough in the tank for a couple of circuits and then the landing, plus what we would need either to get up to the tanker in an emergency, or to fly back to Pax River for a recovery on land.

Fuel levels notwithstanding, we had always planned a 100ft fly-through over the deck prior to climbing back up to 600ft for the final approach. This was to make sure there was nothing unusual going on with the jet that might be spotted from the tower – although I would have hoped the F18 chase pilot would have spotted anything first. We could also check whether there were any wind vortices flowing around the landing area that hadn't been modelled by the simulator and might throw the F35 off course.

'Lightning 65 setting up for fly-through,' I informed FlyCo and was given approval.

'OK, Control, this will be a 100ft fly-through,' I added, 'and, if you're happy, a fairly rapid short circuit to landing for fuel.'

'Copied, Test. We are go for 100ft fly-through,' came the reply.

Wow – I was clear to do this. We were going to go ahead despite the comms issue. I could feel my heart start to beat a tad faster.

This time – travelling at about 100 knots – I got a full view of the deck below me and to my right. It was reassuringly massive and I could see about 100 people standing behind a cordon at the front of the FlyCo tower, among them invited VIPs and the media with their TV cameras ready to record this moment in Royal Navy history. Luckily they had no idea what had been going on in the cockpit during those past few minutes, but I knew I was almost at the point of no return.

The fly-through was as benign as I could have wanted, so I peeled off to the left-hand side of the ship and came back around, outside HMS *Monmouth*. It struck me then that this was going to be one of the last times the imposter 'devil' could play his tricks on me, as I looked across at the F18 and spotted the photographer. 'Holy shit, this is it,' I muttered to myself, knowing that no one else could hear me.

I cleared in for landing with the tower and reduced the speed to 150 knots as I started to come down from 600ft.

'Speed is decreasing, controls are nominal,' I told the test team.

'Roger that. Nominal,' the director replied.

On the deck below me, they were watching the dark, stealthy silhouette of a Lightning II coming in, with all its doors and flaps deployed, the white lift fan door glinting in the sunshine, its gear down, the aircraft banking slightly from one side to the other as I lined up, and looking good for its first-ever landing on a Royal Navy ship.

I was down to 120 knots as I slowly came closer to the carrier. Now it was all about judging my speed, as I came out of normal flight control and hit the deceleration button. My goal was to come alongside the ship and stop while still over the water. Then I would move across to 3-Spot, my target in the middle of the vast deck, one of five designated F35 touchdown points, and bring the jet down from there for a vertical landing.

With the decel button activated, it was now the plane's own control system that was governing my airspeed, as it followed the parameters I had keyed in to match the speed of the ship. At this point the grey bulk of the carrier was growing bigger and bigger and I was starting to see the ocean and the waves. I sensed the faintest outline of a rainbow as the sunlight filtered through the spray being kicked up by the thrust from the engine.

The ship was like a football stadium, as I took the F35 out of auto deceleration, levelled the descent and speed-trimmed it in the hover for position. In the simulator, we had worked on lining up across from the top of the FlyCo tower for height reference, and using a lateral line that ran across the deck through 3-Spot for position reference. We called it the 'bum-line' because, if I was sitting on top of it, then I was in exactly in the right position to start moving across.

Throughout this process, I had been speaking to my test team, updating them on every change in the flight profile, confirming that my F35B was 'nominal' at all times. The seconds ticked by. I was about one wingspan left of the carrier's port side, and I got on the radio again to tell them I was moving across.

'Copied – go for the cross,' the director told me.

Here we go ...

I moved the stick to the right and that rolled the plane a bit as she started moving over the gangway and over the edge of the deck for the first time. Then, as I came up to the white centreline that runs down the middle of the flight deck, I corrected the movement, to stop the jet right on top of 3-Spot.

At that point, the noise was unbelievable, and I was taken by surprise when it ramped up, as the altitude went from 100ft over the water to around 30ft over the deck. It was more than noise – it was the air-shaking feel of massive sound waves as the F35 hovered, seconds from touchdown, with the FlyCo superstructure helping to bounce it all around and augment it.

I was lined up perfectly, both laterally and fore and aft. I glanced inside the control tower and I could see that it was full of high-ranking officers, many of whom had been helicoptered in that morning. Just about every man and his dog had turned out for this one, including some American officers who were on the management team of the F35 programme.

It was time to get this plane on the deck.

'Control,' I said, 'everything looks nominal, temps are good, thrust is good, fuel is good. In position and ready for VL. Go VL?'

'A-firm. Go VL,' came the confident reply.

It is worth recording that even at this point we had planned for failure. If something had started to go wrong – for example, if the deck had begun to disintegrate – I had an emergency routine mapped out. I would have moved back across the side-deck and over the water, immediately converted to get back on the wing, raised the gear and accelerated to full speed. All this would have happened without a word on the radio.

Depending on my fuel state and the condition of the aircraft, I would then have either rendezvoused with the F18 tanker or headed back to Pax River to attempt a conventional landing. In the event of a major aircraft failure that required me to leave the cockpit in a hurry around the carrier, the ship had deployed a rescue helicopter with divers ready to assist if I found myself in the water.

I pushed the stick forward and hit the nose wheel steering button that committed me to the rate of descent selected. The jet started to come down as I laterally checked the stick to maintain the centreline, and speed-trimmed it fore and aft to ensure we stayed on the bum-line. As soon as the wheels hit the deck, the undercarriage suspension absorbed the impact and the aircraft sensed that it had landed. The engine wound down, the nozzles reset themselves, and I slammed on the brakes.

I sucked in a big, deep breath, and thrust my arms aloft in celebration. 'Yes!' I shouted at the top of my voice.

Blackmore joined in on the airwaves. 'Unbelievable!' he exclaimed, both arms raised, from his seat in the tower. 'That was a great landing.'

I couldn't see them, but in HMS *Queen Elizabeth*'s huge hangar, where I had come so close to meeting the Queen nearly a year earlier, almost the entire ship's company were applauding as they watched my F35 come down on live feeds from the flight deck.

This was the moment when two of the most expensive projects the UK military had ever undertaken finally came together, and with it our credibility as a global player in the defence sphere was hugely enhanced.

For me, the main feeling was relief – relief that everyone around me was safe, that I was safe, and that we had achieved what we had set out to do, many months – even years – earlier. But those feelings were already being caveated by the knowledge that I would soon have to move on to the next part of the day's test plan – launching up the ski jump and coming in and landing all over again.

In the tower, the mood was euphoric as the various bigwigs called their bosses to let them know the Royal Navy had finally connected its flagship with its new generation of supersonic jet fighters. Among those receiving calls were the prime minister, Theresa May, and the secretary of state for defence, Gavin Williamson.

I heard later that Ben Key, the Royal Navy Fleet Commander, who was also on hand that day, got on the phone to Keith Blount, Rear Admiral of the Fleet Air Arm, who was busy attending meetings in London.

'I'm delighted to tell you that Nathan's just landed on board, and it's all gone well,' he said.

'Thank fuck for that!' replied Blount.

For the first time, the flight deck operations teams marshalled an F35 around the carrier, as I was directed to my holding spot below the Captain's bridge in the forward of the two towers. There I shut down and began what turned out to be a long wait for the next stage in our flight test plan. All around me the maintainers, plus members of my ITF ground crew, went to work on the aircraft, chaining it down and refuelling it for the first time on the carrier. Everything went off without a hitch.

Above us, the second F35 was preparing to follow me in.

I called Edgell on the radio.

'The approach was nominal, no unexpected vortices and the deck seems to have held up,' I told Andy. 'Fairly easy all round. Good luck, mate . . . and enjoy it.'

I couldn't watch him come in because all I could see from my cockpit, even with the canopy open, was the nose of my jet and the front end of the carrier. But he made a perfect landing 15 minutes after me, and was then moved to his own holding spot behind me.

The first part of our big day had gone more or less to plan. We had overcome the hitch with our communications and had successfully got the first two F35s on the deck of HMS *Queen Elizabeth* in one piece.

24

The plan that had been drawn up, long before we set off for HMS *Queen Elizabeth*, was for Andy Edgell to lead the way with the first launch, using the ski jump at the front of the carrier.

This was a manoeuvre that the Americans hadn't tried at sea because their carriers didn't have ramps, and it was going to be a unique and pioneering event.

We were keen that all the flying 'firsts' were shared out among the test pilot team. Pete 'Wizzer' Wilson, not me, subsequently executed the first shipborne rolling vertical landing on HMS *Queen Elizabeth*, and our sole US test pilot, Marine Major Michael 'Latch' Lippert, would be the first to fly from the carrier with weapons and release them downwind.

But on a day when we had grappled with interference that had interrupted communications between the jets and the test team on board the carrier, we discovered a different problem with the navigation system the ship was using and its compatibility with the jets.

Once we were on deck and had safely shut down, we plugged the ship's positioning system into the aircraft, so the planes would be able to work out exactly where they were and why they were moving forward, as well as rocking from side to side.

But despite our careful preparations, and the painstaking work by computer scientists on the software to ensure the two systems would be compatible, we discovered that the jets would not accept the ship's feed. It lacked the fine tolerances that the F35s demanded. The upshot was that I was sitting there without a horizon on my display, without speed information, and without all the other parameters that are location and motion dependent.

We tried shutting everything down and starting again several times, but to no avail. Eventually we decided to rely on the jet's own GPS navigational system to work it all out itself without any external help. I sat watching the screen until, after a few minutes, I heard the F35's always reassuring 'Bong!' in my ear to let me know it had locked on to the satellites orbiting above us and resolved its position and motion.

I now had everything I needed, and my team confirmed that the ground speed figure I was reading matched that of the ship. It was to take most of the next three months of flight trials to troubleshoot this issue before the ship's feed was routinely accepted by the jets on deck.

We were good to go. But sadly for Andy and his own test team on board the carrier, these issues did not sort themselves out, so I was asked to do the first launch alone.

I said nothing to start with, as I digested this news.

'Do we have to?' I asked the director.

'That's affirmative, Nath,' came the reply, and I could tell by the downcast cadence in his voice they were as disappointed for the other test team as I was.

'We have to – we can go for launch,' he added.

'Roger that,' I said, accepting that we had no choice but to take the lead.

'Ready to break down,' I declared a few seconds later, referring to the chains holding my jet to the deck, which had to be released and removed.

I had been sitting with my canopy raised, responding to the shouts of congratulation from the deck team, with big smiles and repeated thumbs-up gestures after the landing. Now I had to put my game face back on and focus on the first ever F35 launch up a ramp at sea.

'Ready to taxi,' I said.

And then I was moving again and being guided to the launch spot, which was in the middle of the flight deck, about 350ft from the end of the ramp. I noticed how much heavier the F35 felt on its wheels as we trundled around the deck compared to the GR7, the last plane I had used on a ramp, on HMS *Illustrious*.

We had practised the ski-jump launch over and over again both at Pax River and at Warton in the simulator. But we knew the real-world experience at sea could be different, once wind conditions and the movement of the ship were factored into the equation.

This was not the same as lining up in front of the test ramp at Pax, surrounded by grass and concrete. From my cockpit, this ramp looked like a wall. Topped with a precipice over an abyss.

I focused my thoughts on my main area of concern – ensuring that, as we accelerated and then hit the incline, the plane remained on the centreline. A sudden gust of wind, or a lurch to one side by the ship, would require an instant correction as the jet gathered speed. This is something a pilot need have no concerns about when using a catapult launch from a carrier, because it is largely automated and, being attached to the catapult by the launch bar, meant most external influences are irrelevant.

The other issue was the effect the launch would have on the landing gear. We knew the gear would be compressed when the jet hit the climb, and would be released again once the plane cleared the end of the ship. We also knew the moment of impact at the base of the ramp could damage the nose wheel if the compression was too great, which, in turn, was a function of the speed the aircraft hit the ramp at, and fuel weight, and so on. It was those fine margins that governed how far back my take-off run could begin, and we were feeling our way at this point, setting up at what was effectively our best guess and then seeing how the gear performed.

Going up the ski jump was a manoeuvre with few escape options, bar ejecting if something went wrong. Once I was committed, there was no going back, and in this respect it was more dangerous than coming in for a vertical landing.

We had practised for an ejection at Pax, so it was definitely on my mind as I came to a halt at the launch spot. As I always did at the start of any flight, I ran my fingers over the ejection handle to remind myself exactly where it was. The ramp was one thing; I was also aware that just slamming to full power could promote a life-threatening emergency on any fast jet, and I might have to depart even before I hit the bottom of the ski jump.

We had overcome the navigation system issue, but had not found a proper solution to the comms problems that had made life a little more awkward than it should have been on the landing. However, we decided that this was low enough down our hazard spectrum to risk launching using the work-around we had adopted on the way down.

When using a ramp, the F35 goes up it in hybrid form. It generates lift off the wings, but is also being propelled and lifted by thrust from the main engine and the lift fan, in a sort of semi-jet-borne state. In the cockpit it feels quite slow. Whereas using a catapult is like leaving at 'warp speed', this feels laboured, and I always felt the acceleration was more gradual than I ever wanted it to be.

'Ready for conversion?' I asked my team, as I sat waiting to go.

'Go conversion,' came the response.

I hit the button and once again the jet did its Transformer routine.

'Everything looks good. Control? Ready? Are we go for launch?'

'Test, we are go for launch.'

I looked down at the flight deck officer standing alongside the cockpit on my right-hand side in his white overalls and yellow waistcoat, his head encased in a yellow crash helmet. He had done all his checks, and he had seen that the jet had now converted and made sure we were clear back and front. Then, in his headphones, he heard Jim Blackmore, in the tower, give the command: 'Launch the jet.'

This was his moment to go down to the ground on one knee and point his green flag ahead, at the end of his outstretched right arm. It was the unmistakable signal that told me I was 'go' for take-off.

'Slam in three, two, one, now!' I said, as I pushed the throttle forward to full power while still on the toe brakes.

I wanted as much acceleration and energy as I could get and, as I felt the jet start skidding and begin to lurch forward, I released the brakes and we were off. Then it was a matter of adjusting the nose wheel, using the foot pedals to keep her on the centreline, as we rumbled down the deck, hit the base of the ramp and began the climb in a cacophony of noise.

In a few seconds my world of grey was replaced by blue sky and we were airborne. There was no time to celebrate as I counted out the numbers describing the flight profile, and as we gained altitude away from the bow of the ship and then took wing, the F35 released once more in the medium for which it was built.

'Climbing away, all looks good, a nominal launch and a good rate of climb,' I told the team as we rocketed off into the sky above the Atlantic Ocean, the jet roaring at full power.

The flight plan was simple. Raise the gear and convert out. Then fly two circuits of the carrier before coming in for what would be my second landing of the day. We had enough fuel on board to complete this short sortie, plus enough in reserve to get back to Pax River in the case of an emergency.

But from the moment I took off, that script started to be rewritten. The test team discovered that the interrupted comms signal, which had affected the hot mic channel on the landing, was distorting the flow of telemetry from the aircraft.

Their biggest concern was what had happened in the compression and expansion phase to the landing gear at launch because, as the plane hit the ramp, the flow of data being received from the F35 cut out. The result was paralysis, as the team worked frantically to try to piece together enough snapshots of data to get a reliable overall picture.

In the meantime, I was left circling with the gear down, still in converted mode and rapidly hoovering up precious fuel. As I pressed them for permission to land, I was beginning to wonder whether I was going to end this momentous day not on a high, but back at Pax River after one of the shortest 'three-month' deployments to a carrier in Royal Navy history.

'We need to make a decision,' I told the team. 'Either go VL or I'm RTB' – returning to base – 'with gear down.'

A few minutes later I told them we were reaching 'bingo fuel' and I would have to land, come what may. By then they had reached a tentative conclusion that the landing gear may have undergone more compression during take-off than they would have liked, but they decided I could still land.

'OK, we're happy, if you're happy. We're go VL,' the director told me. It was hardly a ringing vote of confidence.

Then he came back on and said that, after further discussion, they had decided that I should execute a soft landing as a precaution, in case the gear was damaged, with the possibility of collapse as the plane hit the deck.

As I completed the final pattern and began my approach alongside the carrier – this time aiming for 4-Spot, slightly further aft than my first landing – I unlocked the flight test section of the computer and reset the landing velocity, cutting it by about half.

There was some anxiety about what might happen when I touched down, but the plane executed the vertical descent like the most well-behaved guest, and we eased onto our three wheels without incident. Taxiing to my parking area, I could feel my right leg shaking, the first time that had happened since my final Harrier flight at Cherry Point seven years earlier.

With the jet chained down, it was finally time for me to shut up shop. I climbed out of the cockpit and found myself being confronted by a whirl of VIPs grabbing my hand and offering congratulations as they rushed towards their departing helicopters. Clearly we had delayed them somewhat with our comms and data issues, about which they knew nothing.

The BBC team were there to record a first quote with the pilot who had completed the first landing and first launch, something I had never intended for myself when I woke up in my hotel that morning. My responses didn't give anything away about the unplanned aspects of either the landing or the launch.

'It was amazing – it was amazing,' I said, my head still encased in my helmet, chinstrap hanging down. 'I feel completely privileged. It all went well, yeah, really, really well.'

I was asked if I had been suffering from first-night nerves and I was happy to admit to those. 'I think we were all nervous this morning,' I said. 'I mean, you are always going to have nerves when you embark on board a ship. It took me back 10 years, to Harrier days.'

This was the cue for a question about Jak. Did I feel that he had been with me that day in spirit, keeping an eye on me? My answer then is exactly how I feel about him now. 'Absolutely. Yes, I do,' I said. 'I think he's always at my shoulder, looking out for me. I think whenever I find myself in awkward situations, or situations that could go wrong, it tends to go right. That is not through any natural ability, and I wouldn't necessarily put it down to luck. So I think he's definitely looking out for me.'

Jim Blackmore had made his way down to the flight deck by then, to grab me by the hand.

'Congratulations, mate,' he shouted. 'You did it. It happened.' It meant a lot to him and to his team to see carrier aviation back on the menu at last.

It was only later, when the BBC documentary was broadcast, that I saw what the ship's captain, Jerry Kyd, had to say as he watched my F35 climbing away from the ramp for the first time.

'Absolutely brilliant.' His face lit up with a big smile. 'The first launch from the Queen Elizabeth, it's just very emotional. It's been a national effort that's gone into this. This next milestone has just happened – that launch of a British naval pilot off a carrier. It's been a wonderful day – the start of the new era of carrier-based aviation for UK defence and the world for the next 20 to 30 years.' Then he added pointedly: 'We're back!'

Once the cheers had died down, I set about the hardest task of the day – to break through the 48-hour comms and media blackout to get a message to Lucy that I was safe and everything had gone more or less as planned. Throughout my career in the Fleet Air Arm, every time I had gone flying I would always send her the same text: 'Off to fly now x.' She would then wait for the follow-up message: 'Landed x.' And if I hadn't sent a message, after being airborne for several hours, she would plan to be on the phone to the squadron.

This time I had no way of contacting her back in England. I still wasn't formally embarked on the ship at that stage, which meant I had no access to email or the internet. I went down to the ship's office, where I explained my predicament. Behind the desk there was a petty officer who came to my rescue. Handing me his phone card, which still had a few minutes for international calling, he said: 'Use this, sir.'

I couldn't have been more grateful, and rushed off to tell Lucy the good news.

That night the mood was upbeat, but again the challenge of the next few days and weeks, and indeed months, when we would continue to push the performance envelope of the F35 from on board the carrier, was already looming large. I came to realise, as I completed scores of sorties from the flight deck, that each of those days was much like the first, the only difference being the absence of the cameras and the VIPs.

As the flying programme continued, I came closer to my final flight for the Royal Navy. I have never been particularly superstitious, but as my last day approached – there was a slight question mark over when it would be, as flying schedules were changed or reassigned – I had to face it. Not only would it be my farewell to the Fleet Air Arm and the Integrated Test Force, but it would also be my last chance to sit at the controls of the truly awesome F35, a plane I had grown to love.

I said nothing to anyone on board the carrier about what was coming up. I have never been one for a big fanfare at watershed moments, and I didn't want to draw attention to it. I knew that last flights had a habit of not going to plan, and they sometimes ended in misadventure, in some cases because pilots took their eye off the ball, or perhaps because they had pushed their luck by one mission too many. So I kept my head down and focused on the job. I wanted to complete those initial flight trials and then start my new life outside the Navy.

25

Three months after the first landing and launch, my final test was devoted to proving that, in an emergency, or when the flight deck was cluttered by other aircraft, an F35 pilot could carry out a vertical landing at 1-Spot.

Right at the front of the ship, this was the most exposed recovery area for our new stealth jets, immediately to the left of the base of the ski jump. The challenge was all about the visuals, because I was putting the nose wheel down only 15–20ft from the edge of the flight deck.

As I moved over in the hover and then came down, all I would see would be water all around me. And until I felt the reassuring bump and bounce of the tyres, there would always be the nagging anxiety that the plane could fall into the ocean. I would be ejecting in that scenario, then having to explain how I lost a national asset worth over $300 million.

The lateral cues for 1-Spot were harder to work off than further back, and I must have practised the approach more than 100 times in the simulator before I finally tried it for real. The key was to place the left-hand corner of the ramp in my vision to the upper right of the nose, and keep it there as the plane came down. There was no margin for error – once the jet started losing height, I would be committed, and it was too late to make last-second corrections.

It was unlikely for 1-Spot to be used in the course of normal operations. But it could be required if five F35s were coming in together, and executing vertical landings one after another, without time for them to be moved off the flight deck. It could also be an option if the other spots were occupied by helicopters, or there had been an accident elsewhere on the landing area.

The goal of the trials was to give war-fighting pilots maximum flexibility. If we could show that 1-Spot was a viable landing location, then, forever after, or for the next 50 years at least, pilots and deck officers would know it was viable, even if it looked like something to avoid.

That day my focus was entirely on executing this high-risk test safely, and delivering for the 40-strong cohort of flight test engineers and specialists watching my every move on their multiscreen displays deep inside the carrier. Repeated touchdowns at 1-Spot were a tall order, and I couldn't keep my nerves completely at bay on what I knew – though almost no one else did – was my last flight in the Navy.

Lucy was aware of what was at stake as I faced the demons that had been ready to pounce ever since the accident. 'Good luck,' she wrote in her daily email. 'I'm so proud of you and love you with all of my heart. Stay safe and come home soon.'

It didn't help that the weather was deteriorating, with increasingly dark, low cloud obscuring the horizon, but I managed to get airborne via the ramp to complete a series of landings right where they wanted them. It was textbook stuff, and I sat with the engines running after each one while the deck crew refuelled the aircraft, ready for another launch.

All my prep work had paid off and, three hours into the test, I was beginning to feel confident. There was only one more iteration to go – the fifth and final landing of my last ever sortie in a military aircraft.

I watched the guys working on the deck around my jet and looked across to the base of the control tower, where the officer in charge of flight deck operations for the day was keeping a close eye on everything we were doing. I was at the heart of an incredible team of dedicated people working in harmony, and soon it would all be in the past. I knew I was going to miss the camaraderie and the collective sense of pride and purpose we all enjoyed as we put this extraordinary new defence asset through its paces.

I lined up ready for take-off, using the ramp one more time to propel my F35 into the rain and low cloud, with the base sitting only 600ft above the increasingly choppy waters of the Atlantic.

I knew serial number BF-05 was the best all-rounder of the test fleet and most suited to this mission. Each of the machines we were using had its own blueprint and detailed history, recording its every move and quirk, and this one was among the most reliable. It had no issues with rain, as some did – they didn't like getting wet, with delicate test equipment on board – and I was confident as I felt its raw power as we ascended the ramp.

Once airborne, F35 engine roaring, I climbed away from the huge grey vessel to conduct a series of medium-altitude tests and burn off fuel before radioing in to indicate my intention to return for the last time.

'Approach, Lightning 65 is now complete and ready for recovery, beginning descent to 1,000ft,' I told air traffic control on the carrier.

As I began my descent, I went through my practised routines – checking altitude, fuel reserves, airspeed, heading – and checked in again with the control room, where the engineers were eager to complete this last test.

'Control, Test is setting up for test point five,' I said. 'Semi-automated approach and VL 1-Spot.'

The controller gave me course and altitude instructions for my final approach.

'Lightning 65, approach, call established at 1,000ft on centreline at 10 miles.'

'Lightning 65, wilco.'

Once again, I would be aiming for a point a fraction outboard of the port side of the bow of the ship, where I'd hover before sliding across and touching down. As I descended into heavy cloud, the weather started to play its part.

The carrier team in the FlyCo tower were reporting an improved picture but, as I got to 1,000ft at a range of 10 miles, I was still in a mass of thick dark cloud, and could see nothing. Travelling at 360 knots, it quickly came down to eight miles, then six miles . . . and I was still in cloud.

I requested a further descent to 600ft, thinking that would finally free me and I'd be able to get sight of the carrier. This was approved, and I dropped the nose. But at two miles' range I was still surrounded by dark, menacing cloud.

It was time to try something else.

I requested an instrument landing, and climbed to 1,000ft to begin a fresh approach. I checked in with my test engineers, again on the continuously open hot mic. We could see the fuel state was a little on the low side, so we decided to abandon our previous plan for me to conduct a fly-through before coming in for touchdown.

Back at 10 miles, and pointing straight at the carrier, I slowed the jet to 250 knots, extended the landing gear, and pushed the conversion button. For the final time I listened as the F35 went through its remarkable automated transformation, from supersonic stealth fighter to jump jet. The conversion light on the instrument panel went out as normal, to signify vertical landing mode had kicked in. Then I heard the tower: 'Prepare for descent . . . descend now.'

From that point on I was committed, using the automated stick in my right hand to maintain heading and flight path.

I spoke to the control room. 'Once I break out of the cloud, I'll continue the approach visually and get to the test point.'

In the bowels of the ship, watching real-time telemetry data on everything from hydraulics, mission systems and landing gear to the jet's power and thermal management system, I imagined them all giving a quick thumbs up to the test director.

'Test, Control – go vertical landing 1-Spot,' came the response.

'Test copied.'

At 800ft, on the glide slope, all was looking good. At 700ft, I checked in with 'Paddles', the landing signal officer, who was in charge of flight operations safety on approach that day. 'Paddles – Lightning 65.'

He came back instantly. 'Lightning 65, Paddles. You're loud and—'

And that was all I heard from him . . .

At that moment my whole world was overtaken by a deafening engine noise – an incredible racket that is normally suppressed by the active reduction system. I'd never heard anything like it before and, as I came to terms with the shock of it, I could feel the temperature in the cockpit rapidly increasing.

At the same time, above the din, I started to hear an audio signal in my helmet: 'Warning, Warning!' it repeated. 'Warning!'

I was sucking on my rubber oxygen mask and getting nothing; the green flight symbology projected onto my pupils from my helmet-mounted display projectors had vanished, the screens on the instrument panel had frozen black and my radios were dead. And the noise . . .

I no longer had contact with the ship. To say it was unnerving would be an understatement. I was so close to safety, but now my plane had turned what was already a challenging approach into a nightmare.

We had trained for total electrical failure. It was identified as part of our hazard spectrum – close to the extreme of the spectrum, in fact – and it was an eventuality we had worked hard to control. I guessed it could be what I was dealing with, but that didn't make it any easier to respond to. I was faced with what looked like a total systems shutdown in dense cloud, with no visibility of the surface I was supposed to land on.

This was naval aviation at its most raw. It felt like I had nowhere to turn.

In the blink of an eye, the highly sophisticated controls of this multimillion-pound aerial super-computer had turned themselves off, and I was right at the cliff edge. Would I find a way back, or fall into the yawning chasm? Was my last flight going to be the one where the game of chance that I had been playing for the last 20 years finally caught up with me? Was it *this* time that the dragons would get me, and turn this into another story of an aviator lost on a final sortie?

I had no contact with the control room. This was up to me. I had only one option, I told myself – stay calm, think logically, continue the approach, and try to keep everything predictable.

Instead of computer displays and automated flying systems, I would have to rely on the small digital attitude indicator set low down on the console, which gave me pitch and roll attitude, speed, height and compass heading. It was still working, thank God, powered by a back-up system. As I checked and rechecked it, I felt like I was reverting to my early training at the controls of a two-seater, prop-driven Chipmunk.

But there were plenty of things the standby indicator couldn't tell me. One of them was my fuel state. I knew I was close to my maximum hover weight – that's what we did in test flying, push the system to its limits. But I now had no way of knowing exactly how heavy my plane was, or how hard the engine was working to slow me down.

The other thing on my mind was the danger that I presented to the people living and working on the floating city I had to land on, and a crash – like a jet smashing into one of the control towers – would make headlines around the world.

As I had done before in moments of crisis in the air, I went through the stress-busting process of speaking out loud a checklist of factors in my favour – what you might call real-time hazard spectrum analysis.

Is the engine still working?

Yes.

Is the lift fan functioning correctly?

Yes. If it wasn't I'd soon know because the jet would start somersaulting, and the auto-ejection system would fling me out of the cockpit before I'd even realised what was happening.

Can I still fly the aircraft?

Yes. But she feels different because the higher levels of automation have dropped out.

OK, just hang in there, I told myself, with standby instrumentation and the ever-faithful stick and throttle.

Still in cloud, and with no forward visibility, landing on 1-Spot was out of the question. It was now about saving this jet, getting it on deck in one piece and walking away.

Then the back-up oxygen supply kicked in, and I could feel cold air filling my lungs. As the canopy began to mist over, I realised that the aircraft pressurisation system had stopped. I immediately began trying to work out the ramifications.

It was all about time. I had to get this aircraft on the deck as fast as possible, before she overheated. With no cooling, the giant computer that is the F35 was going to heat up very quickly, to the point where *everything* would shut down and the plane would fall out of the air.

I pulled my Royal Navy-issue black-leather flying gloves tight to my wrists and instinctively tightened my ejection seat shoulder straps. A chilling thought flashed through my mind – that my career could yet be bookended by ejections, one over land that I survived against all odds, and one over sea, the outcome of which had yet to become clear.

At 500ft I was still looking for that sea, trying to peer through the grey mist to catch sight of a white horse or two that could be a visual cue leading me to the carrier.

At 400ft the waves began to appear from below the cloud. I took my first deep breath since the beginning of the shut-down. Now I could start hunting for the *Queen Elizabeth*. I was aware that my heart was pounding. It reminded me – as if nothing else was already – that I was in a struggle for survival, for me and the plane.

Generally in a crisis, or a particularly demanding phase of test flying, my heart rate rarely rises above 50 beats a minute. But as I start to zero in on the fundamentals, my breathing becomes lighter, to such an extent that I often trigger an oxygen warning alarm, indicating a system problem caused by low demand. This infuriates the flight test engineers who have to explain in their reports, yet again, why the warning was triggered.

But this time my heart rate and breathing pattern were up, which told me the dragons were close. Something else was happening too. Every pilot experiences a physical reaction that alerts them to real danger – for some, the hair on the back of their neck stands up. For others, a metallic taste develops in their mouth. The top of my head goes red hot. Not my face, just my head, and I can tell when it happens – *and it was happening* – because I could feel the heat and see the mist on the edge of my helmet visor.

The demons were back with a vengeance. Is this it? Is my time up? Am I about to lose this plane within sight of the carrier, which would finish my flying career whether I was retiring or not?

I levelled off at 300ft, knowing that if I continued on this heading I should see the ship. But I had to be careful. I might suddenly come upon it and get too close to the rear superstructure, which could lead to me overshooting and being propelled back into the cloud mass, without enough fuel to try again. That was another route to ejection – this time a premeditated one – but something I needed to avoid at all costs.

Time for another deep breath.

I decided to kick a few degrees off the heading to give myself a little more margin for error, and, as I did so, I finally saw the tell-tale wake of Britain's biggest warship. For a few seconds, the stern of the vast carrier drifted in and out of the picture, as I momentarily lost sight of it in the swirling mix of low cloud and breaking seas. Grey-on-grey is all well and good in a tactical environment, but at that moment I would have preferred HMS *Queen Elizabeth* to have been bright orange.

Still with no way of contacting anyone on board, I slowed the aircraft again and tried to establish a 'nominal' approach. Wings level at 100ft, I was aiming for an initial hover position outboard of the centre of the flight deck – at 3-Spot, between the two superstructures, which looked clear and usable. I was making my own decisions and the guys on the deck would have to follow based on what they could see in the absence of radio communication.

I was adjusting my line-up and controlling the deceleration when something magical happened – the canopy began to clear.

'Thank fuck for that . . .!'

Then the cockpit displays started to re-initialise and the oxygen flow returned to normal.

My jet was finding itself again. She was binging and bonging . . .

Relief surged through my veins. The F35 was starting to feel good again and the deafening noise that had alerted me to the shutdown in the first place was being mitigated once more by the automatic reduction system. And now the radios were coming back on stream, and I began to hear transmissions from anxious souls on the carrier, starting with my control team.

'Test . . . Test . . . Test – Control. How do you read?' The director's rhythmic tone and rapid delivery suggested he had been repeating this for the past few minutes. 'Test . . . Test . . . Test – Control. How do you read?'

Then it was the landing signal officer. 'Lightning 65, Paddles . . . Lightning 65, Paddles, radio check . . .'

I needed to silence them both at once and concentrate on my final approach.

'L65 stand by,' I said on all frequencies, doing my best to sound cool and emotionless.

The aircraft had taken a split second to switch off. Now it was rebooting itself with equally remarkable speed, having identified, I later discovered, a momentary stray voltage in the electrical system. It was frightening, no question, but you could argue that the F35 had performed as designed that morning as, all on her own, she worked through and recovered from this glitch. Either way, we had been reminded that even the world's most advanced 5th Gen fighter wasn't immune to a momentary – and heart-stopping – blip.

Hands on the throttle and stick, I nodded my head slowly to the crew to indicate that I was about to move over the deck. They nodded back and ran for cover. Hovering above the landing spot, I realised I hadn't had time to think ahead and assess if there was anything on the spectrum that would affect this manoeuvre. I paused, and then, as if the test team sensed my hesitation, I heard the comforting message: 'Test, go VL.'

I could feel the temperature dropping in my helmet as my visor cleared. I had edged away from the dragons once more, I thought, as I landed and shut down the engine. OK, we had missed that final test point – our last rendezvous with 1-Spot – but we had learnt something new about the aircraft and, most important of all from my point of view, I had got her back in one piece.

After she had been chained and I'd climbed out, I found myself thinking, 'I might as well keep my game face on one last time' as I made my way across the flight deck and through one of the hatches into the superstructure.

I knew I was being watched by the aircraft maintainers and flight deck officers, with everyone craning their necks in the forward and aft control towers. As I made my way along the internal corridors towards the locker room, I batted away the normal polite inquiries from passing sailors and technicians.

'Hey, sir, how was the flight?'

'Yeah, good, thanks.'

'Good flight, sir?'

'Yeah, not too bad.'

In the locker room, I experienced my own unique physical reaction to stress after flying. As I was taking off my G-pants, my right leg started shaking uncontrollably. This had happened after my final flight in a Harrier in the US, and then after I had successfully landed the F35 on the carrier for the first time. I stood there watching it tremble, waiting for it to burn itself out, as my body expressed the emotion that my mind would not allow.

I had got away with my last flight, but I knew how close I had come. Now I had reached the end – it was the last time I would even touch an F35, and the last time I would take part in carrier aviation, the most demanding flying of all.

I finished taking off my flying kit and headed to the flight control centre, where the engineers were waiting to start what turned into a lengthy final debrief. We concentrated on the data and remained unemotional throughout. Overcoming near misses is part of being a test pilot. There were a few handshakes and a few comments along the lines of 'That was interesting' and 'Well, that didn't exactly go to plan,' but other than that the team was focused on identifying the cause of the shutdown. It was a problem in the electrical system and something that was unique to the experimental test aircraft I was flying. Once they had concluded the investigation, the aircraft was released from its quarantined status, ready to fly again.

The following day, Jerry Kyd invited me up to see him, a lovely touch by a man who was enormously respected by his ship's company, on what would be his last posting at sea. He later became Commander United Kingdom Maritime Forces and then had a final stint as Fleet Commander.

As we sat and chatted about the whole trials programme, I remember thinking the cabin felt more like a small library than the captain's quarters on a ship. He was a great person to talk through my decision to leave with.

'If you feel it's the right time to make the leap, then it's the right time,' he told me. 'I completely respect and understand that. It's all about leaving at the top of your game. If you're on a high, take that leap and use it as a springboard and then keep going.'

It was sound advice that bolstered my confidence to start the transition from service life to civvy street. Before leaving, I presented him with a set of wings which had been in my pocket when I completed the first landing and launch from his ship what already seemed a lifetime ago.

A few days later, as I stepped off the carrier in Norfolk, Virginia, and we prepared to head back to the UK to start our new life outside the Royal Navy, I found myself looking back to the day a seven-year-old boy had stared up at that 747 with the Space Shuttle on its back from the back garden of his home in Stoke-on-Trent. He couldn't have imagined the flying career I was lucky enough to have. I had defied my teachers' advice that I should stay earthbound, and achieved my dreams as a pilot. I had flown at least 40 different aircraft, all over the world, had been privileged to help our war effort in Afghanistan, and had finished by helping to establish Britain's newest maritime air asset on the Queen Elizabeth Class carriers.

And in an ever-changing world, I had learnt that if anybody

tells you that you're not meant to do something, based on your background, they're simply wrong.

Whatever you can do, or dream you can, begin it. Boldness has genius, power and magic in it.

Johann Wolfgang von Goethe (attrib.)

Epilogue

December 2022

The twentieth anniversary of the accident was a beautiful winter's day at RAF Wittering, just as it was in December 2002 when I lined up in my Harrier for a short take-off with Jak in the instructor's seat behind me.

There were almost no clouds in the sky and it was cold and crisp. The airfield on the border of Cambridgeshire and Northamptonshire was dotted with its ever-present residents, a parliament of strutting crows filling the silence with their calls.

Andy Neofytou – aka Scrabble – and Simon Rawlins – aka Scranbag – and I had come to mark the passage of two decades since Jak lost his life, and I miraculously escaped with my own, in the freak accident that formed the introduction and backdrop to my military flying career.

Our idea was to have a little get-together that we thought Jak would approve of, to remember him and acknowledge his legacy, something we had also done at the first-year and tenth-year anniversaries. We brought two bottles of white wine, as well as a packet of Jak's favourite Marlboro cigarettes, and had received permission to drive onto the airfield and head for the crash site at the base of the windsock.

I was also carrying a small bouquet of flowers in tribute to a man who has always kept a protective eye on me and whose memory is never far from my thoughts. Jak would have probably laughed at the flowers – being the archetypal toughie fighter pilot that he was – but I did my best in an area that is definitely not my strong suit. All I know is that it was a colourful bunch that included tulips and a few other bits and bobs.

We met for lunch at the Tobie Norris pub in nearby Stamford – an old drinking haunt from our Harrier days at Wittering – and drove in convoy to the base, through security and to the gate that leads onto the airfield. The place looked pretty run-down, it has to be said, with abandoned hangars and no aircraft on the flight line.

Since our days at Wittering, when it was buzzing with activity as the home of Harrier training, the airfield has been re-tasked as an RAF logistics and transport hub. The only aviation that takes place now is air experience flights for young cadets in small prop-driven machines, and the activities of local university flying clubs.

It felt subdued as we drove past the main accommodation block, where I spotted the window of the bedroom where I was staying on the morning of the crash. We went past the old hangar and the flight line where I had started the Harrier that day, and on past what was then the new GR7 Harrier squadron hangar, which now looked quite derelict.

When we got to the gate onto the airfield, Scranbag, who was leading, stopped and got out. We were at the 'FOD check' – a blue painted square on the road where we had to check our tyres for any foreign objects that could end up on the runway. This was a measure that had been implemented in the wake of the accident, to help prevent similar disasters in future.

Then we were on the airfield, driving with our hazard lights on as required by the base authorities, who had given us permission to make this little pilgrimage on a day when no flying was scheduled. We drove over the main runway and onto the northern taxiway, where Jak and I had come in to land, in preparation for our fateful short take-off run.

Driving along that taxiway, I spotted the woods on the right-hand side where I had thought Jak might have ended up, and from where he would emerge laughing and joking after ejecting. I passed the point of take-off. And then – at this point, barely moving – I was on the section of tarmac above which the engine of my Harrier had exploded, and I could almost feel the shock of being violently thrown forward in the cockpit as the power cut out and the plane started to roll.

Once again, Scranbag had stopped and got out, and was walking back towards my car. I opened my window and felt a blast of cold air, bringing me abruptly back to the here and now.

'I'll let you lead from here, Nath,' he said, 'because you know where it is.'

Well, all I knew was to head for the windsock, but when we got there, we weren't sure we were in the right place. We needed to find the small section of perimeter fence that had been replaced. This was where Scrabble had ordered the firemen to cut it, so they could carry me from the field where I had landed to the waiting ambulance.

It took us a few moments to realise that we had gone too far and, after reversing down the taxiway, we eventually found the section of wire that had been fastened in where the cut had been made. It was still a subtly different grey to the rest. It was the only physical sign that something had happened here on the morning of my sixteenth training flight in a Harrier all those years ago.

Alongside us, the field had been ploughed, ready for the next season's crops, as it had been 20 years earlier, something that undoubtedly saved me from either being killed on impact or suffering serious long term-injury. It occurred to me, as I stood there surveying this scene once more, that I had never met the farmer, but that perhaps on a day like this in the future I will.

We were now close to the spot where I had sat dazed and stunned, watching my Harrier burn in the distance, and our mood – that up until then had been the normal diet of fighter pilot banter – turned more sombre as we walked towards the fence in silence.

It was time for our ritual to begin. I climbed the fence and leant over to post my flowers through the chain links from the field side. I didn't want them to be, in any way, a potential danger to planes operating on the airfield. Scranners lit a cigarette and placed it on the ground for Jak and I opened the wine. We all took a swig and toasted Jak before pouring the remainder on the ground for him.

We each spoke about our recollection of what had happened that day and I was struck particularly by what Scranners had to say about what he had seen from the cockpit of his jet as he prepared to take off over a mile away.

He said he saw my Harrier begin its take-off run and thought nothing of it initially, as he focused on his own upcoming training sortie. Then he remembered thinking that something slightly weird had happened, because my aircraft appeared to be leaving the ground with afterburners lit, and Harriers don't have afterburners.

Scranners saw what he thought were flares being fired, and it crossed his mind that it was extremely unsafe for someone to be doing that on an airfield where a plane was taking off. But it started to make sense when he saw a black shape shoot across the horizon with a streaming parachute following it. As it disappeared behind the distant treeline, he clocked the jet coming down and exploding.

'I think that aircraft has just crashed,' Scranners told his instructor sitting behind him.

'Did you see any chutes?'

'I saw one.'

'D'you think he made it?'

'Don't think so, no.'

After telling the tower what he had seen – informing them that the crash did not look 'survivable' – Scranbag taxied back in. As he did so, the crash alarms sounded on the airfield and the emergency response teams went into action, led by Scrabble, who dashed from the authoriser's desk to the Popemobile. At that stage, as Scrabble drove at high speed across the airfield to reach me, Scranbag was certain that both Jak and I had died.

We agreed that those events, which had changed all our lives and those of others who witnessed it, felt like they had happened only yesterday. But we only had to look at each other – now greying and middle-aged – to see that was not the case. It was disconcerting to think that we were now slightly older than Jak was when he died; at 43, we used to think of him as one of the 'old and bold'. We certainly didn't consider ourselves as old on that anniversary at Wittering, even if our bodies were telling us something different.

It also struck me that day how lucky the three of us were to have come through our careers in the Navy unscathed, something that sadly cannot be said of several of my friends and colleagues who lost their lives in flying accidents.

From my perspective, it felt right to say hello to Jak and to be at the crash site again. It felt right to refresh my memory of it because it had faded and it felt wrong for it to fade. And it was right to be there with those two guys, who were so intrinsically part of what had happened. I felt I could connect – or reconnect – with them and with Jak: it felt like another opportunity to 'rebalance' my life.

But it was weird, in a way, to stand there pouring wine onto the ground and knowing that in the air – 50ft or so above me – I had confronted the threshold between life and death, the angels on one side and the Grim Reaper on the other. As I listened to Scrabble and Scranners, it felt like they were talking about someone else and someone else's story, as if this were not a real experience. Is this really where it had happened? Is this the fence that I went shooting across? And is that the field that I landed in? All of it was familiar but surreal at the same time.

By now the sun was setting and the cold was intensifying as the beginning of another clear December night edged across the airfield. Inspired by Jak's hell-raising reputation, and led by the irrepressible Scranners, we raced each other back along the runway *Top Gear*-style, just as we had 10 years earlier, and then stopped at the old ski jump which we'd used to practise carrier launches in the Harriers. Now it was fenced off and covered in moss and weeds. We got out and climbed up it and, standing at the top, agreed to do this all over again in five years' time.

On the long journey home, I thought about why that little ritual always works. I have to admit I find it hard to be at Jak's grave at the Fleet Air Arm cemetery at the Church of St Bartholomew at Yeovilton. I go there most years and stand and talk to him, but it feels very different going to the crash site, which is not accessible under normal circumstances. If it was, I would be there every year, because there I can touch the ground and feel it all and process it all again. That overwhelming and monumental experience becomes more real, and it's the place I can connect to Jak – it's where his memory resonates most powerfully.

I have indeed grown to know Jak London far better in death than I knew him in life. He was killed on my first flight with him, and up until then I had only spent a few hours in his company, chatting over a beer in the mess bar at Wittering. But his guardian presence has always been there and the idea of that – that he has looked after me ever since he left us – is something his family shares too.

This was never better expressed than in a letter I received from Jack's older brother, Andrew, a retired solicitor from Helston in Cornwall whom I met at the funeral and again at the inquest. Sixteen years later he wrote to me out of the blue.

'Dear Nathan,' he wrote,

> you may vaguely remember me. I am Jak's brother ...
> and I hope you do not mind me writing to you. I was
> so pleased and proud to see, both on Sky News and
> BBC News, that you were the very first pilot to land
> an F35 on the new carrier, HMS *Queen Elizabeth II.*
> It must have been a tremendous thrill for you after
> all you have been through, and I would like to think
> that perhaps Jak was with you, when you made that
> landing. My sister Helen and I will continue to follow
> your career with interest and we both wish you every
> success in the Fleet Air Arm.

I will always be grateful for that message. He captured
my thoughts exactly.

Acknowledgements

I would like to thank so many truly amazing and remarkable people I have been lucky enough to meet on this exciting and at times turbulent adventure we call life.

Firstly, thank you Chris Terrill, my fellow green beret, I'm truly honoured to call you a friend and without your natural gift of curiosity the seed for this book would never have been sown.

To Mark, an extraordinary gentleman who has guided me patiently though this process. I have learnt so much from you and will be eternally grateful for your belief in a boy from Stoke.

Ed, a master of your craft, we have shared so much venturing into unchartered and at times bumpy territory. What a journey! Thank you so much and I hope to now learn more about your incredible adventures.

A big thank you to the Headline team for your enthusiasm and encouragement. A special thank you to Martin and Holly for being great at what you do; I always felt in safe hands.

Scrabble, it took huge courage to drop everything and run to be by my side after my ejection. I cannot thank you enough and your loyalty during that time has remained with me, I couldn't ask for a better wingman.

Scranners, from commissioning to retirement we've been together, shoulder-to-shoulder, and your camaraderie has been a reassuring constant. You are a true friend and someone I'd follow into any merge . . . carry on!

Gazza, thank you for your leap of faith that got me back into the cockpit. I am eternally grateful to you for trusting me to fly with you on, what was, your last Harrier flight – knowing that now makes it even more meaningful. I feel very lucky to have you as a dear friend.

To Sparky, you stuck your neck out in supporting my quest to become a test pilot and I'll be forever thankful for your part in shaping my life's arc; I'm proud to know you.

Maria and Jak's family, thank you for the grace and kindness you have always shown me. My only worry throughout this process has been to make sure Jak's legacy is honoured. He was and always will be a legend.

To all of my friends and colleagues in the Navy, Air Force, Marines and beyond. Thank you for all that you do. I continue to be humbled by the selflessness and bravery that you display every single day. I'm privileged to have served alongside you.

I owe my life to the incredible team at Martin Baker and GQIrvin Parachutes. Without your fierce intelligence, dedication and innovation I wouldn't be here to tell my story.

Mum, thank you for your unwavering love and support, even during the tough times when I'm sure you would have preferred my feet to have been firmly on the ground. Dad, for always encouraging me to achieve my dreams by keeping a space open on the pottery bench next to you – thank you.

To my family, thank you all for your support. From sitting

with me for hours in front of a cardboard cockpit in the living room to words of encouragement when they were needed most. Thank you for having faith in my seemingly impossible dream.

Lucy, it is impossible to put into words what you mean to me. Thank you for your unconditional love and support throughout and for being my rock during the highs and lows – none of this would have been possible without you. Your light shines so brightly. I love you.

Image Credits

Page 6
Andy Neofytou – UK Ministry of Defence © Crown Copyright 2023
Gary Langrish – UK Ministry of Defence © Crown Copyright 2023
Simon Rawlins – UK Ministry of Defence © Crown Copyright 2023

Page 7
HMS *Queen Elizabeth* and HMS *Monmouth*
  © Lockheed Martin photo by Dane Wiedmann
F35 launch © Lockheed Martin photo by Dane Wiedmann
F35 landing © Lockheed Martin photo by Dane Wiedmann

Page 8
FA2 and F35 © Lockheed Martin photo by Dane Wiedmann
Ski jump base, RAF Wittering © Andrew Neofytou
With Lucy © Nathan Gray